'A fascinating portrait o  what happens when forg hatred and division. Inte Henry Olonga, artist, r international cricketer

'Astonishment! What a name! What a gripping and moving story – one which relives the experiences of many Zimbabweans and former Rhodesians in a crucial, dramatic period of the country's history.'
Rt Rev Dr Chad N Gandiya, retired Bishop of the Anglican Diocese of Harare, Zimbabwe

Astonishment

Laying Ghosts in Mugabe's Zimbabwe

Graham Jones

instant
apostle

First published in Great Britain in 2019.

Instant Apostle

The Barn
1 Watford House Lane
Watford
Herts
WD17 1BJ

British Library Cataloguing-in-Publication Data

A catalogue record for this book is available from the British Library.

This book and all other Instant Apostle books are available from Instant Apostle:

Website: www.instantapostle.com

E-mail: info@instantapostle.com

ISBN 978-1-912726-10-3

Printed in Great Britain.

For Lynda
my extremely patient wife

Author's Note

Many of the names in this story have been changed, either to spare people's feelings or simply to respect their privacy. And for narrative convenience, some of the details of the two trips to Astonishment's home patch have been reordered. Childhood memories have been checked wherever possible, but many of those who can verify them are no longer alive and their accuracy is inevitably subject to the passing of time.

Acknowledgements

Thanks go to Astonishment and Bridget Mapurisa, their family and friends, the staff of Matthew Rusike Children's Home and the many other Zimbabweans who have welcomed me to their country and facilitated the writing of this book. I must also thank my wife, Lynda, who shared my travels; Alison Hull for her encouragement and knowledge of the publishing world; Louise Bryant for her comments on the text; and Len Kynaston who helped fill out my memories of our African childhood.

Graham Jones

Contents

Preface

The man in the Mazda sedan tightens his grip on the wheel and flicks an anxious glance at the rear-view mirror. He's heading north on the N1 highway, eating up the miles through the flat grasslands of South Africa's Limpopo Province. In a couple of hours, so he hopes, he'll reach the Limpopo River and the border crossing at Beitbridge. If he makes it through Zimbabwe's labyrinthine immigration procedures in reasonable time – three hours would be good – he'll be home by midnight.

His destination is Matthew Rusike Children's Home on the outskirts of Harare where Astonishment (for that is the man's unlikely name) is responsible for 150 AIDS orphans and other child victims of the economic meltdown in Robert Mugabe's Zimbabwe. It's early 2009 and Zimbabwe's inflation is the worst in history. It takes a billion Zimbabwe dollars to buy a tomato, a suitcase of notes to go shopping, though most of the time there's little to be had on Harare's supermarket shelves.

Hence Astonishment's latest foray south to buy supplies for the children in his care. Homeward bound, his car boot crammed with bread, cooking oil, mealie-meal flour and cartons of tinned food, Astonishment watches Polokwane city with its proud new World Cup-ready football stadium receding to his left. Shifting his gaze to the spooling ribbon of road behind him, he wonders again why the dark blue Toyota Corolla hasn't overtaken. It's riding dangerously close.

The last ragged outskirts of Polokwane slide away and ahead is open veldt. Now there's movement in the rear-view mirror. The Toyota looms closer, swings to the right and comes alongside, matching the speed of the Mazda. The passenger window slides open and an arm signals to Astonishment to stop. He senses danger and accelerates. The arm withdraws and a shotgun takes its place. With another glance to his right, Astonishment sees it nodding to tell him to stop. It then points directly at his head, the muzzle a metre from his ear.

He pulls over, taking care to leave the engine running. The Toyota swerves left and blocks him in. Two men get out. They fling open Astonishment's door and haul him to the ground. He's on his back on the tarmac, shielding his face against the blows and the kicks. It's over very quickly. With three or four stamps on his head, the men flee – one to the Toyota, one to the Mazda. Through slit, swollen eyes, Astonishment sees the Mazda and its cargo and 2,500 US dollars donated by well-wishers disappearing down the straight, empty road towards Polokwane. He's aware of grit in his mouth and a crushing pain in his ribs. He tries to stand, but sags onto the tarmac and lies still.

Scroll back forty years to an earlier roadside scene in Zimbabwe, then called Rhodesia. This same Astonishment is a child, aged two. Barefoot, dirt poor, dressed in ragged shorts, he's walking the dusty verge with his Uncle Chengeta near the town of Chivhu – or Enkeldoorn as it was known in those distant colonial days. A 1962 Ford Anglia flashes by. Through the dust thrown up in its wake, Astonishment catches sight of a white boy in the passenger seat, his feet on the dashboard and his elbow on the sill of the open window. The car and its occupants are gone in a moment, but it's like a glimpse of another world. Astonishment has never been in a car. He's rarely seen a white person. To him, *varungu* are another species, insulated by wealth and privilege from the hardships of ordinary life.

While the car-jacking at Polokwane is real, this second scenario is imaginary. But it could have happened. As a white Rhodesian teenager, I saw many a roadside urchin blanketed in dust as the family car flew by. With a slight geographic adjustment (our home was in another part of the country), my first encounter with Astonishment could have been on an African dirt road in the late 1960s. We might even have exchanged looks across the cultural divide – car-cocooned white boy to roadside *piccanin*, as he would have been called.

Assuming it didn't happen quite so, our paths crossed only after I'd returned to Zimbabwe nearly forty years after leaving it. Partly I wanted to show my family where I'd grown up. Partly I was looking for my own childhood, or whatever vestiges might still be there to be recaptured. I also wanted to see what had happened to the beautiful but flawed country I knew as Rhodesia and which was now the Zimbabwe of Robert Mugabe.

On that visit, it took another child on the streets of Victoria Falls Town to lead me, unexpectedly, to Astonishment. In meeting and getting to know this inspiring man, I started to see my own upbringing through new eyes. As he told me his story from childhood destitution to saving the lives of Zimbabwean orphans, it turned out to be not only his story but the story of Zimbabwe itself through the period of my long absence, from liberation war to new nationhood and the tragedy of its more recent past.

When Astonishment and I eventually stood with 300 mourners at Uncle Chengeta's tribal funeral not far from Chivhu, I felt a chasm had been bridged.

Part 1

2008
The Return

1

A Sunlit Childhood, Far Away

I paused at the top of the gangway, eyes screwed against
the African sun, and took in the scene.

Ahead of me, a low, white terminal building bore the
message, *Welcome to Victoria Falls*. On a square of lawn
between two palm trees, the Zimbabwean flag-of-many-
colours lifted and fell in the breeze – green for farming,
gold for mining, red for blood spilt in the war of liberation
and black for the people. Superimposed on the Communist
star, a yellow Zimbabwe Bird, the country's emblem,
seemed impervious to the new arrivals. The Comair flight

was just in from Johannesburg and the passengers ahead of me were crossing the tarmac to the immigration hall.

My last views of Zimbabwe had been thirty-nine years earlier as I mounted the gangway of an Air Rhodesia flight at Bulawayo Airport, flew to the capital, Salisbury, and caught an onward flight to return to boarding school in England. A photograph taken by my father that same day from the rooftop viewing terrace in Bulawayo shows a gangly sixteen-year-old in a school blazer, duffel bag in hand, taking a last look back at his childhood home. Then as now, the Zimbabwe Bird had fluttered on the terminal flagpole – not on a Marxist red star, but flanked by two sable antelope on the green-and-white flag of Ian Smith's rebel regime. In the photograph, the Bird appears again on the tailfin of the turbo-prop Air Rhodesia Viscount, stretched and stylised to make it look airborne. It might have been a trick of the light, but the name on the fuselage appears to have lost some of its letters and reads A R RHOD S A.

The memory of that long-ago departure filtered back as I watched my wife, Lynda, and our three sons making their way down the gangway at Victoria Falls. With it came a jumble of half-remembered sensations – the fine, white sandiness of dirt country roads; the abrupt grandeur of the granite outcrops in the Matopos Hills; luminous evenings filled with the scent of wood smoke and the crowing of cockerels; the drumming of African rain on corrugated iron roofs; the rude cry of the *go-way* bird and the black, shiny-backed *chongololos* – the monster-millipedes that crawled out after the rains and crunched as you rode over them on your bike. The memories flooding back were those of space and freedom and the sunlit, Californian lifestyle of white Rhodesia in the 1950s and 1960s.

Still on the gangway, I struggled to connect the country I was now entering as a British tourist to the place in which I'd grown up. Childhood always seems like another land, and so it did now. But when the country itself no longer exists, when even its name has been expunged, the gulf seems achingly unbridgeable. Mixed with the thrill of being back was a dash of sadness that this was not, and never could be, the same country.

Of course, it hadn't all been idyllic. I recalled how the shadows had lengthened across that far-off, sunny childhood as I grew older and came to understand the injustices on which my carefree world was built. Colonial Rhodesia was one of history's dead ends and its fall was inevitable, but it left me nostalgic for a place and a time I thought could never be recaptured.

In the air a few minutes earlier, I'd pressed my head to the window and watched with excitement as the African scrubland rose to meet us and the spray from Victoria Falls appeared like a wisp of cotton wool on the brown landscape. It had felt like coming home. Now, as I disembarked into Robert Mugabe's Zimbabwe, my thoughts turned to recent headlines. This was the terrible election year of 2008 when Mugabe, losing the first round to his rival, Morgan Tsvangirai, had unleashed such a tide of violence that Tsvangirai had withdrawn to avoid more of his supporters being killed. Mugabe, defying the result, had been sworn in again as President just a few weeks earlier.

Coming home? I wondered if I was.

My parents hadn't intended to wind up in Rhodesia. My father, a conscientious objector in the Second World War, had spent the duration driving a supplies lorry in China for Nationalist forces fighting the Japanese. Returning to England after the war, he got ordained as a Methodist minister and was sent back to Hong Kong by the Methodist Missionary Society in preparation for a China posting. The timing could not have been worse. When the Communists came to power that same year under Mao Zedong, Western missionaries were banned and those already in the country were forced to leave. Foiled, Dad had the task of welcoming expelled missionaries coming over from the mainland. One of these was my mother who'd been teaching in Canton. They married more or less on the spot, came back to England and asked where else the Missionary Society would like them to go. The Society weighed up their experience of the Far East and my mother's knowledge of Cantonese and despatched them to Southern Africa.

Geoffrey and Margaret Jones travelled out by Union Castle steamer to Cape Town, took the slow train up through Bechuanaland – now Botswana – with a three-month-old baby (me) and moved into a rambling, colonial home in Bulawayo. There I spent my first five years (joined by my Rhodesian-born sister, Christine, after two years) in what seems now to have been a blissful succession of long, sunny days.

The house on Bulawayo's Abercorn Street forms the backdrop to my memories – the red-polished *stoep* with its white, wooden balustrade draped in bougainvillea; the corrugated iron roof, originally blood-red but faded pink in the African sun; the brown, prickle-carpeted garden, dotted with frangipani and poinsettia where I rode my tricycle, played with my Dinky cars in the dirt and splashed about in a tin tub on hot days. I also, allegedly, had a habit of setting off down Abercorn Street in my pedal car and was regularly intercepted by neighbours who soon got to know where to return me.

Away from home, I played with little Ndebele children in the dug-out foundations of the schools and churches that Dad was in charge of building. Then there was what we called On Trek – family camping trips of a week or more to remote Methodist outposts in our mud-coloured 1940s Chevrolet Bakkie with the box rear end (a model popular on Rhodesian farms because the box made a handy container for transporting your workers). Ours had been inherited from Dad's predecessor and came with a bullet hole in the roof where a passenger cradling a gun had fired off accidentally when it hit a bump.

My mother found a teaching job in Bulawayo, so much of the time Christine and I were in the care of our Ndebele maid, Elsie. I remember Elsie's beret and blue dress, her African way of sitting straight-legged on the ground, ankles crossed, and her kindly, soft-spoken presence around the house. Devoted as she was to *Mufundisi*'s kids, she clearly wasn't on duty the day a herd of cows ran amok on Abercorn Street. At the age of three, I was sitting on the sun-baked steps of the *stoep* when a long-horned cow crashed over the hedge from the street, galloped past me with heaving flanks and thudding hooves and disappeared through the gate. I don't think I was frightened. I must have been trusting enough of the world and its ways to think that this kind of thing was normal, and I casually mentioned it to my mother when she got home from school. She didn't believe me until I led her out and showed her the hoof prints a few inches from where I'd been sitting. She was even more contrite when the Bulawayo *Chronicle* the following day carried the story of stampede mayhem on Abercorn Street.

The tin tub in the garden features again in the memories when I decided to add some excitement to the daily splashing about by building a diving board. Rootling in the garage, I found a couple of oil drums and a plank with which I constructed a diving board long and high enough to give a good run and a satisfying plunge. Unsurprisingly, it collapsed on the first attempt. Instead of the cool splash I'd been expecting, all I felt was the sickening jolt of a broken wrist as I hit the ground.

My best friend, Micky, had broken his own wrist a few days earlier. I don't remember how he did it, but I do recall being impressed by his gleaming plaster and massive, triangular sling. There was an injury to inspire respect. Now I, too, had a plaster, but was mortified when all I got was a pitiful length of ribbon – I think the torn edge of a sheet – to keep my wrist attached to my neck. I pleaded for a sling like Micky's, but my mother refused to go back to the clinic to ask for an upgrade.

Micky was with me on my first day of school at Baines Kindergarten, named, as most schools were, after one of Rhodesia's Victorian pioneers. I was hugely proud of my crisp, new uniform, as is clear from the beaming face in my first-day-of-school photograph. It consisted of khaki shorts and shirt, an elasticated belt with an S-shaped snake buckle, a striped school tie held in place with a very grown-up clip and, bizarrely for a five-year-old, a trilby hat. The effect was like a walking mushroom – or two walking mushrooms, as Micky and I set off for school together. (To my parents' embarrassment, I insisted on wearing the hat when we came back to England the following year, and recall a Birmingham bus driver whipping it off my head, sticking it on at a jaunty angle and gurning at the other passengers. *What's so funny?* I thought in my odd, colonial way. *Haven't you seen a school hat?*)

The final item of uniform was the green school blazer. Micky had one, naturally, but my mother knew we'd be back in England on leave within the year and was reluctant to spend the money. This is where Elsie stepped in. Seeing my disappointment, she took up my case: 'Please, madam, let him have a blazer like his friend.' My mother compromised. Instead of the official blazer, she found something near enough (and cheap) in Hassamal's emporium down at the Indian end of town and sewed on a Baines School badge. I don't remember anyone objecting, so it must have been near enough.

Somewhere in all of this, there's a memory of standing at the side of a road with other small children, all of us in crisp, Sunday best, knees and faces scrubbed, hair slicked down and hands clutching Union Flags on sticks. Then excited cheers and lots of waving as a large, black car rolled by with someone very important inside. I now know it was the Queen Mother on her visit to Bulawayo in July 1957. She must have liked Rhodesia as she'd been before in 1953, just after the Queen's Coronation, to help mark the centenary of the birth of Cecil Rhodes. On that occasion she'd brought Princess Margaret with her, supposedly to distract her from her doomed romance with Group Captain Townsend. When they arrived in Bulawayo, my parents left their nine-month-old with Elsie and went to the garden party organised by the mayor in honour of the royal visitors. Earlier in the tour, Bulawayo's black citizens had entertained them with tribal music and dancing. In the spirit of the times, the garden party was whites only.

2

Premonitions of War

After a year's leave in England, we returned to Rhodesia in 1960 – now with the addition of my second sister, Sheila. Moving from Ndebele-speaking Matabeleland to the Shona-speaking end of the country, the first stop for my parents was Shona language school at Nyakatsapa Mission in the Eastern Highlands near the border with Mozambique. My memories are of mist-covered, wattle-forested mountains, manila envelopes delivering each week's correspondence course for home schooling and meeting the family who became my parents' closest friends and colleagues.

The Reverend David and Marjorie Kynaston were fresh out from Manchester and also learning Shona before taking up a Methodist Church appointment. Their son, Len, was slightly older than me and his sister, Brenda, a little younger. Dad and David found common cause as smokers – Dad with his pipe, David a cigarette smoker. Much time was spent looking for places to indulge without being caught by the formidable American lady-principal who regarded smoking as only slightly less evil than native witchcraft. For some reason, Len was spared the correspondence course. His parents did what you'd do in

Manchester and enrolled him in the local school. So at eight years old, he found himself the only white kid at Shona-speaking Nyakatsapa Primary. It didn't worry Len – nor the school, apparently – but it horrified the education authorities when they found out. White children were not permitted to go to black schools and after three weeks Len was made to leave – possibly the only child in colonial Rhodesia ever to be expelled from school for being white.

Shona school over, we moved to the capital, Salisbury, and the Methodist Church manse in Belvedere. The names of Salisbury's white suburbs – Belvedere, Avondale, Mabelreign, Greendale – now seem oddly displaced as though the city's late-Victorian founders, settling in the land of the kudu and the crocodile, had tried to replicate the English Home Counties. At the time, though, it was where we lived and this pastiche of England in the African bush didn't seem incongruous. Nor was it remarkable that Africans lived in tightly packed townships with names like Budiriro, Mufakose, Kuwadzana and – one that stoked particular anxiety – Harare. Before it gave its name to the capital and was relabelled Mbare, Harare was just another Salisbury township and somewhat prone to rioting. If you saw trucks full of police or reservists screaming through the suburbs, it was usually to Harare to quell unrest. But no one ever went to Harare, so we didn't think too much about it.

I say no one, meaning no one white, but that's not quite true. The churches maintained links across the divide to the point where some of the ladies from the all-white Trinity Church where Dad was minister started giving European-style cookery lessons at black Methodists' homes in Harare. And these weren't domestic servants wanting to be able to cook to the satisfaction of madam and the *baas*, they were upwardly mobile Harare residents looking for a taste of the white lifestyle. And why not? My mother was one of the group that drove to the township once a fortnight, struggling to turn lumps of trek ox into something resembling boeuf bourguignon or traditional roast with all the trimmings.

Driving home one night, she and her passengers found themselves surrounded by a crowd of Harare kids throwing stones. In the confusion it wasn't clear who or what was the target, but they were forced to stop. Before they knew it, a truck bristling with armed police pulled in behind and another appeared in front. A white officer bellowed at Mum to stay close and the two trucks escorted this inconvenient carload of church ladies to safety. My mother explained later that she wasn't frightened *of* the kids, more *for* the kids if they got too provocative and the police responded with force. If reported at all, the riot was possibly a couple of lines in the next day's *Rhodesia Herald*. No whites were injured, after all.

The Belvedere manse, a long, low, white-painted bungalow, occupied a dusty plot on the corner of Princes Road and Snowdon Road with a hessian-coloured lawn, a broken-down iron gate and a circular dirt drive bordered by whitewashed rocks and verdant granadilla plants. Drawn up under the jacaranda trees would be a white, bench-seated, Mk II Ford Zephyr with fins and chrome grille – the car Dad used and which I always thought was pretty classy for a minister, certainly an improvement on the Bulawayo Chevy – and the dumpy, brown Ford Prefect that was Mum's. Separate from the house but linked by an open brickwork wall was the concrete *kaya* for the use of the servant. This was built to a standard Rhodesian design with one bedroom, a toilet (the so-called *piccanin kaya* or PK) and a fireplace for cooking. Not that it was ever occupied. My parents thought it demeaning to ask anyone to live there, so, unusually for a white family in Salisbury, we got by with neither housemaid nor gardener on the premises. That might have been the first hint that my missionary parents did not entirely go along with the prevailing culture.

The lack of an on-site servant had its advantages because the empty *kaya* made a perfect base for playing Cowboys and Indians with Harry, Glynn, Ivan and a horde of other kids from Snowdon Road and the streets off. We fought with cap guns and home-made bows and arrows (hours were spent trying to find the perfect bow stick and tying and retying the string for maximum tension) and the *kaya* wall provided a great defensive position for whichever side had possession. Or if it wasn't Cowboys and Indians, we raided Dad's garage for planks and nailed up a succession of lopsided platforms in the branches of the wide-spreading msasa tree that stood on the plot between the *kaya* and Snowdon Road. When we'd had enough of fighting and construction, we cycled down Montgomery Avenue to spend our pocket money *tickies* on fizzy drinks and ice lollies from the local garage.

A highlight of the week was after school on a Thursday when I pedalled beyond the garage to the Belvedere shops and spent ninepence (three whole *tickies* from my shillinga-week pocket money) on *The Valiant*. It was three weeks out of date by the time it reached Salisbury, but Captain Hurricane and The Steel Claw were no less thrilling for that – Captain Hurricane, in particular, for his ability to take out five Germans with one sweep of his fist (they conveniently stood in an arc and said '*Himmel!*' or '*Donner und Blitzen!*' as the fist made contact). The feeling of let-down when I got to the back page and had to wait a week for the next issue remains with me still.

One blistering afternoon when the heat seemed to drop from the sky under its own leaden weight, Harry, Glynn, Ivan and I decided for no particular reason to build a fire in the clearing under the msasa tree.

'I know,' said Glynn as the sticks began to crackle and we wondered what to do next. 'Let's cook some potatoes.'

'Hey, *lekker*, man. Let's do it.'

I collected four potatoes from the kitchen and we poked them into the hot centre of the fire. None of us had any idea how long potatoes took to bake, but we prodded them optimistically until they turned sooty. Glynn then spoke again.

'Got any cold drinks?'

'Don't think so,' I said.

'We got stacks in the fridge at our house,' said Harry.

We agreed that a cold drink would be just the thing to wash down our feast. The question then was whether to bring the drinks to the potatoes or vice versa. Harry suggested the latter and found an empty cornflakes box. We scooped the embers and potatoes into the box and pushed through the shoulder-high grass towards Snowdon Road. Then Harry yelped as a tongue of flame scorched his fingers. He and Ivan let go the box. It disintegrated into an orange ball and the flames roared up the bleached, dry grass stems. We ran like startled animals, racing for open ground. We must have found some bamboo branches, because we then ventured back and tried flapping at the flames. But there wasn't much that four small boys could do and the fire by now was crackling towards the road. Cars pulled up and stopped. People got out and joined the beating with branches and bits of sacking. Appalled, but also secretly thrilled, we stood and watched what we could no longer control.

Eventually, the fire was either beaten out or ran out of grass to consume. Did we own up? I honestly can't remember.

School was Selborne-Routledge Primary, a short cycle ride up Snowdon Road and named, like Baines, after early explorers. Built barracks-style with classrooms in parallel rows, it educated the local white children to a surprisingly high standard – or maybe that's not so surprising, given that for every pound spent on white education, the government spent pennies educating black children. How much education did you need to be a garden boy or to count cattle on a farm?

We sat at neat rows of double desks, the girls in pink-and-white gingham and we boys in much the same khaki uniform I'd worn at Baines. (As I turn up the old photos, I see we looked alarmingly like Hitler Youth.) Instead of the Baines trilbies, however, we had felt caps emblazoned with the school crest – a complex design involving ox wagons, something resembling a pair of cheese graters (the cheese graters of learning?) and the school motto: *Forward together*.

With a few exceptions like South African Mr Van Der Byl, most of the teachers at Selborne-Routledge were British expats, eager to bring an international point of view to our narrow, colonial minds. In one of those barracks classrooms, I once listened to our Standard Six teacher, Mrs Mackay, debating with my good friend Stephen the status of the groundsman watering the lawn on the other side of the open window.

'Do you not understand, Stephen? He's a human being like you and me.'

Stephen attempted to get his head around this concept but it proved too much. 'You mean the *munt*?'

'That's not a word I want to hear, Stephen.'

'OK, the *kaffir*. The boy. No, he's not a human, Miss, he's a animal. He's quite intelligent, but he's a animal.'

Repellent as it sounds today, the view was not unusual in 1960s Rhodesia. Even though many of us had had more contact with black nannies than with our parents as we'd grown up, the urban Rhodesian eight- or nine-year-old had somehow learned to be repulsed by black skin.

'Watch it,' I once heard someone say at the school drinking fountain. 'I saw a *kaffir* using that.'

'Agh, sis! You swear?'

'*Ja*, man.'

'Yugh. Where we supposed to drink, then?'

The attitude must have been instilled from an early age. Once at a children's party as the black servant stood by in his starched white uniform, a friend's mother remarked that she didn't mind giving *munts* a lift in the car sometimes, but not for too long. "Cos after a while they start to smell, don't you find?' Like a cow, the black man in your kitchen or watering your lawn did not have feelings. If you did have to transport your blacks, the least unpleasant way to do it was in the back of a pick-up.

I must have known that something here was wrong, but I don't recall being perturbed by it until I looked back later and understood the racism for what it was. Back then, I accepted that my friends thought one thing, my parents thought differently and that's the way things were. If anything, the problem was my parents' oddness in standing out against the culture. When you're eight, nine and ten, you want to fit in and their un-Rhodesianness was sometimes perplexing. Their English accents aside, they didn't even talk like other people's parents. To them, an African adult male was a man, not a boy. Black people were Africans, not *kaffirs*. It was all somewhat disorientating.

Or it would have been if I'd thought about it much. When I joined the First Salisbury Boys' Brigade and the leader instructed us to 'get your boy to polish your cap badge', his assumption that we kids each had a personal valet didn't seem incongruous. For children who didn't know the word 'racism', there were more important things to worry about – like winning back the marbles you'd lost at break time or learning to wrap your swimming cozzie so tightly in your towel you could play rugby with it all the way to the pool without it coming undone.

Along with the blacks, the other object of revulsion in the Selborne-Routledge playground was English pommies. Poms said 'milk' with a tight 'i' instead of the lazy

Rhodesian 'moolk'. And 'deown' instead of 'darn', as in 'Darn Sarth', also known as Sarth Efrica. Poms had strawberries and cream complexions and effeminate, Beatles-style hair, not the macho Rhodesian crew cut that the rest of us sported. Worse, they wore appalling pommy shorts that flapped around the knees whereas true, tough Rhodesian guys wore their shorts so short the points of the pockets peeped out below the hem.

Mrs Mackay once introduced a plump, rosy-faced new boy from England. His name was Jeremy, pronounced Jewemy. That alone was enough to set off splutters around the classroom. 'What a pom!' When he spoke like a lisping English toff, the mirth was audible. He seemed oblivious to the shame. A little later I heard Stephen (him again) attempting to explain the differences between poms and local boys: 'Us Rhodeezhans, we tough, you hya? Not like you English. Jew understand?' Jeremy seemed happy to agree.

I don't recall what happened to Jeremy: coward that I was, I probably kept my distance to avoid taint by association. Maybe he came back to England: I can imagine him becoming a Surrey stockbroker. Or conceivably, he and his immigrant family embraced the life, became more Rhodesian than the Rhodesians and propped up the regime to the last as many incomers did.

Selborne-Routledge combined British schooling as it might have been in the 1950s with lessons reinforcing our self-perception as intrepid pioneers. We studied European cavemen and medieval castles, and Mrs Mackay's class performance at the end-of-year concert was a medley of Scottish folk songs. In flat Rhodesian accents, we sang about skipping gaily over the hills for red-cheeked Mairi's wedding, all the while twirling our tartans and doing pointy kicks. Most of the class sang, anyway. Mrs Mackay once told me my face was lovely, but please would I not sing on the high notes – one of those throw-away teacher's comments that can still sting fifty years later.

Nearer to home, we learned about the Pioneer Column and the Matabele War and King Lobengula whose capital near Bulawayo meant *Place of Slaughter*. Our hero was Major Allan Wilson, our very own General Custer, whose Shangani Patrol died gallantly at the hands of the savage Matabele in 1893, allegedly singing 'God Save the Queen' as they were speared. As for Zimbabwe Ruins down near Fort Victoria, there was no way these could have been built by the primitive Shona whose mud and thatch *kraals* we used to glimpse through the scrub and flying dust as we drove out of town for picnics at Lake McIlwaine. Although it was a mystery who the builders were (theories ranged from the Portuguese and the Arabs to descendants of the Queen of Sheba), they were clearly a 'great civilisation' as opposed to 'these people'.

'These people' was shorthand for the feckless blacks, usually said in a tone of exasperation and indulgence that you might adopt for children. 'Hey, mind that boy,' said my driving instructor when I later came to have lessons and an elderly African on a bike wobbled out in front of me. 'Agh, these people, hey? We'll never understand them.'

The counterpoint to 'Mairi's Wedding' was Jack Watson's 'We Who Follow' which won a competition to become the national song. It spoke of pioneers marching into the wilderness to found a country and bequeathing it to us who followed. Mrs Mackay would thump out the tune on the school piano while we kids sang along, lustily vowing to guard and cherish our Rhodesian homeland. To our young minds, the song fed the narrative that this was our country, carved from the bush by our fathers and grandfathers who in the process had brought the benefits of civilisation to mud-hut savages. Schools, roads, hospitals, running water, beer halls... what was there for the natives not to be grateful for? We thought it extraordinary they persisted in eating that disgusting, traditional mealie-meal porridge called *sadza* when so much else was available – but that was the natives for you. As we dimly became aware of unrest in the townships in the early 1960s, it was unthinkable we'd ever hand Rhodesia to people whose own fathers and grandfathers had been barefoot goatherds.

Did we children know back then that cherishing the homeland would one day mean war? I doubt it, though the signs were there. From the Belvedere manse on Saturday afternoons, we could hear the cadet force at Prince Edward High School going through its drills with commands and marching tunes wafting over from the playing fields. Even if rarely voiced in that comfortable decade before the war got under way, there must have been a premonition that one day we'd have to defend our African paradise against the black hordes. So the Prince Edward band pomp-pomped away on a Saturday afternoon and we sang along as we played at cowboys in the *kaya*, oblivious to the real significance of what was going on:

I'm in the army now.
I learned to moolk a cow.
The cow let off and I took off.
I'm in the air force now.

To such accompaniment, Prince Edward's finest were toughened up for the coming conflict. And the cult of the tough Rhodesian existed even in primary school. Stephen's lecture to Jeremy the Pom was mainstream thinking among the bigger kids and even some of the staff. While matronly Mrs Mackay taught us Scottish country dancing in the school hall, Mr Van Der Byl could always be relied on to give permission if you wanted to beat up a foe during break time. The rule was that both of you had to apply.

'Please, Sir, Mr Van Der Byl, Sir, can me and Jeffrey go out with the gloves?'

'*Ja*, sure. I'll book you in.'

The news would spread. At break time on the appointed day, we'd abandon the games of marbles and British Bulldog and cluster round the square of concrete by the back gate that served as a boxing ring. There we'd cheer as Norman and Jeffrey or Will and Dirk thumped each other for ten minutes. Sometimes there was blood. Once, I either challenged or was challenged and underwent a pummelling. As something of a swot in class and often ribbed for my knock knees (a constant dilemma there: go for tough-guy micro-shorts and expose them, or wear something pommy style and make them less obvious), I must have thought a bloody nose would be worth it for some playground credibility.

In the Salisbury school holidays, a treat for my sisters and me was to stay at Chibero Mission near the small farming settlement of Norton. This was the country posting where the Kynastons had ended up after language school at Nyakatsapa, unlike us Joneses who always lived in town. As one who never lost his light Manchester accent and was more at home playing comic songs on the piano than taming the bush, the Reverend David Kynaston made an incongruous frontiersman. But he took to it, pulling teeth as required after church on Sunday and on one occasion shooting a wounded leopard that was threatening local *kraals*. Who else would do it, if not *Mufundisi*? And when the gardener's brother wanted to strike a blow for the liberation struggle, which white home should he choose to petrol bomb but that of the Kynastons? As he said at his trial, it was the only one within reach.

For the liberally minded Kynastons, it must have been troubling when their daughter, Brenda, became best friends at Norton School with the daughter of 'Boss' Lilford, the millionaire rancher and the money behind Ian Smith's racist Rhodesian Front party. At the age of ten, Brenda would spend weekends at the Lilford ranch, riding horses and skimming the veldt in light aircraft. Each time, according to her brother Len, her parents worried at the views she might be absorbing on the place of Africans in society. Tellingly, Lilford was later murdered on his ranch by a gang of assailants.

Since his aborted career at Nyakatsapa Primary, Len, like his sister, was now experiencing school life at the die-hard end of the political spectrum, in Salisbury as a Prince Edward boarder. His fellow boarders were mainly the sons of tobacco farmers whose families had carved their considerable wealth from the bush and whose way of life depended on cheap, plentiful black labour. This cohort had the greatest stake in preserving white rule and became the mainstay of the cadet force. Hardness was all at Prince Edward. Len talks of being beaten for a minor infringement, then beaten again when his father saw the bruises and complained to his house master. As a missionary kid and head chorister, once playing Mabel in a Prince Edward production of *Pirates of Penzance*, Len was not natural Prince Edward boarder material. On Sunday afternoons, he escaped and came to us at the Belvedere manse, grabbing a few hours' respite from the regime of beatings and character-hardening that had to be endured from Monday to Saturday.

For a town boy like me, Chibero was exciting for being country. The mission station residence was a tin-roofed, white-painted house with burglar bars and a *stoep*, set in a chicken-clucking yard and looking out on empty veldt – a landscape you might have called monotonous but which always spoke to me of adventures to be had beyond the rusty wire fence. On hot afternoons, Len and I would sometimes pick up Len's air guns and set off down the sandy track that led past the school and the thatched church and into the *bundu*, the empty grassland that stretched as far as you could see. We persuaded ourselves we were tracking guinea fowl or gazelle. In truth, the only tracks we ever spotted were the imprints of our own *tackies* as we trudged home empty-handed. Occasionally we'd fire off pellets at a crow on a telegraph wire, but the only harm we ever did was oblige it to flap disdainfully to a new perch.

Chickens were a different matter. When Marjorie Kynaston once happened to mention she needed a bird slaughtered for supper, Len and I selected our victim from the chicken run, loaded our weapons and opened fire. As its scrawny body filled with lead, the chicken launched itself at the fence, exploded through a gap in a cascade of feathers and somersaulted into the compost pit. We stopped firing, alarmed at what we'd done. This was messy, not the quick kill we'd expected. The chicken continued to flip and tumble in the pit until Patience the maid came out with a bread knife and sawed its head off. Supper that night, eaten as always by the dim light of hissing Tilley lamps, was more pellets than chicken.

After that we fired at targets drawn in crayon on sheets torn from a school exercise book and tied to the fence – except for the time we got bored and persuaded my sister, Christine, to stand with her legs apart to see if we could hit the target by shooting between them. Bedtime revealed a weal on the side of her neck, probably caused by a ricocheting pellet. Credit to Christine, she never snitched – though years later when she worked for British Airways and could nominate three family members for cut-price air fares, she chose my parents and my younger sister, Sheila. If that was punishment for shooting her, I guess it was deserved.

In the Kynastons, my parents found allies in trying to push back at Rhodesia's increasingly racist culture. The gestures were often small and must sometimes have felt futile. David and Marjorie initially resisted having a servant until one of the Methodist high-ups suggested that employing a housemaid would not only provide a wage but would raise the social standing of the girl in question and enhance her *lobola* – her future bride price – because she'd worked for a white *baas* and madam. So they relented. Later, someone told them they ought to have a small bell at the table to summon said girl. A bell was acquired, but Marjorie could never bring herself to ring it. Instead she would walk to the kitchen door and enquire politely, 'Patience, would you mind coming in?'

'Why doesn't madam use the bell?' demanded Patience.

Unspoken answer – because it's demeaning and I feel as if I'm surrendering to this racist culture if I use it. To Patience, it was what madam was supposed to do.

My parents, too, mounted quiet resistance and took a stubborn pleasure in being provocative. When an American Methodist minister – black, with a doctorate – came to stay, he asked my father to take him into town to buy a lens for his camera. Like my school friend, Stephen, struggling to comprehend that the gardener was human, the white lady shopkeeper wouldn't have it that the reverend doctor could speak for himself.

'What does he want?' she asked my father.

'Well, ask him.'

With some reluctance, she entered the uncomfortable zone of speaking to a black man as a customer wanting service rather than a servant to be given instructions. She was surprised at how much he knew about cameras. But even the American voice failed to persuade her that he was any different to the boy in her *kaya*.

Later, when a conference brought black and white clergy together at Salisbury's Trinity Church, Dad took the unprecedented step of arranging for the delegates to eat together. Ida Price – third-generation Rhodesian, congregation stalwart, her sun-weathered face as brown and wrinkled as a walnut – found out what was happening only when the African clergy started filtering into the church hall. She came to Dad in a fluster. 'Don't you think,' she whispered, 'that these blecks would be heppier if we just gave them *sadza* outside?'

Lulled by its cultural blindness and its sense that all was normal, white Rhodesia continued to entrench as the wind of change blew down through the rest of Africa.

3

The Citadel Crumbles

1964 and another departure on leave. This time, when my parents and sisters returned, I stayed behind at boarding school in England. This arrangement had been talked about for some time, so it never occurred to me to object. Not that I would have done. The parting was hard at the age of eleven, knowing I'd only be going home once a year in the English summer holidays, but the thought of living in two countries rather than one had a certain appeal. Britain, home of The Beatles and The Rolling Stones, was where things were happening in the mid-1960s while backwater Rhodesia didn't even get the latest Elvis until weeks after its UK release. I remember Dad pausing at the postbox in Salisbury and asking for my final OK before releasing the letter that accepted my school place in Bath. I said yes.

What I didn't realise at the time was my parents' prescience that had I gone to secondary school in Rhodesia, I'd probably have been called up to fight in Ian Smith's army. They could see the way the political wind was blowing.

For this their third tour, my parents returned to the original home in Bulawayo – the corrugated roof now a little more faded, the timber balustrades slightly more termite-chewed. And Elsie, who came with the house, was there again to greet them. This is where I returned every July for my six-week school holiday through the second half of the 1960s.

Forbidden from crossing black Africa at the height of apartheid, the South African Airways 707 that bore me home each year was obliged to take a detour down the west coast of Africa and to refuel at Luanda in friendly Portuguese Angola on its way to Salisbury. After economic sanctions were imposed on rebel Rhodesia, I usually took some item that the family couldn't buy any more. Most times it was Mars Bars which went in the fridge in Bulawayo and were carved into thin slices to make them last. Returning to school at the end of the holidays, I'd fill my case with cheap Rhodesian cigarettes for selling to my smoker friends. A few shillings profit at the start of term was one of the perks of the two-country arrangement.

One disadvantage was the pom factor. I worried that each school year in England was turning me into another Jeremy. The accent could be adjusted, the hair could be crew cut and the facial tan was usually passable at the end of an English summer term. The real problem was the paper-white knees which would scream 'Pommy!' as soon as I stepped outside the garden gate. So every holiday, freshly arrived from England, I'd spend the first few days in a deckchair in the back yard, pointing my knees at the sun to try to undo the damage of ten months encased in long school trousers. Only when the dumpling white had pinked and then browned could I re-enter Rhodesian youth society with any credibility.

These things are important when you're thirteen.

Within this society, at least the narrow segment that I knew, Africans remained alien and unknowable – a presence on the periphery of our lives, sometimes benign, as with our nannies, but more often to be feared. Sure, there were gardeners and housemaids who lived and moved among us, but they only ever went by their first names with no sense, to us, of a life beyond their role as servants. The lack of curiosity among my circle of friends was almost total. Though it was good to see Elsie again, I was ignorant of her surname until long afterwards. She didn't live in our *kaya*, but disappeared every afternoon to... where? Somewhere in the black townships, but which one and how far away it was and how she got there and what time she had to get up in the mornings to reach our house on Abercorn Street were questions I never thought to ask. Elsie was just there – cleaning, polishing, sweeping, cooking and making tea between the hours of seven and two, like thousands of other servants in the white suburbs.

I speak for myself here, but I suspect my parents knew more of Elsie's backstory. When she needed medical treatment on one occasion, my mother signed as her employer to classify her as 'Coloured', not 'Black', so she qualified for the better-resourced, mixed-race hospital rather than the one for Africans. Her skin tone just about made it credible, so why not?

Had we wanted to employ more servants, we could easily have done so. In both Salisbury and Bulawayo, we were constantly opening the back door to men in worn-thin suits who would simply announce, 'I want-y wek.' The demeanour was nearly always resigned, expecting rejection at best or the dogs at worst. (Yes, dogs were sometimes trained to see off black people who ventured onto the property.) Sometimes the caller would dig into a pocket and produce a fragile piece of paper, brittle on the folds, stained from much handling, and present it for inspection. It typically read: 'Sixpence is a reliable boy and can be trusted for gardening and other duties.' Underneath would be the signature of a former white madam who had no further use for his services.

A newspaper advertisement at the time summed up the social and racial hierarchy. It concerned a motorised lawnmower. On the drive in the background, two cars – one large and flashy, the other slightly more modest. In the foreground, a grinning, black gardener sitting proudly astride the lawnmower in question, a corner of the *kaya* visible at the side. The caption: 'His. Hers. Mine.'

The one time our Bulawayo *kaya* was used was to house Kennedy, a star pupil at Mzilikazi High School where my mother taught science. Kennedy was the son of a domestic servant and for that reason had been able to live with his father and so qualify to go to secondary school in town. But then his father lost his job and had to go back to his rural home. To keep Kennedy in education, my mother swept out the *kaya* and invited him to live there.

'If I'd had the courage of my convictions,' she said later, 'I'd have given him a spare room in the house. But that would have broken so many taboos.'

I met Kennedy just once as I was cleaning out the family hamster cage in the yard where I used to brown my knees. Kennedy silently materialised at my shoulder. I knew of his existence and I'd seen him through the burglar-barred windows of the house, coming and going across the yard. But I never expected to meet him, still less have to talk to him. He smiled and asked me what I was doing. I guess he was lonely. I shrugged him off and finished the job as quickly as I could so I could escape into the house.

Was it embarrassment at having to make conversation with a black boy of my own age? Or the culture that said it didn't matter how I reacted because he was only an African? Either way, I treated him shamefully. Looking back now at the fourteen-year-old hunched sullenly over the hamster cage, I regret having added one more brick to the wall of hostility between the races.

Kennedy later got a high-tech job in the Gulf States and once visited my parents after their return to England. This time, they gave him a bed in the house.

On the move to Bulawayo in 1965, Dad transferred from a white circuit of the Methodist Church to a rural black circuit. That meant that most Sundays he was out in his little Ford Anglia (a come-down from the Salisbury Zephyr), rattling over corrugated dirt roads to lead services in places with evocative Ndebele names like Mzinyati and Nyamandhlovu. Back in town, Mum, Christine and Sheila would walk to church down Abercorn Street and Main Street, thoroughfares broad enough to turn an ox wagon and a full span of oxen as Cecil Rhodes had decreed they should be. I would go, too, when I was home, usually making some excuse to cycle to avoid the teenage cringe of parading to church in full public view. The route took us down jacaranda-lined avenues, past colonial Meikles Hotel and under the statue of Rhodes himself, swaggering atop his plinth and gazing north as he contemplated British rule from Cape Town to Cairo. From there it was a short step to the all-white Main Street Methodist Church – a red-brick, tin-roofed edifice with gothic arches street-side and a tall pulpit and polished pews inside.

Sunday services were a slice of England from the Ladybird books – the men in 1950s suits with Brylcreemed hair and Clark Gable moustaches; ladies in floral crimplene and Sunday hats, hymnbook in white-gloved hand. And in the bank of pews under the organ pipes, facing the congregation, the boarders of Evelyn Girls' School – farmers' daughters, mainly – who piled noisily in at the last minute in their blazers and straw boaters. At least sermon time could be spent trying to decide which was the prettiest.

One of Dad's African church members said to him once: 'What would happen if I put on a clean shirt, and came with you to Main Street?'

'Let's try it,' said Dad.

On one of the Sundays when he wasn't out in the country, Dad accompanied Remington Dube to the front door of Bulawayo Main Street. In some alarm, the steward issuing the hymnbooks put a hand on Dad's shoulder.

'Is he...' he whispered, glancing furtively at the black face. 'Is he coming in here?'

'Well, I think so,' said Dad.

'For the service?'

'Uh-huh.'

'Well, could I ask you, please, to take him down to the empty pews at the side? We don't want him upsetting people.'

Shades of Ida ('Let them eat *sadza*') Price. That said, the churches often took the lead in challenging the racist government and behind the scenes there was inter-racial bridge-building going on that I knew nothing about. So I can't be too sniffy about Main Street. Or maybe just a bit.

Churchgoers or not, Rhodesia's whites were conventionally Christian, much as in the southern states of the USA, which you could see as a cultural parallel. This caused problems when Gibson Kumalo, the choirmaster at one of Dad's African churches, found himself in jail in Bulawayo for some mix-up in his paperwork at the border with Zambia. Dad went to visit him and found him guarded by a white prison officer. Before he left, he suggested they pray together. The guard's face twitched with conflicting emotions. If praying was to be done, it was only right that he as a good Christian should join in. But praying with a black man? Rhodesia's prison officer training was no doubt thorough, but it didn't seem to have covered this particular scenario.

Through the 1960s, Rhodesia's whites retreated further into the *laager* at every election. In 1962, the newly formed Rhodesian Front of Ian Smith and Winston Field, bankrolled by the previously mentioned 'Boss' Lilford, defeated Edgar Whitehead's more moderate United Federal Party. In 1964, Smith ousted Field to become the first Rhodesian-born Prime Minister – a man, in other words, with nowhere else to go if white rule crumbled.

From then on, fear of black takeover became the dominant political theme.

Armistice Day 1965 brought the Unilateral Declaration of Independence (UDI) which slammed the door on black majority rule and pitted Rhodesia against the world. 'We are a courageous people and history has cast us in a heroic role,' intoned Prime Minister Smith on the radio after signing the Declaration beneath a portrait of the Queen. 'We have struck a blow for the preservation of justice, civilisation and Christianity.'[1]

The *Rhodesia Herald* of 12th November 1965 led, naturally, with *UDI: RHODESIA GOES IT ALONE* and carried white oblongs where government censors had been at work. Otherwise, life continued unruffled. The same issue carried advertisements for Castle lager, Rothmans cigarettes, the new Ford Taunus and other appurtenances of the good life. Salisbury's crew-cut, teenage band, The Astronauts, promised to make your *braaivleis* go with a swing. On the letters page, one writer rejoiced at the calibre of recent English immigrants ('I should like to welcome all new Rhodesians to this wonderful country of ours') while another made the case that Salisbury women (I think he meant white ones) were prettier than those in Europe. In other news, a Rhodesian team had won an ocean fishing contest in Mozambique and an unnamed African woman had been killed in a collision with a car in Mufakose township.

An advertisement for a career as an army officer was the sole hint of any conflict to come.

---

[1] The *Rhodesia Herald*, 12th November 1965.

Although serious hostilities didn't begin until 1972, there was low-level activity through the late 1960s. During my post-UDI school holidays, the Bulawayo *Chronicle* occasionally reported bands of terrorists, or 'terrs', coming over from Zambia. Regarded as little more than poorly armed garden boys, they'd be swiftly seen off by our brave Rhodesian troopies whose tally of terrorist dead or 'floppies' was closely tracked and cause for celebration. In those early stages of the war, the government line was that plucky Rhodesia could counter any threat emanating from the so-called 'chaos to the north of us' – shorthand for those comically inept, black-ruled regimes that were daring to challenge white supremacy south of the Zambezi.

What we faced, we were told, was Communist-inspired terrorism intent on destroying Christian values and Western civilisation. The Rhodesia we were gearing up to defend was Britain as it once had been in a golden age loosely located in the nineteenth or early twentieth century before it lost its moral fibre. The nation that had given birth to Major Allan Wilson of the Shangani Patrol could now produce no better than his risible namesake, Prime Minister Harold Wilson. Britain had tragically degenerated while Rhodesia, alone, preserved the ideals of decency, hard work and fair play exemplified by Edwardian England.

For all Rhodesia's sense of going it alone, we were not without friends. Mozambique was on our side until the Portuguese quit in 1975 and handed over to black rule, triggering a new and more intense phase of the war. We also had South Africa. Our friends Darn Sarth kept the petrol flowing as economic sanctions took effect and we repaid the favour with jaunty *Dankie Suid Afrika* stickers on our car bumpers.

The fighting, such as it was, remained remote. I only ever encountered one Rhodesian army roadblock as Dad was driving us out of town on his way to a conference for black clergy at Mzinyati Mission. Mum leaned cheerily out of the window and joshed with the white soldier, 'If I was a terrorist today, I'd be wearing a clerical collar.' From his blank stare and slowly revolving, gum-chewing jaws, I don't think he got the reference. Terrorists in the late 1960s were a minor hazard, on a par with lions or crocodiles if you ventured too far from civilisation. Local comedian Wrex Tarr used to entertain white audiences with a comic lament about a stupid 'terr' swatting away the tsetse flies and pining for a beer in the hot Zambezi Valley.

But even within the city limits, things were stirring. My mother, who cycled every day from Bulawayo's white suburbs to teach physics to black pupils at Mzilikazi High School, found one day that the green and white Rhodesian flag had disappeared from the flagpole. Nobody would say where it was. All that could be gleaned was that someone had threatened trouble if the school hoisted the white oppressor's flag. In time, my mother noticed a change of attitude among her students. Previously eager to be educated, many were now asking, 'What's the use? The whites will never hand over power. What recourse do we have?'

Dad's colleagues, too, began to voice support for the armed struggle. One such advocate was a young Methodist minister, the Reverend Canaan Banana, who had a habit of slipping away without warning – probably, Dad suspected, on political business. His agenda became clear when he allied himself with Robert Mugabe and became Zimbabwe's first President at independence. The Methodist Church also nurtured Joshua Nkomo whom Dad interviewed and formally approved as a lay preacher. Nkomo later headed the liberation movement as founder of ZAPU (Zimbabwe African People's Union). During the war he made common cause with Mugabe's ZANU (ditto, ditto, National Union), then suffered the fate of most of those presuming to challenge Comrade Bob. Shortly after independence, Mugabe branded him 'a cobra in the house'[2] and accused him of plotting. Nkomo fled the country and ZAPU was folded into ZANU to create ZANU-PF. Nkomo died in 1999.

But this is running ahead. Back in the 1960s, Ian Smith's government was reassuring us that the terrorists – murderous, certainly – were a futile force because the Africans understood the benefits of white rule. (As the common mantra ran, 'We've got the heppiest blecks in Efrica.') The Ministry of Information issued brochures with pictures of Kalashnikov-toting guerrillas looming over peaceful African villages. Inside were close-up photographs showing black people shot, beaten, burned and mutilated. The aim, we were told, was to expose the true nature of these 'liberators' and rubbish the claim that they represented an oppressed people.

With an eye on international opinion, the government issued ready-written air letters extolling Rhodesia as a land

---

[2] https://web.archive.org/web/20070107095908/http://www.swra dioafrica.com/pages/Nkomo_letter.htm (accessed 31st January 2019).

of sunshine, wide horizons and a standard of living unattainable in Harold Wilson's benighted, strike-ridden Britain. The idea was that we'd readdress these letters to our kith and kin abroad and so do our bit to reverse the white exodus which by then was gaining pace. With only a quarter of a million whites in a country of 5 million blacks, every incoming European bought more time for the regime. For a while, the Rhodesia Broadcasting Corporation's morning radio programme even welcomed new arrivals by name.

It was different along the borders where the war was real and the Rhodesian army was starting to take casualties, but to us townies with our comfortable, servant-equipped homes and lifestyles centred on the swimming pool and the *braai*, it seemed inconceivable that Rhodesia would fall. Hadn't Ian Smith promised there'd be no sell-out? On Bulawayo's colonnaded Main Street, the shop windows displayed portraits of Smith looking as heroic as his oddly immobile features would allow against backgrounds depicting his war service in the RAF. His expressionless face, reconstructed with skin grafts and plastic surgery after he crashed his Hurricane in 1943, reproached the perfidious British who were determined to bring Rhodesia to its knees while ignoring 'the chaos to the north of us'. More in sorrow than in anger, Mr Smith – Good Old Smithy – expressed Rhodesia's disappointment at our betrayal by the Christian West.

With the media under government control, the only alternative source of information was the BBC World Service. It was an evening ritual in our Bulawayo home to gather round the radio for the BBC news, starting with the sonorous announcement: 'This is London'. Then came the 'Lilliburlero' signature tune and the pips, washed over by waves of static that made London seem like the far side of the moon. In fact, the broadcasts came from a relay station in Francistown, a hundred miles away in Botswana. According to the government, the station was part of a plot by the British to eavesdrop on Rhodesia's communications and beam BBC propaganda into the country. Broadcasts were jammed from within Rhodesia, so listening to the news required dexterous twiddling of the dial to catch the words through the electronic quacking that filled the airwaves.

Still the white citadel stood. I have a yellowing copy of the Bulawayo *Chronicle*, bought during my last school holiday in the country. The date is 21st July 1969. Apart from the headlines – the moon landing and predictions of manned exploration of Mars by the 1980s – not much has changed since the UDI *Rhodesia Herald* of four years earlier. Rhodesia State Lotteries announces a £20,000 draw, there's a sale at Wyn's Boutique and Gwelo Sports Club has beaten Shabani at rugby. But there is one difference – advertisements for Glens Removals and no fewer than four airlines including TAP Portuguese Airways and BOAC. Signs, maybe, that the white exodus was becoming a stampede.

Two weeks before I left Bulawayo for the last time, Dad asked if I'd like to go with him to visit some of his furthest-flung churches and schools among the Batonga people near Lake Kariba. Eager for a final African adventure, I said yes. Setting off before dawn in the Ford Anglia, we headed north over the dry Bembezi riverbed, past the tin-shack *dorp* of Lupane and the Half Way Hotel (half way from Bulawayo to Victoria Falls) and turned east towards Binga on the shores of Lake Kariba. In three hours we'd passed one vehicle – a listing, smoke-spewing African bus, its roof piled high with rope-lashed bundles, bicycles, sticks of furniture and chickens in hooped cages.

Off the main road, the surface turned to Rhodesia's ubiquitous strips – double tarmac ribbons that required you, dangerously, to shunt one set of wheels onto the rough, gully-riven margin in order to pass or overtake. When the strips ran out, the road became dirt corrugations which each successive vehicle made more jarring for the next: by some law of dynamics, the ridges seemed to be spaced for maximum vibration. The technique here was to drive fast enough to skim the tops while fighting the judders to keep the car on track and avoid slewing to the side. Slowing down to keep the dust off any passing villagers was not an option.

Lowland baobabs started to dot the landscape like bulbous turnips. Children ran out from desiccated *kraals* and waved as we passed.

The bridge over the Gwaai gorge provided a hundred yards of welcome tarmac before the corrugations began again. We passed the Pioneer Trading Store and laid another coating of road dust on its rust-streaked Coca-Cola sign. Beyond the mining settlement of Kamativi, we pulled up at a barrier resting on an up-ended oil drum. The tsetse fly control. An old man in a ragged khaki uniform leaped from his chair, saluted toothily and crept round the car with a butterfly net. Satisfied we were clean, he saluted again and waved us through.

The road turned from corrugations to barely discernable track across the veldt. A Land Rover approached, driven by a white man. The badge on the door announced him as the Binga District Commissioner. He leaned out as he came alongside.

'Howzit? You going far?'

Dad explained we were travelling to see the Methodist minister at Siabuwa village.

'Reverend Sibanda? He's a good man. Does good work darn there.' He clunked into gear and moved on. 'You mind out for terrorists, hey?'

For a townie white kid, those three days hosted by Joseph Sibanda and his wife in their tiny, tin-roofed, dust-bowl house were the closest I had come to African village life. From a world bound in by the culture and mindset of one-twentieth of the country's population, this was an exposure to the other 95 per cent – territory into which I'd never ventured. On the first night, I stood mesmerised as the people of Siabuwa village mourned a child who had died two days earlier. To the beat of drums, eight or nine children kicked up the dust in the firelight and blew into cattle horns to emit a hypnotic, piping lament. The ceremony would go on all night until the burial in the morning. Nearly fifty years later, the shuffling bodies and flickering shadows came vividly back to life when I stood at another tribal funeral and again sensed a door being opened on to another world.

The next day, feeling fraudulently important, I drove with Dad and Joseph Sibanda to inspect Siabuwa School –

two or three thatched, mud-brick buildings with holes in the walls for doors and windows, and ragged children so tightly packed on their mud benches that those on the ends were constantly sliding off. Selborne-Routledge this was not. Only the top class had desks. Those with no books squatted outside and wrote in the sand.

From the school we returned to the village to pay our respects to the chief. His sun-scorched *kraal* at first seemed deserted except for a small knot of women dancing at the grave of the dead child. An old man emerged from a hut and informed us that Chief Siabuwa was drinking beer. A child was found and sent to fetch him. He arrived, cigarette dangling from his fingers and displeased because 'today there was no beer'. Someone produced some carved wooden stools and we sat with the chief and his men in the shade of one of the huts. With Joseph translating, Dad and the chief discussed the rainfall, the crops, how to get more parents to send their children to school and the need for a tin roof for one of the classrooms. When Dad estimated that a new roof would cost £100, the idea was politely laughed off.

I asked if the chief would mind a photograph. Without a word, he upped and disappeared into his hut. I wondered if I'd offended. A moment later he reappeared in his full regalia of office – a blue and crimson robe, a pith helmet and a brass crescent on a chain around his neck. Pinned to the robe was a badge with the word 'Tokyo' and a rising sun emblem.

'Where did you get that?' asked Dad.

The chief answered in a tone that suggested, *Where do you think?*

'He says Siabuwa store,' translated Joseph.

Bumping home along a tortuous dirt track in Joseph's Land Rover, we passed a barefoot, elderly man who was nearing home after walking the fifty miles from Binga. All he had in his hand was a Fanta bottle with a few precious drops of water. We gave him a lift for his last three miles. It turned out that this man had converted his entire village to Christianity. 'We have no church in our village,' he explained. 'The whole village is a church.' As we drove in, we gathered a plume of excited, scampering children, kicking up the dust behind us. The people of the village crowded round to shake hands African style – palm to palm, then grasping the thumb – and to offer the Chitonga greeting, '*Mwapona?*' How are you?

'We must pray,' said our hitchhiker.

An impromptu service took place under one of the village's few trees, Joseph Sibanda presiding.

On the morning of our departure, Joseph asked if we could give a lift to Binga to a girl who worked for the family. He told us two of the bridges up the road had been destroyed and the bus couldn't get through. At the height of the dry season, this was unlikely to be floods. I wondered with a nervous thrill if insurgents had been at work, but missed my chance to ask. I never did find out. In the end, Maria failed to turn up but we detoured to Binga anyway to tell the District Commissioner we were leaving his patch.

Here was a world and a way of life that I'd barely encountered except through car windows. The old man walking the highway apparently miles from any habitation; the children who ran out from *kraals* and waved as we passed; the women waiting at country bus stops, bundles on their heads and babies on their backs; the small boys pushing toy cars made from coat hanger wire along the side of the road – these and the other vignettes that characterised 'these people' and were part of the visual backdrop, so familiar they barely registered, had briefly become individuals. And just as this door had inched open, my Rhodesian life was over. A few days after our return, I and my duffel bag boarded the A R RHOD S A flight to Salisbury for the last time.

I wish now that I'd been more aware of what was happening during those brief 1960s school holidays. I wish I'd understood that this sunny, comfortable society, this preserved-in-aspic replica of a bygone, leisured England, was sliding towards the cliff edge and would soon be gone forever. Half in it, half out of it, I lived the life unthinkingly, as teenagers do, with little effort to retain the memories. Soon, memories were all there were.

My parents left Rhodesia soon afterwards as the opposing pressures became harder to bear. Distrusted by Africans because their faces were white and by white neighbours because they worked in black churches and had African colleagues, they found themselves shunned by both sides. When white friends were seeing their sons drafted into Ian Smith's army and black colleagues were sending their children to join the guerrillas, their sympathies were torn.

What was Dad to do? Come out in support of the armed struggle, or keep his head down and work towards a nonviolent resolution? But how was that to be done in the face of an intransigent government and a white population gearing up for war? Where to place his sympathies became more complicated when a mixed-race couple, friends who taught at Tegwani Methodist School near the Botswana border, were murdered in a raid. A random crime or another punishment meted out by terrorists on perceived 'sell-outs'? It was never clear, but tensions ratcheted higher. The possibility loomed that association with white missionaries was now turning my parents' black colleagues into targets for the guerrillas.

Eventually, the conflicts became impossible to reconcile and my parents decided the best way to advance majority rule was to leave. They'd already taken some of the Rhodesia out of me by sending me abroad to school and they felt that my sisters, too, deserved a different education to the one they were getting at Evelyn Girls' School. So in 1970, they pulled up stumps. The plot of land they'd bought for a retirement home on Bulawayo's Essexvale Road was sold for half what they'd paid for it and they started life again in England.

In the decade that followed, Ivan and Harry and Glynn and the rest of my Selborne-Routledge contemporaries were, I assume, called up to fight. For several years, Ian Smith's efficient little army – the so-called 'best counter-insurgency force in the world'[3] – held the line and exacted heavy losses on the enemy. The trouble was, there were more of them and they kept coming. Over time, the funerals of young reservists became more frequent: Prince Edward School alone lost more than fifty of its old boys including some, no doubt, whom I'd heard being drilled

[3] Peter Godwin and Ian Hancock, *Rhodesians Never Die* (London: Macmillan, 2013).

on those far-off Saturday afternoons. The war moved closer in and whites driving out of town could only do so in armed convoys. Month by month, more territory was ceded and the white *laager* was dismantled like that A R RHOD S A logo. The 'chicken run' of departing whites increased the military and economic burden on those left behind.

A final strategy for shoring up white rule was to share power with the compliant Bishop Abel Muzorewa and clumsily to rename the country Zimbabwe-Rhodesia. It failed, opening the way for the election victory of Comrade Robert Gabriel Mugabe in March 1980.

Such were the thoughts and memories swirling through my head in August 2008 as I emerged from the Comair flight to Victoria Falls and paused on the gangway to take stock. But I'd delayed long enough. Down on the tarmac, my family was waving to me to get on down. I hurried to join them and stepped into Zimbabwe for the first time in four decades.

4

A Message in Stained Glass

What was it that took me back? Curiosity, I guess. A middle-aged quest for a distant childhood, something to stir the memories of what had been. And wondering if it might still be possible to reconnect after all this time. Through all the years of getting on with life, that sunlit country south of the Zambezi had morphed in my mind into something shimmering and insubstantial, a far-off land as unreachable as a mirage. Sometimes I wondered if I'd ever even lived there. From time to time it hit the news – the heady days of early independence followed by the rumours of massacres in Matabeleland, the takeovers of white-owned farms and the crumbling of the economy – but from 6,000 miles away it felt like a foreign country and the thought of returning barely registered. Or if it did, it was something I'd get around to sometime. So while I was concentrating on other things, half a lifetime went by.

Then our eldest son, Alasdair, announced he was getting married to his university girlfriend, Abi. I knew that if I didn't bring Lynda and the boys back to Zimbabwe to show them where I'd come from, I'd have lost the chance. Just as I'd always wanted to know more about my own father (his tales of driving a charcoal-fired supplies lorry over mountain passes in wartime China had never got beyond a few tantalisingly incomplete anecdotes), I hoped in turn to fill in some family background for Alasdair, Gareth and Edward. And where to go to see Zimbabwe at its most spectacular? It had to be its number one tourist attraction, Victoria Falls.

It was a bad year to make that decision. The presidential election of 2008 was when Mugabe came tantalisingly close to being toppled. The first round in March had him out-voted by Morgan Tsvangirai of the MDC (Movement for Democratic Change), but the ruling ZANU-PF party refused to release the results. As weeks went by with no official announcement, rumours circulated in Harare that Mugabe was acknowledging defeat and would soon be gone after nearly thirty years in power. Such hopes were dashed. Conceding Tsvangirai's narrow lead and the need for a second-stage run-off to be held in June, ZANU-PF launched a campaign of terror and intimidation with the aim of smashing the MDC and rendering it impotent ahead of polling day. Hospitals filled with the victims of beatings and 're-education'. Rather than see more of his supporters tortured and killed, Tsvangirai pulled out and returned the presidency to the old man.

One day in April, with the violence at full spate in far-off Zimbabwe, I spent a morning hillwalking in the Yorkshire Dales. My hike took me through the high countryside of Langstrothdale, up the valley from Kettlewell. It was a cold spring day with a buffeting Yorkshire wind harrying the clouds across an ice-blue sky and ruffling the coats of the new season's lambs. But I scarcely noticed the landscape for the churning in my mind. The holiday to the old homeland was now booked. But such was the post-election turmoil, the British Foreign Office was warning tourists not to travel to Zimbabwe. As I trudged, I wondered if this back-to-the-roots idea was such a good one. Maybe I should cancel and take the family to somewhere safe and sensible, like Spain. I knew, of course, that my anxieties were nothing compared to the suffering in election-weary Zimbabwe and I told myself not to be so timorous. Still, though, I couldn't shake off my indecision. The question clouded my thoughts: *To go or not to go?*

I descended the track to the hamlet of Hubberholme where the twelfth-century church of St Michael and All Saints sits by the tumbling River Wharfe. I turned aside through the daffodils bobbing in the churchyard, walked up to the gnarled porch and clicked open the door. As I did so, my eye was caught by a laminated, A4 sheet of paper, freshly drawing-pinned to the woodwork. It carried a computer-printed verse from John's Gospel. I knew it well – the words of Christ to His disciples at the Last Supper: 'Peace I leave with you; my peace I give you … Do not let your hearts be troubled and do not be afraid' (John 14:27).

I stepped inside. The low-roofed interior was heavy with the atmosphere of eight centuries of prayer, the air almost palpably thicker. The same text on another A4 sheet was pinned behind the font as if drawing me further in. I picked up a mildewed information sheet and started reading in the dense, thrumming silence. J B Priestley liked it here, apparently: his ashes were scattered in the churchyard. And on the north wall, so the sheet informed me, was a marble plaque that would repay attention. I walked over for a look. It turned out to be in memory of George Hobson, a Victorian engineer whose claim to fame was designing the Victoria Falls Bridge across the Zambezi gorge. Perusing the Hobson family window alongside, I noticed with a start of surprise a leaded pane the size of my palm with an image of the bridge itself – a postcard from Victoria Falls in stained glass. The traditional postcard greeting flashed into my mind: *Wish you were here.*

Not what I'd expected to find in a Yorkshire country church – and what you make of the incident will depend, I suppose, on what you believe. For me it swung the decision. The anxiety dissipated like weights dropping from my shoulders and the holiday went ahead.

With a nod to the fluttering Zimbabwe Bird, I followed my family across the tarmac to the immigration hall. There we joined the queue of tourists waiting to give up fifty-five US dollars each for entry visas (the British ones, anyway: other nationalities untainted by colonial misdeeds paid less). Next came the scrummage around the baggage bay where the cases were hurled in from the runway apron. Finally, we emerged onto the airport verandah where a dozen Matabele warriors in leopard skins whooped and pounded the floor to welcome us in.

The fifteen-kilometre minibus drive to Victoria Falls Town through scrub woodland began to reveal some of the contrasts of Robert Mugabe's Zimbabwe. Roadside hoardings advertised whitewater rafting and helicopter trips above the Falls for those who could afford them. The road itself, however, was almost empty of vehicles. That's not to say it was deserted. Like a Lowry stick-man painting transplanted to Africa, the verges teemed with people on the move – boxes and baskets on heads, babies on backs – all walking the unhurried African walk that knows it will get there if one foot keeps being placed in front of the other. Leaning my head against the minibus window, I wondered what they thought of us – if the camera-snapping Chinese or European tourist was the new white *baas*, flashing by in motorised comfort while the mass of the population did what it had always done and walked.

Victoria Falls Town baked soporifically under its corrugated iron roofs, the shadows dense black beneath the verandahs, and the shops and houses shabbier than the trim little settlement I remembered from family holidays. Even in winter, as it was now, the afternoon heat of the Zambezi Valley drove residents and tourists into the shade and reduced the pace of life to a crawl. At the newly built Kingdom Hotel, designed like a Great Zimbabwe theme park, we parted from a gaggle of tourists from China. Then on to our own destination, the fabled Victoria Falls Hotel.

For nostalgic, colonial perfection, I don't believe there's anywhere to match it. I harboured childhood memories of tea on the terrace when, as poor missionaries, we'd stayed in the cheap, self-catering rondavels out in the town and ventured into the hotel for a treat. Now, as booked-in guests from England, we entered surroundings little changed since Edwardian times when visitors alighted at the railway platform a short step from the entrance and followed the porters into an African version of Claridge's. The mahogany and chintz and leather, the potted palms and slowly churning ceiling fans, the chunky brass and porcelain and the zinc shower heads as big as dinner plates, even the hotel logo with its politically incorrect white hunter seemed miraculously to have survived the fall of Rhodesia and the deprivations of ZANU-PF. And yes, you could still take tea with scones and cakes and cucumber sandwiches served by white-liveried waiters while looking down from the terrace at George Hobson's famous bridge and the rising spray of the Falls behind it.

But along with my childlike delight at finding the colonial dream intact was a feeling that such a survival could not have happened had it not been in ZANU-PF's interests. How many of our holiday dollars were propping up a regime that had so recently been slaughtering its opponents to stay in power? In the few days of our stay, Zimbabwe's miseries were never far away. Lynda, who can glean someone's life story on the briefest acquaintance, discovered that multilingual Mary on reception was sending all her salary to Harare to support her unemployed family and disabled brother. Each trip out of the manicured grounds tipped us into a world where the victims of a wrecked economy and 200 million per cent inflation hawked anything and everything to scratch a living. A ragged man on Victoria Falls Bridge sold me a souvenir 50 billion Zimbabwe dollar note for two US dollars. Later I noticed I could get the same note for one US dollar – either a 50 per cent devaluation in half an hour or a sign of people's desperation for currency that didn't crumble through their fingers.

We toured the Falls, its age-old roar reassuringly constant against the uncertainties of life in modern Zimbabwe. The guide who led us along the spray-soaked rim of the gorge opposite the tumbling sheets of water was as smiling and animated as any Zimbabwean we'd met – except, that is, when he stood aside to let us take in the view and a look of intense sadness fell across his face. A man there who has suffered, we thought. When we asked what he made of the recent election, he spoke warily of 'a season' which Zimbabwe was enduring before God brought better times, as surely He would. Similar sentiments came from the riverboat skipper who took us for a tourist sunset cruise on the Zambezi. Lynda (naturally) discovered that Mika was both a boatman and a church pastor at the uncompromisingly named Soul Winning Ministries. He told us many of his congregation were starving.

Wandering out from the hotel entrance on the second day, I noticed a railway carriage standing alongside the station platform. The years fell away as I recognised the brown and cream livery of Rhodesia Railways in whose wood-panelled sleeper compartments I'd made many a slow, creaking journey between Salisbury and Bulawayo or from Bulawayo through Mafeking and Kimberley to Cape Town. I crossed the deserted platform for a closer look. The Rhodesia Railways name had long ago been painted out, but each window still bore the etched, overlapping RR logo I remembered so well. Hand shielding my forehead, I pressed against the glass and took in the plump, green, leather seats and steel washbasin of one of the compartments. An evocative moment. I could almost hear the xylophone dinner gong that the steward used to beat as he tramped along the corridors to announce dinner in the mahogany-lined dining car.

Inside, someone was clanking about with a bucket. Eager to re-experience a little piece of childhood, I gripped the handrail and mounted the steps. The cleaner looked up from his mopping. I apologised for the interruption and asked if I could take a look. Without a word, he stepped back and nodded down the carriage.

In one of the seats, busy on some paperwork, sat a large, crew-cut white man, the back of his neck spilling over his collar, and his thighs almost bursting from his khaki shorts. Without meaning to, I found myself slipping into the accent.

'Oh hi. I'm from the UK, but these old carriages... I remember these from way back. Jew mind if I look around?'

He put down the cellphone he'd been about to dial and leaned back. 'So you from Rhodeezha?'

'*Ja.* A long time ago, like I said.'

'And you're art from England?'

'S'right.'

'Boy, you must be wondering what's happened to this country. Whole place is falling apart. Can't even get a working locomotive up to the Falls. Not like the old country, hey?' He looked past me at the cleaner. 'Hey, Champion. Make sure you clean under the seats, hey?'

Champion didn't exactly say 'Yes, *baas*' as he might have done circa 1962, but the scene nevertheless produced a moment of flashback. I could have been ten again, waiting for the steward to unhook the leather bunks and make them up with crisp, white, RR-monogrammed bedlinen as the wheels clacked rhythmically and night descended on the slowing passing *bundu*. This ex-colonial could have been Stephen from Selborne-Routledge, now bulked out, like me, into middle age. If so, what did he now make of his black fellow citizens? The nostalgia that haunts the old Rhodesian jarred in my mind with a sense of rightness – relief, even – that the old, racist culture no longer held sway.

Champion resumed his mopping and the man turned back to me. '*Ja*, sure,' he said with a sweep of his hand. 'Take a look around.' He smiled ironically. 'Welcome to Zimbabwe.'

If that encounter took me back in time, the next, later that morning, pointed me forward and had a more profound effect than I could possibly have imagined at the time. Without it, I would not be writing this book.

Once again venturing out of the hotel, we walked as a family into town for a look around the curio shops. As we slowly returned along the shimmering streets, the noonday shadows tight against the walls, a barefoot little boy in ragged shorts and a torn T-shirt appeared alongside and slipped his hand into Lynda's. The story calls for a cute face and limpid eyes, but I honestly can't remember what the child looked like. I turned around and there was Lynda holding hands with some kid. What follows is how she described it afterwards.

'Hello, Mama,' said the child.

'Hello,' said Lynda, guessing his age at six or seven. 'What's your name?'

The mumbled answer sounded something like Zondiwe.

'Hello, Zondiwe. Shouldn't you be in school today?'

'Ah, no. I don't go to school.'

'Oh. But what about your parents? Don't they send you to school?'

'Ah, no.'

'No?'

'My parents, they are not here.'

Not here? wondered Lynda. *Meaning dead? Or not in Victoria Falls?*

'They are late,' added Zondiwe. Having divulged this puzzling information, he adjusted his grip and he and Lynda walked on together in silence.

'Are you going to your hotel, Mama?' he said eventually.

'Yes, we are, Zondiwe. Are you going to play?'

He looked up with serious eyes. 'Ah, no. I do not play.' With this, he seemed to run out of things to say and detached his hand. 'Well, goodbye, Mama.'

'Goodbye, Zondiwe.'

Lynda looked down at his doleful face and the little shirt falling off his shoulder and felt a wrench of pity. Wishing she could do more, she handed him the only money she could find, which happened to be a US dollar note. He seized it. With no serviceable pockets among his rags, he held it tight in his fist as he disappeared.

For all we know, Zondiwe was somebody's Artful Dodger for extracting dollar bills from tourists. If so, good for him. He did it endearingly. But that short encounter continued to dog us. Everywhere we looked in Victoria Falls Town from then on, we saw more ragged Zondiwes roaming the streets, alone or in packs. Cushioned in the opulence of the Victoria Falls Hotel, Lynda and I agreed that our tourist bubble, wonderful as it was, needed a corrective. Sooner or later, we had to come back and acquaint ourselves, if not with Zondiwe, then with some of the many million other Zondiwes in Robert Mugabe's Zimbabwe.

5

Mugabe's Zimbabwe, 2010

So, thank you, Zondiwe, if that is your name. It's because of you that Lynda and I found ourselves flying into Harare two years later, having sought out a children's project to become involved in and discovering Matthew Rusike Children's Home.

It was my widowed mother, now retired to the Lancashire coast near Blackpool, who pointed us in that direction. She told us that the Reverend Matthew Rusike had been a country Methodist minister during our years in Rhodesia and that she and my father had known him slightly. In 1950, a group of villagers near his home in Makwiro, west of Salisbury, had held an all-night beer-drinking session. The village huts had caught fire and a number of the drinkers had burned to death. The following day, Mr Rusike found a huddle of orphaned children on his doorstep. He took them in, and from those beginnings grew the children's home that carries his name – now run by the Methodist Church of Zimbabwe and relocated to the shanty suburb of Epworth in south-east Harare, directly beneath the airport flight path.

We made more enquiries and discovered that the home was run by the improbably named Astonishment

Mapurisa. *Astonishment?* we thought. *Who calls their child Astonishment? Astonishment that the new arrival had turned out to be a baby? Astonishment that the child had been born at all?* It then emerged that Astonishment would shortly be in the UK on a fund-raising tour. We fixed to meet him at the Hampshire home of Paddy and Jenny Coles – he being the treasurer of a UK charity called the Friends of Matthew Rusike Children's Home, which was hosting this man's visit.

Astonishment turned out to be a stocky, round-featured man in his early forties, his eyes crinkly with much laughing and the corners of his mouth constantly atwitch as if about to erupt into more laughter. Even as we stepped through the door of the Coles' home, Astonishment's laugh came bubbling through from the kitchen over some business to do with lunch. He might have been asking Jenny if the *sadza* was ready. He emerged, still chuckling, and greeted us with pumping handshakes.

We began our pitch tentatively in the Coles' comfortable drawing room. After our Victoria Falls experience, we told Astonishment, we were interested in working with deprived children in Zimbabwe. Was there any opportunity at Matthew Rusike for a teacher of emotional intelligence (Lynda) and, less obviously, a commercial hack and ghostwriter (me)?

The notion that he'd need time to think about our proposal didn't seem to cross Astonishment's mind. 'Yes, yes, yes! You must come. There is so much you can do. Lynda, our children need you. This is exactly what we need. And Graham… yes… we will definitely find work for you. This is perfect. I thank God we have met. Please book your flights now, now, now.'

We parted not with handshakes but with hugs, convinced we'd be meeting again very soon.

We returned in August 2010. After the violent election of 2008, ZANU-PF had agreed to share power with the opposition MDC – cynically keeping the security, defence and justice ministries and handing the MDC the poisoned chalices of finance, labour and social welfare that would make them unpopular as soon as they needed to rein in expenditure. Nonetheless, the MDC had made some progress in putting a wrecked economy back on its feet. Replacing the worthless Zimbabwean currency with the US dollar had killed off inflation, even if the same battered notes now went round and round to the point of disintegration and the lack of coinage meant that nothing cost less than a dollar – a real problem in a country where millions still lived on a dollar or two a day.

Off the plane in Harare, we queued at agonising length for our visas at fifty-five US dollars apiece, passing the time with a rancher's wife whose property had been seized in the takeovers of white-run farms in the early 2000s. She was coming back for the first time to find out what had happened to it. We wished her well.

Astonishment was waiting on the concourse. Back home and free to be fully African, he sprang from the waiting crowd and threw his arms around each of us in turn. His laughter rang across the exit hall.

'Welcome, my friends! Welcome! Welcome! We've been praying for you to get here safely, and look! Now you are here! Thank God. Thank God.'

He took our cases and led us to the car park where his Toyota seven-seater stood flaring in the eye-watering sunlight. On the short drive to Epworth, windows down to cool the interior, he enthused about what we'd be doing for the next two and a half weeks.

'Lynda! Yes! You will be teaching our children. There is so much we can learn from your expertise. Graham! Ya! We will definitely think of something. But first you must rest. It is the weekend. You are welcome, welcome.'

From the car, I looked out at the Salisbury of my childhood – Africa's 'garden city' as it styled itself in colonial times. Much was strange. The faces in the streets had turned from white to black with not a *murungu* to be seen once we were clear of the airport. The road was potholed and jagged-edged where the tarmac had crumbled, but among the smoke-spewing buses and battered pick-ups I noticed more than a few top-end BMWs and Mercedes. ('Oh ya, the politicians,' explained Astonishment. 'Or businessmen. Often it's the same.') At every traffic light, a swarm of vendors moved along the line selling oranges, groundnuts, sunglasses, cellphone chargers, puncture repair kits, potato crisps. As we crossed the city boundary, an ebony beauty smiled down from a billboard, her lips seductively brushing a glass of cola. 'City of Harare welcomes you,' purred the caption. 'Enjoy our friendly environment.'

Through the disjoint of the unfamiliar, some things were sufficiently the same to tug at the memories. The jacarandas still bloomed and the humanoid sculpture atop the Pearl Assurance building still dominated what I remembered as Jameson Avenue – now Samora Machel Avenue. The road to Epworth passed through suburbs that would once have housed white families, and white families only. *Where were they now?* I wondered. The outlines of that old, comfortable lifestyle were still discernable, but the houses looked rundown and overbuilt with stucco extensions, ugly perimeter walls and litter-strewn frontages. For better or worse, the trim, prim neighbourhoods of the 1960s had stopped worrying about how they looked.

Astonishment swung the Toyota off the main Chiremba Road and onto the strip that wound through Epworth township. Music jangled from a score of tin-shack stores as we negotiated our way past donkey carts and cyclists and in through the gates of the Matthew Rusike compound. Strewn with granite boulders that looked as though they'd rolled loose from Epworth's famous balancing rocks, the compound enclosed a rough expanse of bush with a low, red-roofed office block and a cluster of jacaranda-shaded homes where the children lived in families with their house mothers. As we drove up the track from the gate, we passed a group of boys returning from the borehole with buckets of water on their heads. They waved. Other children kicked about in the dust with a football made of plastic bags stuffed into more plastic bags. Driving on, we circuited the water tower and came to a stop at Shamie's house where Lynda and I were to stay.

Shamie – full name, Chishamiso – was a soft-spoken, gentle-faced lady in her thirties, housemother to eight of

Matthew Rusike's 150 orphans. She introduced us to her children. We met Faith and Barbara, shy, sad-looking sisters whose mother had succumbed to AIDS at Epworth Medical Centre and whose relatives back in Mutoko district couldn't or wouldn't have them back. Both were HIV-positive. Two other sisters, Marigold aged nine and six-year-old Enid, had been made homeless with their sick mother after Mugabe's 2005 *Murambatsvina* ('Clear out the rubbish') campaign to bulldoze the tin and cardboard shacks of ex-farmworkers driven off the land and into the towns by the farm takeovers. House and possessions destroyed and with nowhere to live but out in the open, their mother had died of AIDS soon afterwards. Another of Shamie's charges, three-year-old Tsitsi, had been found in a forest as a baby, attempting to eat the dirt at the spot where he'd been abandoned.

Similar stories came from other households on the compound. A toddler suffering from scabies had been abandoned at the gate with a note from his mother: 'Please make sure my child goes to Matthew Rusike Children's Home. I have no work and my husband has deserted me, so I cannot keep him.' Another, barely old enough to lisp his name, had been left standing on the driveway with nothing but the clothes he wore and an orange in his hand – a poignant last gift from a mother who no doubt wanted the best for her soon-to-be lost child but could manage no more than this tiny gesture. New-born babies regularly came to the home from Harare's Chitungwiza Hospital after their mothers had given birth and walked out, unwilling or unable to bear the cost of another child.

Then there was Beauty, the girl from the cesspit. She'd been born in a long-drop toilet in Harare and had either fallen down the shaft by accident or been thrown in by her mother who then fled. Passers-by heard the baby crying and broke down the cement structure to get her out of the bubbling, foetid soup into which she was sinking. Someone took her to hospital from where the police brought her to Matthew Rusike. Unnamed and her parentage entirely unknown, this baby from the poo was christened Beauty to mark her rebirth.

And so the stories went on – most the result of Zimbabwe's AIDS epidemic (which turned one in seven of the population into an orphan child) and its 85 per cent unemployment rate which made it excruciatingly hard for families to feed and educate their children. Conditions at Matthew Rusike were rudimentary, but vastly better than the life from which most of the children had come. And whether they arrived malnourished, abused, abandoned, orphaned by AIDS or HIV-positive themselves, what each child unfailingly received was love. It's remarkable that simple love can be such a healer, one that even the smallest child instinctively knows if it's getting and knows how to give in return. And here the love was almost tangible. The home with its chronic lack of resources and its staff who often went for months without being paid had an atmosphere all its own that you sensed as you walked the poinsettia-lined drive from the gate. An atmosphere of lightness and laughter as the grind of Epworth township faded behind you. Out of nothing, it seemed, Astonishment and Shamie and their many devoted colleagues contrived to give security and the hope of a better future to their damaged children.

And despite the circumstances from which most had come, the children responded. On our second or third evening, Lynda and I sat on a rock as the sun sank in a tangerine blaze behind the eucalyptus that lined the dirt playing field. In the cool of the evening with the pods of the flamboyant trees snapping like gunshots over our heads, four children – two boys and two girls – came out to play. The light was fading, so all we could see was their silhouettes against the pale sand. The four shapes pirouetted and cartwheeled and raced in circles like Matisse dancers liberated from the canvas and taking on a life of their own. Their exuberance and abandonment and sheer joy of play were breathtaking. By some miracle, the miseries of Mugabe's Zimbabwe had been transmuted into rare, sublime happiness with only Lynda and me to witness it.

The first Monday after our weekend's rest was National Heroes' Day, the public holiday to celebrate the fallen in the war of liberation. After three days in which the power had run for roughly two hours in twenty-four (close to the average, so we were told), the holiday brought a full day's electricity. Which meant the entire population could tune in to Radio Zimbabwe. (When Shamie explained this connection, I thought: *Don't people have battery-powered radios?* I can only say that when I later tried to buy a torch battery, it was harder to find than a dollar note that wasn't thumbed and worn to the texture of old tissue paper.)

Heroes' Day began with Shamie skipping down the corridor chanting 'Electricity! Electricity!' and switching on her antique radiogram. (After she died of tuberculosis the following year, her song to welcome the electricity remained a poignant memory.) The day's output from Radio Zimbabwe consisted mainly of monologues from the President, extolling those who had given their lives in the struggle against the white oppressor (*Does he mean me? I thought*) and vowing that Zimbabwe would never again submit to British colonialism. In a flashback moment, I recalled huddling around a radiogram of similar vintage, listening to Ian Smith on Radio Rhodesia telling us there'd be no sell-out to the blacks. The accent was different; the message was the same, simply with the colours reversed.

The politics of the day were interrupted at intervals by dance music. With each new tune, three-year-old Godfrey gyrated across the cement floor of Shamie's living room, hips wiggling and fingers clicking like a dance pro. When we admired his style, he shimmied up to Lynda and said gruffly: '*Mukadzi muchena, tamba!*'

Shamie snorted with laughter. 'Do you know what he's saying?'

'No.'

'He's saying, "White woman, dance!"'

So Lynda did.

Heroes' Day aside, each weekday morning began with devotions for the staff – a Bible reading, a hymn in Shona and a thought for the day, mainly in Shona but with key phrases in English for the benefit of visitors. Astonishment, who hadn't been around much since our arrival, took his turn at leading on the third or fourth day. He bustled in with his customary chuckle and the small gathering looked up expectantly. Astonishment was about to tell one of his stories.

'Ya, this you will not believe. You know what I saw last week?'

A murmur suggested that people didn't.

'Out on the road to Chitungwiza. Near the airport, last Monday. I was in the car and in front of me was this truck full of workers in the back. Suddenly, these guys started screaming and jumping over the side onto the road. While the truck was still moving! I thought, *how could they be so stupid?* But you know what it was?'

More murmuring and wagging of heads.

'An eagle had flown over with a live snake in its talons. But the snake must have been fighting back, because the eagle dropped it right there in the back of the truck. So these guys suddenly found a very annoyed snake at their feet. Out of nowhere! Snakes from the sky! No wonder they got out so quick!'

The chuckles went on for some time while Astonishment embellished the scene.

'He always has a story,' said Astonishment's secretary as we filed out afterwards. 'You never know if he's making them up, but he makes us smile every time.'

That was the day Astonishment drove Lynda and me to Harare where he had business at the Methodist Church head office. But first he had a surprise for me – a detour down Samora Machel Avenue, a wiggle onto Herbert Chitepo and then a right turn into a rough, meagre little street whose rusty signpost announced it as Snowdon

Road. The Snowdon Road I'd raced up and down on my bike half a century ago – then a broad, smooth thoroughfare, now disappointingly rutted and overgrown and so much narrower than I remembered. How much of the change was real and how much was in my head I didn't have time to consider, for a minute later we drew up at the gates of Selborne-Routledge Primary School. The pioneer names had survived. I didn't expect that. The listing metal sign behind the fence bore the same crest with its ox wagons and cheese graters of learning and its *Forward together* motto. Behind it were the same barrack-like classrooms.

Astonishment, who we soon discovered can talk his way into anywhere, announced to the gatekeeper that his friend from England used to be at this school and could we come in for a look? The old man's suspicious face broke into smiles, as usually happens when Astonishment gets to work. He opened the gate with a squeal of hinges and we were in.

There were no children at school this late in the afternoon, but the secretary's office was busy. Black faces, of course, where once they'd been entirely white.

'I can't believe you're so old you were here nearly fifty years ago,' laughed one of the ladies, flatteringly. 'Sure, you can look around.'

Walking the grounds with Lynda and Astonishment, I tried to pick out what had changed. The lawn the groundsman had been watering while Stephen and Mrs Mackay debated his status had been paved over. And there was now a small swimming pool, albeit cracked and empty. But the hall where we'd Scottish danced, the spreading tree under which we'd played marbles and the concrete square where we'd biffed each other with boxing gloves were all intact. I recognised the steps where we'd sat for class photographs – a memory in monochrome, suggesting it derived from the black and white prints in my mother's album rather than from reality. Surrounded by the past, I nonetheless found it hard to connect. The buildings had lasted, but so much else had changed. I had changed. The country had changed. The old faces were long gone – some, like me, quitting the country and dodging the draft; others, in all likelihood, going off to fight for Rhodesia. I felt I was walking among ghosts.

The feelings were similar when Astonishment drove us further down Snowdon Road to the manse, still owned by the church and now lived in by the Methodist Bishop of Zimbabwe. He and his wife were out, but their teenage children shyly allowed us to look inside. Another house now occupied the plot we'd set on fire and the verandah sported a security grille, but the rest still stood as remembered – *kaya* included. I tried hard to insert myself back into the scene with Glynn and Harry and Ivan, but the gulf was too wide to bridge convincingly. It seemed that childhood tugged strongest while the places themselves were unvisited. Finally being there was vaguely deflating. I didn't feel what I expected to feel. If I was looking to reach back and touch the country I once knew, to feel its texture between my fingers, it wasn't happening. The past remained elusive, just beyond my grasp.

Modern Zimbabwe broke in the following day when Tapiwa, ardent Arsenal fan and Matthew Rusike's accountant, showed us more of the sights of Harare in the home's wheezy minibus. (Tapiwa was also the resident butcher, called upon whenever a cow was donated and needed to be slaughtered.) From the city centre, he headed through the smart suburb of Borrowdale to get as near as he could to Mugabe's fabled palace. Built by Serbian contractors to a Chinese design and one of Africa's most luxurious residences, it's said to include three acres of accommodation, marble imported from Italy and blue-glazed tiles all the way from Shanghai – not to mention the concrete underground bunkers and riot-police unit on permanent standby. Way before we reached it, the traffic seemed mysteriously to thin out and armed police stepped forward from the verges to keep us moving.

'Not a place to break down,' smiled Tapiwa, urging the juddering van to keep going beyond sight of levelled guns. Then a few minutes later he swerved to the side and hit the brakes.

'What's up?' I asked as we slewed to a halt.

Tapiwa nodded forward. All the other vehicles on both sides of the road were crowding into the sides.

Over the rise ahead of us came two police motorbikes, lights flashing and sirens screeching. They must have been travelling at 100kph – a dangerous feat on a road as potholed as this one. Close behind was an open-backed truck, overflowing with armed guards in *Star Wars*-style helmets. Then came a line of expensive 4x4s and a blacked-out Mercedes limousine, followed by another gun-bristling, bobble-helmeted truckload of guards. Bringing up the rear was an ambulance.

I raised my camera, but Tapiwa motioned it away. 'Don't,' he said. 'They'll probably shoot you.'

The motorcade was gone in seconds, the sirens fading behind us.

'Was that who we thought it was?' asked Lynda.

'The President? Ya, ya. Whenever he travels, the road has to clear immediately. It's the law. We get used to it.'

Known locally as Bob Mugabe and the Wailers, the screaming presidential cavalcade had long been terrorising the road users of Zimbabwe. Getting hurt was a serious possibility. Over the years the Mugabe juggernaut claimed a number of casualties – drivers or pedestrians who didn't get out of the way fast enough, or outriders killed and injured by accidents happening at high speed on Zimbabwe's appalling roads.

'Ah, that motorcade,' said Astonishment later. 'Once in Kuwadzana, it passed some people selling fish by the roadside. Instead of cowering, they waved their fish at the President as if mocking him to buy some. Before evening, a truckload of soldiers arrived and started beating up the vendors. Some people ended up in hospital as a result.'

We watched the President disappearing to his concrete bunker. *A man truly in touch with his people,* we thought.

About a week in, Astonishment dropped by at Shamie's house for lunch. The electricity had been off all day, so Shamie had prepared her stew and rice on an open fire behind the house. We were near to finishing the meal when a knock came at the kitchen door. It was Miriam, one of the other housemothers. After the greetings, she explained her business to Astonishment. 'You know those two little brothers who arrived last month?'

'Oh ya. Oliver and Edson.' Astonishment knew every child in the home by name and background. 'The younger one,' he explained for our benefit, 'he's very sick from AIDS. These brothers have a stepmother who badly abused them and this child has a crippled hand from where she burned him.' He turned back to Miriam. 'So how are they doing?'

'Ah, this is the problem,' she said. 'They're stealing food from the larder and I don't know how to stop them. There is no lock on the door. Maybe we should put one on.'

Astonishment looked thoughtful. 'No, don't do that,' he said after a pause. 'I have a better plan. We have to consider why these boys are stealing. It's because, with their stepmother, they were never sure when they would get fed. If they're confident there's food available, they won't do it. So what you do is this. You tell the boys that they are in charge of the larder. It's their responsibility to make sure all the food is accounted for. Set them as guards.'

Miriam looked dubious, but agreed to give it a try.

'Will that really work?' asked Lynda, after she'd gone.

'Oh ya, I think so. You see, I know how a starved child thinks. I was such a one myself. So when I look at these children, it's me that I see and I recognise the potential for change. That's because...' He paused as though reluctant to say it. 'That's because, when I was very young, my relatives sold me as a slave.'

A slave? We pressed him to say more, but Astonishment was late for a meeting in Harare.

'It's true,' he added. 'Before you leave this place, I'll tell you a story of hunger and rejection and exploitation – the story of my childhood.'

A few days later, Astonishment announced that he needed to drive to Bulawayo at the weekend. Would we like to go with him?

'Of course,' we said.

The night before we left, Astonishment explained an extension to the plan. Down at his rural home near Chivhu on the main road to Beitbridge, he intended to slaughter one of his family's cows to provide meat for the Matthew Rusike children. We could make a detour out from Chivhu, do the deed, stay at his rural home and continue the journey to Bulawayo a day later. Like me, it turned out he had memories to exorcise, ghosts to be laid to rest. The tract of country between Chivhu and the bush town of Buhera, seventy kilometres to the south-east, was the landscape of Astonishment's childhood – a childhood just as improbable as his name, as we were soon to learn. If my quest in coming to Zimbabwe was to relive my childhood as a little white boy, Astonishment was intent on doing the same as a little black boy on the other side of the racial divide.

'Many of these places I haven't seen for over twenty years,' he told us. 'I'll show you where I grew up. Bring that recorder of yours and I'll tell you my story. There might even be a book in it.'

We loaded the Toyota at dawn, the horizon a ribbon of pearly pink before the sudden upthrust of the sun. Epworth township was stirring with cocks crowing and the smell of woodsmoke wafting over the compound wall. The last item to go in was a live chicken in a cardboard carton, intended as supper that evening once we got to Astonishment's rural home. I recalled my father coming back from taking services in country churches with a similar gift of a scrawny, quivering fowl, legs tied and wings flapping feebly in the boot of the Ford Anglia. Seeing these chickens ineptly put to death remains a vivid memory. I guess Elsie, the Bulawayo maid, must sometimes have done it out of sight. In the absence of an Elsie or an air gun to fill its skinny carcass with lead, the technique was to lay the chicken on its back, place a foot on each outstretched wing and saw its squawking head off with a kitchen knife.

Maybe this particular fowl sensed its fate, because it refused to lie quietly in its box. Nor were its feet tied. By the time we reached the end of the drive, it was beating against the lid of the box, then working its head through the flaps as if to demand an explanation for this appalling treatment. We were moments away from a displeased chicken erupting from its box and smashing around the inside of the car. Astonishment stopped and found a length of string. Throwing open the tailgate, he pushed the protesting bird back into its box and tied down the flaps.

'No more dancing, chicken!' he chuckled.

Squawks and the thumping of wings accompanied the drive as we left Harare and hit the Beitbridge road heading south.

Once free of the suburbs, somewhere south of Chitungwiza, Astonishment stretched back in his seat and let out a long, thoughtful 'Hmmm'. It suggested an arranging of memories and a wondering where to begin. I guessed what was coming and clicked the button on my recorder.

Part 2

2010
Murambiwa

6

Rejected

'Picture the Mukarati homestead,' began Astonishment. 'It lies in the middle of the bush, not far from the country town of Buhera. Like a thousand other *kraals* in Zimbabwe, it's a circle of mud and thatch huts built on bare earth. Going back to the 1960s, it's home to Peter Mukarati, his wife and their six children of whom the oldest is a boy called Calisto. There's a pen for the ten or so cows, a rack made of branches for storing maize, a prickly thorn hedge to keep out wild animals and a shallow well near the little river that runs to the east of the homestead. In the dry season when the river disappears and the well fails, the only water comes from digging in the sandy bed of a larger river some two kilometres distant. The women bring it back in twenty-litre buckets on their heads. The water is dark brown, but drinkable if you let it settle and take from the top of the bucket. In all, a place of extreme poverty in a poor, dry, neglected part of Zimbabwe.'

I had, of course, seen many such homesteads, typically at a distance across the *bundu* from a passing car. Astonishment's description took me back to Siabuwa, my closest experience of what he was talking about. As for how life was lived in these places, my ignorance was almost total.

'Calisto Mukarati is sixteen but still in primary school – which is not unusual. In the same school is Lonia Ndiya, a lively, pretty girl of the same age whose equally impoverished homestead is a few kilometres away at Chirimudombo. They get together. Lonia becomes pregnant.

'At sixteen they were only kids and in no position to get married. So the two families came to an agreement whereby the Mukarati family gave three head of cattle to Lonia's family. Effectively they were saying: "We acknowledge responsibility, but our son is too young and cannot take care of your daughter and her child. So we offer these cows in compensation."

'The cows were transferred soon after the baby's birth, which took place in a hut in the Mukarati homestead on 22nd August 1967. When Lonia delivered her son onto the mud floor, the only other people present were Calisto's mother and Lonia's elder sister, Angela. Such was the poverty, Angela had to rip up her petticoat to keep the baby from the cold. And that's how I arrived.'

So where was I on the day Astonishment was born? August would have been a school holiday out from England. I was fourteen and back at the Abercorn Street house in Bulawayo – 350 kilometres away in distance but a world away in culture and circumstances. On the day of his birth, I was probably sunning my knees in the garden to work up a tan.

'Why Calisto's homestead?' asked Lynda, from the back seat. 'Wouldn't your mother have given birth at home?'

'Ah no. You see Lonia's mother, my grandmother, no longer lived at the Chirimudombo *kraal*. Her name was Naomi, by the way. She'll be very important later in the story. Her husband, Shadrach, had six wives, of whom Naomi was the second. As is often the way in these families, she'd had a falling out with wife number three, a lady called Jasmine. Polygamous husbands always favour the newer wife, so Naomi had quit the homestead a few years earlier and gone to live with her brother, Ngobho Mazvito, who worked on a white man's farm, Moolman Farm, near Chivhu – though then it was known as Enkeldoorn. That meant there was no mother at home to look after Lonia in her pregnancy.

'There had previously been an older brother at the Chirimudombo homestead. He was called Chengeta, but he'd also left before I was born and gone to join his mother at Moolman. That left three younger siblings, Elizabeth, Martha and Elison, who now depended on the pregnant Lonia to look after them. Otherwise, the Ndiya homestead had nothing to offer Lonia but a bunch of unsympathetic half-relatives.

'A week after my birth and with heavy heart, Lonia took her new baby boy back to the Ndiya family at Chirimudombo. By then she'd named me Murambiwa, which is Shona for "Rejected". It signified my rejection by my father's family who preferred to part with three cows than have any involvement in my upbringing.'

Lynda was appalled. 'She really called her own child "Rejected"? That's terrible. I can't believe it!'

'Oh yes. Murambiwa is quite a common name in Zimbabwe. The Ndebele in the west would use the name, Zondiwe.'

Zondiwe! My mind flashed back to a shimmering street in Victoria Falls Town and the ragged, beguiling *murambiwa* who'd been part of the chain linking us to Astonishment. A different name, but another reject.

Astonishment pressed on. 'Being at home with a young baby was tough for Lonia – motherless, taking care of her little sisters and brother and having to share a hut with Jasmine who'd already driven Naomi out of the homestead. But one good thing came of it. Jasmine had a son called Justice who grew very fond of the new baby boy and said to the rest of the family: "This child of Lonia's – we cannot let him go through life being called 'Rejected'. He's a gift from God and one to be welcomed. We didn't think we'd like him, but we do. This child has surprised us.

More than surprised us. For this reason, we should call him Astonishment."

'So that was the end of Murambiwa,' continued Astonishment. 'For the time being, anyway. It's strange that Justice chose the English word, Astonishment. But then, Justice was an educated man and maybe he wanted to show off his English – his name being English, too. Unfortunately, I never knew him. He went to join the liberation struggle, one of six Ndiya boys who first trained in Mozambique and then fought in the war. Of the six, four returned and two were killed. Justice was one of them.'

Justice's story brought to mind those Rhodesian government news reports with their tallies of terrorist 'floppies'. So one of those statistics was the man who gave Astonishment his crazy name. I wondered if Justice, to whom names were obviously important, had been inspired by his own name when he took up arms against the white oppressor.

'My mother and I remained at the Ndiya homestead until I was eighteen months old,' Astonishment continued. 'For her, still a teenager, it was eighteen months of back-breaking toil – pounding grain, grinding maize, fetching water and cooking meals for the rest of the family, all with her baby son bundled on her back. Eventually Lonia grew sick of the tensions and arguments with her stepmother and was desperate to be reunited with her real mother. But how could this be done? A distance of seventy kilometres was a serious obstacle to a country girl who didn't have the money to travel by bus and whose only option was to walk.

'The answer came when Naomi returned for a short visit and left her a dollar that she could ill afford herself.

One morning, Lonia pretended to be visiting the neighbours and walked twelve kilometres with me on her back to the nearest bus stop. The only one to see her leaving home was Martha who was up at sunrise pounding rapoco. She wanted to come too, but Naomi's dollar would only cover one bus fare. Martha had to stay.'

A question occurred as Astonishment was talking. Father's family name – Mukarati. Mother's name, Ndiya. Where did Mapurisa come from?

Astonishment chuckled. 'It's a complicated story.'

This didn't surprise me.

'Ya, ya, like much to do with African families. Before she married Shadrach Ndiya, my grandmother's family name was Mazvito. But her brother, Ngobho, had previously been a constable in the old colonial police force and that gave him great status in the community. Given the fluidity of these things in Africa, his name expanded to take in the Shona word for police, which is *mapurisa*. It was a term of great respect, so he kept it. Mapurisa Ngobho Mazvito was the name he proudly carried.'

A crazy name just got even crazier. 'So you're really called Astonishment Police?'

Astonishment slapped the steering wheel and threw back his head with a laugh. 'Yes, yes, yes. Not a common name, I grant you, but perfectly true.'

'So how did Mapurisa pass to you?'

'Well, later, this policeman took it on himself to register his nephew – my uncle Chengeta – and in the process decided to give him the Mapurisa name. Uncle Chengeta then did the same for me, even though he himself uses Ndiya and Mapurisa interchangeably.'

I was struggling to follow. 'How does this Uncle Chengeta come into it?'

'Ah. My mother's brother, the one who left the Ndiya homestead before I was born. First he joined Naomi, his mother, at Moolman Farm. Then he found work at Coetzie Farm nearby. He married a lady called Bianca and they took my grandmother in to live with them. This was the set-up that greeted Lonia when she and her toddler son finally made the break from the Ndiyas and caught the bus to join them in 1969. As the man of the family, it fell to Chengeta to register his nephew and that was the name he decided to give me when he eventually got around to it. That's why I no longer carry my father's name. Instead I have the name of my uncle's uncle, the colonial-era constable.'

A complicated family, to say the least – and a name that seemed to owe more to other people's whimsy than to Astonishment's own parentage.

Astonishment fell silent as he picked his way past a bus that was listing precariously on the dirt verge, disgorging passengers. A man in a torn shirt was busy on the roof, unlashing bundles and bicycles and suitcases and passing them down to their owners. We were through the mining town of Beatrice, just past the spot where a car crash the previous year had injured Morgan Tsvangirai and killed his wife, Susan – one of many mysterious road accidents to have befallen Mugabe's opponents over the years. We cleared the bus and picked up speed.

In the bustling town of Chivhu, we turned east off the main road opposite the green Dutch gable end of Vic's Tavern – a reminder of the time when Chivhu was the

Afrikaans outpost of Enkeldoorn. Astonishment pointed it out with a tilt of his head. 'When I was little, Vic's was a hotel for white people,' he continued. 'You had to be white to eat there – either that or a brave black person with lots of money.'

I asked Astonishment what else he remembered of the Ian Smith years.

'You know, there was no official apartheid in Rhodesia, not like South Africa, but we Africans were well aware of segregation. In Salisbury, smart shops like Meikles had a separate window for black people to buy things through so they didn't go inside and upset the white customers. Even some parts of the city were out of bounds. To be in First Street, you had to have a note from your white employer to say you were there with his permission.'

'I knew people who trained their dogs to chase black people,' I added.

Astonishment chuckled. 'Ah yes. As a country boy, I never entered a white suburb in colonial times, but we heard stories of those dogs. Sure, white people didn't trust us. It even went as far as which beer you were allowed to drink. To be seen drinking clear, European-style lager, you had to have a pass issued by the authorities. You couldn't buy a Lion or a Castle without such a pass. Otherwise, Africans could only drink home-brews or Chibuku-brand sorghum beer. I think it was to stop blacks and whites socialising. Whites would never drink African beer, like they'd never eat *sadza* – so, if you stop Africans drinking European beer, you prevent the races fraternising.'

I was aware of the South African pass laws under apartheid, but Rhodesia? I asked Astonishment how far Rhodesia had copied the system.

'Not so much, officially,' he replied, 'but something like it applied in the towns. When you started a job, if you were black, you had to hand over your pass to your employer to stop you bunking off. If he wanted to fire you, he'd tell you to collect your pass from the windowsill. There's still a saying in Shona, "Your pass is on the window." It means you're fired!

'It all goes back to the 1930s when the colonial government allocated two-fifths of the country to 1 million blacks and three-fifths – the most fertile areas – to 50,000 whites. Blacks were then barred from taking skilled jobs and from taking up residence in white areas. But they still had to pay the hut tax. In any homestead, the number of huts was an indication of the owner's prosperity and therefore the amount of tax he owed the government. But in a culture with no money, only cows, you could only pay it by leaving home and finding work in the towns or on commercial farms. So that way, the government got its taxes plus a ready supply of cheap, black labour. Even though many people worked only until they'd covered the tax and then went home, there was still a constant influx of workers.'

Lynda cut in. 'So how did people manage, leaving their wives and children in the country and moving to the towns?'

'It was very hard. Men would often have one or more wives in the country and another in town. If they couldn't afford buses or couldn't cycle those long distances, they often didn't bother going home and you ended up with broken families. For black people, poverty became the expected way of life. That's how the law was designed.'

From some recess in my memory, a picture came to mind – a long, straight strip road, shimmering in the heat somewhere outside Salisbury or Bulawayo. Through the windscreen of the family Ford, I see a lone figure forming in the distance. The dancing mirage solidifies into a middle-aged man in a threadbare suit, pedalling a sit-up bicycle. We lurch onto the dirt to pass him. He's gone and forgotten in a moment. Back then I had no idea where a man might be so laboriously cycling in an empty landscape, and nor did I trouble to ask. I wondered now, was he pedalling to a distant rural home, having earned the few pounds' hut tax that now had to be paid to the District Commissioner?

'The same kind of thinking applied to black education,' said Astonishment. 'If you worked on a farm, you had to be educated enough to measure out chemicals and count livestock. So the government provided enough education for that, but no more. Even so, parents who wanted to send their children to school had to toil to raise the fees, keeping themselves in poverty to give the next generation a chance.'

The eastbound road out of Chivhu took us past sun-faded, deep-verandahed shopfronts where it wasn't hard to imagine the long-gone, khaki-clad, bush-hatted Boers of Enkeldoorn parking their *bakkies* and stocking up on beers and *biltong*. About a kilometre after the shops petered out and the bush resumed, Astonishment took a right onto a dirt road. The hum of the tarmac gave way to the sloughing of sand beneath the tyres. A plume of dust rose in our wake.

'Now about here – yes, I think it was here, this is the place where I got arrested.'

I couldn't imagine Astonishment being arrested for anything.

'It was that tense time right at the end of the liberation struggle. Round here we were subject to a curfew – no black people out after 6pm. One night at about 7pm, my good friend Kariba and I were crossing the road right here to get back to our compound when this white guy drove by. We ducked down in the ditch to avoid being seen, but we weren't quick enough. He stopped and shouted at us, demanding to know why we were out after curfew. Neither of us spoke much English, so we couldn't explain that we were just walking home and hadn't realised the time.

'"You! *Iwe!* You're breaking the law," he shouted. Even though we barely understood, we could guess what he was saying. "Get in the car, you cheeky *munts*. I'm taking you to the police." Then he bundled us in.'

'Single-handedly?' I said. 'But there were two of you. Couldn't you have resisted? Or run?'

'We were terrified. For all we knew, he thought we were insurgents. If we'd resisted, that could have brought the army out to hunt us down. No, it was safer to do as he said.

'So we got in and he drove us to the police station in Enkeldoorn. He laid the charges and left and we slept that night in the cell. The black constables on duty were fully aware that this was just a mistake, but they didn't have the authority to release us. It was only when a white officer turned up the next morning that we were finally given a warning and allowed to go.'

Astonishment drove on, the Toyota pitching and listing on the rutted road like a ship on an ocean swell. From the rear, a beating of wings in a cardboard box reminded us we had a restive passenger who wasn't enjoying the ride. Away in the distance, a smudge of movement resolved itself into a donkey cart advancing in our direction. Astonishment slowed as we approached, then pulled up alongside and wound down the window. While the donkey twitched its ears against the flies, an old man leaned forward with a ragged, tooth-deficient grin. Astonishment's face lit up and he grasped the man's hand. The greetings went on for several minutes with much chuckling and slapping of palms. 'Hello, Uncle … Hello, my nephew. How is your family? … Ya, they are well. How are my aunt and all the children?' And so on. Eventually Astonishment crunched into gear and pulled away.

'My uncle,' he explained.

Your uncle! We pass a random donkey cart on a dirt road in the middle of nowhere and the guy turns out to be your uncle? It became a running joke that every other person we met from farm workers to shopkeepers was a relative of Astonishment's. As he later unpicked his tangled family relationships in the telling of his story, we realised the encounter with the donkey man wasn't so improbable.

'So where was I?' resumed Astonishment. 'Ah, yes. My mother and I have left the Ndiya homestead and joined Granny Naomi, my uncle Chengeta and Chengeta's wife, Bianca, at Coetzie Farm, a few kilometres down the road from where we are now. Coetzie was the official name, but all commercial farms had an unofficial name which the white people knew nothing about. Because the owner was a nice, calm, placid kind of man, it was called Zinyoro Farm which means all those things in Shona.

'So now we're a family of farm labourers. In Rhodesia in the 1960s, commercial farming was about ensuring your workers had enough food to stay alive and be productive – but no more. Workers couldn't survive on their wages alone, so the owner supplemented the pay with milk and mealie-meal. But that still kept the workers in poverty. In truth, the workers at Zinyoro were not really employees at all – more like tenants. Their labour was payment to the owner for the privilege of living on his land and being allowed to tend their smallholdings when they weren't working for him.

'There was a shop at Zinyoro where you could get things like sugar and cooking oil on credit and the money was deducted from your already meagre wages. Come payday, you went and collected your cheque – not a cheque that gave you money, but a breakdown of where your money had gone.' He laughed. 'People would come back and say, "I've just got my cheque. I have no money!"

'Occasionally a very old cow would be slaughtered and the workers would get some meat. Otherwise, farm labourers like us lived on the fringes of survival.

'Some of the farms in the area had schools for workers' children, but not Zinyoro. People who wanted to send their children to these other schools were free to do so, but my mother couldn't afford it. Instead, when I was six, I was put to work on the farm. My main task was chasing away the birds with a cowhide whip – a *sjambok* – which produced a fine, satisfying crack if you flicked it right. From Monday to Friday I carried out my duties on my own. At weekends, the kids who'd been at school during the week came and helped.

'There were other tasks, too. I weeded the maize fields and shelled the cobs when they were picked. Everything was paid by results, even for a six-year-old. For weeding lines of maize, I got twenty cents for every hundred metres. At harvest time, I stripped off the husks and put the maize in sacks. The sacks would then be weighed and I'd be paid accordingly. If you didn't produce, you didn't eat.

'Around that time, I started to notice that my pretty mother had a new gentleman friend. His name was Job and he worked at Kadzedzewa Farm, about eight kilometres from Zinyoro. I remember a tall, slim man in his early thirties, newly divorced and turning up now and then on a bicycle having clearly made an effort to look smart. He and my mother used to engage in long, private conversations in my mother's hut. And more, it seems, because she soon became pregnant. One evening I came into the hut from the fields and found her packing her few belongings in a cardboard suitcase. With her was her cousin, Mrs Hwete. This was worrying. Shona custom dictates that any woman eloping must be accompanied by an older relative. Here was the relative. There was the suitcase.

'"Mama, what are you doing?" I asked.

'"Goodbye, my son," was all she said.

'"But where are you going?"

'"I have to leave." There was no further explanation. I trotted behind her, tugging at her skirt as she headed for the road, her case balanced African-style on her head.

When the Enkeldoorn bus rattled into view, she told me to be good for my grandmother. Then she stowed her case on the roof among the chickens and the bicycles and climbed aboard. Did she look back? I was too much in shock to notice. I must have stood for many minutes, gazing at the slowly receding bus and then at the column of dust that marked its progress once it was out of sight. When the last wisp had blown away, the last visible connection to my mother, I stumbled back to the *kraal*, numb and confused, tears running down my cheeks. I cried the whole night. Granny Naomi did her best to comfort me, but there was no disguising the truth. My mother had left me and I had no idea when or if I would ever see her again.

'To me, at six, this was one more inexplicable event in a life in which I had no control over anything. Adults made decisions for reasons I could not comprehend, and all I could do was live with the consequences.

'When I asked my grandmother what had happened, she told me my mother had married Job Magondo and gone to live with him in Mhari, down off the Buhera road in Chikomba District. Mhari was not that far away – I now know it's about two hours' drive in a car. But as far as I was concerned, it might have been at the other end of Africa.

'I didn't see her again for another six years.'

7

Morrison Farm

A few kilometres on, Astonishment stopped and killed the engine. Silence fell, broken only by the chirping of cicadas in the dry grass. Ahead of us, the sandy ribbon of road shimmered in the mid-morning heat. To our right, at the far end of a stubbly field, I picked out a cluster of derelict mud-and-pole shacks, their roofs collapsed and their walls crumbling into the soil. To the left, behind a line of gum trees, the tin roof of a farmhouse. Astonishment nodded towards the ghost settlement.

'My childhood home,' he said.

He stepped out of the car and Lynda and I followed him across the field. Standing at the edge of the ruins, he paused and took in the scene. For a few moments, the only movement was a lizard darting over a lintel.

'Ya, this is it. Shortly after my mother left us, Granny Naomi and I plus Uncle Chengeta and Bianca moved the short distance from Zinyoro Farm to the one we're standing in now.' Astonishment pointed to the farmhouse behind the gum trees. 'That was Morrison Farm, or Onion Farm as we called it for the simple reason that it grew onions to sell in the shops in Salisbury. And here...' He walked over to the nearest of the shacks and laid his hand on a ribbed and weathered doorpost. 'This was our compound, built by the farmer for his workers but abandoned sometime after 2000 in the farm takeovers.'

Even in ruin, the buildings looked familiar. Though the materials were more primitive, they could have been suburban *kayas*, transplanted from colonial Salisbury and set down in the bush. The white view of what black workers needed for accommodation was obviously a standard one.

'Ya, there were no comforts here. These were merely places to wake up and start labouring. Again my task was to work in the fields, weeding and scaring off the birds. Tedious work, I can tell you. But the dipping and dehorning days were exciting. We barefoot kids would trot behind the men in their tattered overalls and torn gumshoes as they rounded up the semi-wild cattle, drove them to the dip tank and forced them through with a lot of shouting and cracking of *sjamboks*. Then came the dehorning to stop the animals damaging each other – or more to the point, damaging their market value. Like monkeys, we'd perch on rocks or in trees to watch the entertainment. The workers would grapple the steers with their bare hands, one at the head and one on each leg, wrestling the beast to the ground so the horns could be sawn out. After the sawing, they applied a hot iron, pressing it deep into the flesh. You can imagine the frenzy and the dust as the beast fought back. And all the while, the white farm manager in his shorts and bush hat would be sitting on the rails of the pen, shouting instructions. "Grab it, you lazy boneheads! *Bamba! Bamba!* Hold! Hold! You, boy! Hold that leg down. Harder, you stupid *kaffir*."

Anyone not putting in the effort could expect a painful flick from the *sjambok* which dangled from his wrist.

'I remember one steer, down on the ground, lashing out and kicking a man called Stefan in the leg. Bleeding heavily, he fell over and let go the tail. The manager hopped off the fence, rushed over and delivered a hefty boot on Stefan's backside. Then for good measure he smacked him on the ear. The poor man quickly grabbed the tail again.

'I can still picture that manager, though he's long dead now. His name was Greg, but we called him Kachasu after a vicious, home-brewed beer that could floor you before you could say, "Yes, *baas*." That stuff certainly made you forget your poverty. You could tell the *kachasu* drinkers because they were the ones with teeth as brown as sticks.

'Kachasu Greg not only terrified the workers, he also came after us kids. To him, we were no different to his employees, just smaller versions. One day, five of us little ones had climbed a tree to watch oxen being castrated. One of the animals escaped in mid-procedure and galloped away. We thought we were hidden among the leaves, but Kachasu spotted us and ordered us down to catch it. We tumbled out of the tree and ran in terror, driven equally by fear of the white man with his *sjambok* and fear of the escaping steer. I don't know what we'd have done if we'd caught up with it, but we lost it when it ran into some woodland. We sneaked back to the compound, dreading the growl of Kachasu's approaching Land Rover, the snap of his whip and his angry voice demanding to know what we'd done with his half-castrated beast.

'But you know, for all the poverty and hardships, the workers here at Morrison knew how to have a good time. We had our own entertainment – boxing matches, for instance, often starring Uncle Chengeta who was no mean brawler in his prime. He used to box in beer halls when they ran competitions. Whenever there was drinking here on the compound, it wasn't long before Chengeta was on his feet and challenging others to a fight. He was tough as cowhide, that one, but fun-loving underneath. You could hear his belly-laugh from way across the fields. On the other hand, he could easily develop grudges for no particular reason if someone persuaded him. He liked his drink and he liked his women. His father, Shadrach, had six wives and I think Chengeta wanted to emulate him. He managed three before members of the family persuaded him that enough was enough!'

Astonishment paused as though the years had rolled away and he was six again, watching his Uncle Chengeta squaring up for a fist fight. He stood with a slight smile, lost in his memories.

'You know, here was where I made my first childhood friend. Surprisingly, he was white. Dave was about my age, the grandson of the farm owner. Unlike the white adults, Dave was a familiar face around the compound where people called him *Piccanin Baas*. I got to know him when he came by on his bike from the farmhouse and saw me in shorts that were so torn and tattered they were almost nonexistent. He pedalled back home and returned with a pair of freshly ironed shorts of his own. He understood a bit of Shona, but the only English I knew were the orders I heard from Kachasu. Somehow we managed to communicate. I couldn't believe that this well-dressed white boy from the big house was actually giving me a pair of his own shorts. They were good shorts, too. For years they were the only ones I possessed. I wore them until they fell off in shreds.

'So Dave and I became friends. Having fitted me out with a decent pair of shorts, he then found a spare bike back at home and taught me to ride it. He'd cycle down to the compound and, if I wasn't needed in the fields, we'd take off together for the day. We shot birds with his air gun. We swam in the dam on the Sebakwe River. It's infested with crocodiles even now, so no adult would ever have let us go if they'd known. But we sneaked out all the same. I never saw a crocodile, but once we got a massive scare when we came across two pythons thrashing about in the water – playing or fighting, I don't know. We didn't stay to find out. Or if it was too cold for swimming, we'd find one of those forty-four gallon oil drums that white people used to saw down the middle lengthways to make a *braaivleis*. Of course there were no *braais* for us, but the half-drums made good troughs for cattle and were lying around everywhere. It wasn't hard to find one and turn it into a boat. Two small boys could fit in comfortably.

'But the most amazing thing of all was when Dave took me back to the farmhouse. The Shona maid preparing lunch in the kitchen was horrified when the little *baas* turned up with a ragamuffin from the compound and invited him in. She protested that I'd mess up her clean floors, that I stank of woodsmoke, that the big *baas* and the madam would be furious if they found out. Dave was unperturbed. He ignored her protests and led me into the house. As I followed him from room to room, still watched by the glowering maid, my eyes must have stuck out on stalks at the luxury I saw around me. A single room was the size of many huts put together. I'd never slept in a bed, always on the floor. In fact, the first time I slept in a bed was when I was nineteen. But here were soft, bouncy beds with springs and covers that Dave and his family slept in every night. This was beyond my comprehension. I knew white people were wealthy, but I'd never imagined their lives could be like this – so different, so easy, so comfortable.

'Eventually Dave's parents found out about the friendship. They could have banned it, but they didn't. Because Dave accepted me, they accepted me. I even started having meals at the farmhouse, eating European food served up by the still-hostile maid. I had no idea how to use a knife and fork, so I ate with my fingers as if I were eating *sadza*. Dave thought this was a great idea, so he ate with his fingers, too.'

I tried to reinsert myself into the old Rhodesian mindset. How would Ida ('Wouldn't these blecks be heppier...?') Price have reacted had a *piccanin* turned up in her dining room and started eating with his fingers at her table? I suggested to Astonishment that Dave's parents must have been unusually enlightened.

'Not entirely,' he answered. 'They were fine when it was just the family, but if they had white friends in the house, then contact was banned. I guess that was a step too far – too many taboos. Dave was happy to play with me when he was on his own, but even he withdrew in the company of other white people. Still, that didn't stop us having some wonderful times together when no one else was around.'

Astonishment began pacing among the ruins, recalling who had lived in which of the tumbledown shacks. 'Ya... ya... this one belonged to Finish.'

'Finish?'

'Yes, Finish, the deaf and dumb tractor driver who chose to take all his wages in beer and could only ever mutter one word: "Finish." No one had any idea what he meant, but that became his name. And this one, this was where my friend Kariba lived, the guy I got arrested with.'

The name launched Astonishment on another trail of memories. 'Kariba. Ah! That wasn't his real name, but he was such a live wire he was like electricity. So we called him Kariba... like the dam... where the hydro-electricity comes from. We used to scare birds together with our *sjamboks*. I remember once, after we'd had a busy morning, we decided to take a break. While I snoozed in the shade of a tree somewhere near that little hill over there, Kariba picked some maize and built a fire to roast it. Still dozing, I heard the crackle of dry sticks, quickly followed by a shout. The fire was spreading and Kariba was stamping on it – barefoot, of course, but when you've never worn shoes you develop a plastic-like shell on the soles of your feet that can even put out fire. I laughed at the sight of him hopping and dancing on the flames that were eating up the grass along the edge of the field. "Oooh, ah, ah, ah, ah!" he gasped, trying to keep pace as the brown grass smouldered and blackened. In a few moments, the flames were licking at the mealie stalks. With a massive whoosh, they leaped to shoulder height and tore through the field.

'We fled like frightened impala. Looking back, we saw Finish coming over on his tractor and some of the others following behind. At the height of the dry season there's no water, obviously, so the only way to put out a fire is to beat it with sacks and branches. Eventually the adults got it under control, but not before it had destroyed about half a kilometre square of mealie field and bush – roughly from that hill to the road and over to the rocks that you can see in the distance.

'"People are saying it was you kids that started it," said one of the workers back at the compound that evening.

'"Are they?" I replied. "What gives them that idea?"

'The man looked at me suspiciously, but said nothing. And that was the last we ever heard of it. We never let on to anyone what really happened.'

I told Astonishment how I, too, had started a bush fire as a child, but conceded that his was probably more impressive. 'And I never owned up either.' We agreed that if he went public, so would I.

We walked back to the car and continued driving. Astonishment took a few minutes to collect his thoughts, then picked up his story.

'Soon after my mother's marriage and departure to Mhari, Uncle Chengeta took it into his head to return to Buhera, to the Ndiya homestead he'd left a few years earlier. His wife and children went with him. That left me in the sole care of my grandmother. Despite the harsh working conditions at Morrison Farm, this was the short, golden period of my childhood. To other members of my family, I was still Murambiwa, the rejected one, but not so to Granny Naomi. She called me Asi, her pet version of Astonishment. Of all my relatives, she was the only one who ever showed me unconditional love. She adored me, and I adored her in return.

'Whenever Granny Naomi went shopping in Enkeldoorn, she would take me with her. Hand in hand, we walked into town from Morrison Farm down the road we've just driven – and when she'd done her business, she'd buy me a bottle of cola and an iced bun. I loved that! I *loved* it! That was my special treat. On the walk back to Morrison, I could feel the fizz in my stomach. Even today, a sip of cola takes me right back to being six or seven in the general store in Enkeldoorn with Granny Naomi.

'She also introduced me to beer. Like most people, she enjoyed the strong, home-brewed, country beer made from maize and rapoco. Whenever word went out that beer was being brewed on the compound or in one of the nearby villages, she'd hurry over with one hand holding on to mine and the other clutching a half-jar of peanut butter. Before she settled down to drink, she'd add some beer to the jar, mix in some *sadza* and feed it to me. It's amazing how quickly a slug of beer and peanut butter *sadza* can put a child to sleep!

'It always distressed her that she couldn't afford to send me to school like some of the other farm children. She was uneducated herself, but she did the best she could – which consisted of teaching me to count to ten in Shona. *Poshi, piri, tatu, china, shanu...* I can't say the words without thinking back to my grandmother squatting in the shade of her little shack at Morrison, laying down sticks in the sand to help me learn. But more important was what she taught me about life and relationships. Hers was a life of constant hard labour, but she showed me that there's dignity in work, that humility is to be valued, that there's more to be gained from giving preference to other people than from seeking your own interests. She was a wonderful woman. I wish God had kept her until I could have taken care of her in return. I'd happily have carried her on my back for the rest of her days.

'Granny Naomi continued working for a year or so at Morrison until she became too old and weak to go on. In Zimbabwe, your children are the only insurance policy you have – which is why people value big families. With no way of supporting herself and me, she had no choice but to follow Uncle Chengeta back to Buhera and become dependent on him. I was then aged eight and of course I had to go with her, leaving behind Dave and Kariba and all my other friends. We got a bus for part of the way, then walked the rest with my grandmother carrying our few belongings in a bundle on her head. For our first night on the road, we relied on country hospitality and found a family of strangers willing to take us in. For the second night we lodged with Granny's daughter, Angela – the one who tore her petticoat to wrap me in as a newborn and who now lived with her husband, Sullivan, at a homestead not far from the Ndiyas. I remember she cooked us a chicken, which was not something anyone did lightly. It tasted sensational.

'Eventually we reached the Ndiya *kraal* at Chirimudombo. There we learned that Uncle Chengeta had quit the village and had set up home a few kilometres further on. We carried on walking and found where he lived. We were not exactly welcome. Chengeta's hut was little more than a hovel. He had no cows, so was poor even by African standards, and was already supporting his wife and four children. Now, to add to the burden, he found himself saddled with his aged mother and eight-year-old nephew, two extra mouths that he could ill afford to feed. That said, our arrival wasn't all bad news. Aunt Angela's husband, Sullivan, still owed Naomi a cow as part of Angela's bride price. Honourable man that he was, he turned up soon after we arrived and handed it over. Even better, it came with a calf. Chengeta's homestead at last possessed some cattle, even if only two.

'There was much mending of relationships to be done. The Ndiya homestead had never had happy associations. It was from here that Naomi had fled to escape the antagonism of her husband Shadrach's third wife, Jasmine; here, too, where Lonia had found life so trying as a young mother. I remember Jasmine turning up to check out Naomi's intentions concerning Shadrach. Was she here to reassert her position as wife number two? When Naomi made it clear she had no interest whatsoever in rekindling anything with Shadrach, I think there was some degree of reconciliation. That didn't stop Shadrach himself pitching up to see if Naomi was for reclaiming. By then, though, he was very old and nearly blind, so possibly couldn't even see what she looked like. Even though some of the neighbours tried to get them back together, Naomi remained adamant. In the end, the two old people agreed to stay separate, meeting only on beer-brewing days when Shadrach invariably hobbled over to Naomi's to sample her latest batch.

'While the Ndiyas patched things up to an extent, there remained the ongoing resentment at my father's family, the Mukaratis, who had cast me off at birth and contributed nothing beyond the original three cows. The Ndiyas felt they'd been exploited and loathed the Mukaratis as a result.

'My father, Calisto, was by now working in Salisbury and was out of contact, but the rest of his family still lived close by as they had done when Calisto and Lonia were at school together. Sometimes Granny Naomi would take me to visit Aunt Angela at her homestead nearby. The route took us past the Mukarati *kraal*. As we approached, my grandmother would cue me as to what to say if we met anyone: "Go away! I don't want to see you. You never wanted me. I despise you."

'I was unclear why I was supposed to hate the Mukaratis. It was simply what all Ndiyas did. My Mukarati grandfather was reckoned to be not so bad. It was said he had a soft spot for my mother and would have kept her within the family if he'd had his way. The real villain in the Ndiyas' eyes was his wife. They claimed she'd been instrumental in booting my mother out of the homestead just a week after she'd given birth, so reserved their harshest venom for her. I recall funerals at which both families were present and the Ndiyas literally barked in derision when my Mukarati grandmother appeared.

'At least moving back to Buhera meant a chance to start school. Matsvai Government Primary lay midway between the Ndiya and Mukarati homesteads, a walk of a few minutes across the bush. When my grandmother took me to apply, the head at first refused to take me. At nine, I was too old for the entry year, Standard One, for which the Government of Rhodesia Education Department said you had to be six. But realising I had no alternative, he relented. Joining a class of six-year-olds, I entered the exotic and unfamiliar world of education. I was expert at herding cows, but I couldn't read or write a single letter.

'My schooling lasted three weeks. This was 1976 and the war of liberation had reached Buhera. As the freedom fighters advanced westwards from Mozambique, the reclaimed territory was declared to be liberated and therefore no-go for any government activity. That included government schools. Communication with Salisbury was severed. Teachers, being government employees, could no longer collect their salaries. Schools in the liberated zones had no option but to close.

'To drive home the message that colonialism was finished, the comrades took apart the Matsvai Primary buildings. From the Ndiya homestead, we could hear them hammering and sawing to remove the timber and the zinc roofs. Asbestos, too – that could be used again. The villagers helped. Dismantling the buildings was symbolic of dismantling the white regime and if the materials could be put to use in people's houses, so much the better.

'So thanks to the comrades,' sighed Astonishment, 'my education was over in less than a month. It was only after four more years, four years of conflict, that I saw the inside of a classroom again.'

8

The War Comes to Buhera

Again Astonishment fell silent, navigating the boulders of a dried-up river course that cut across the track. The sun-baked veldt rocked slowly by, the midday glare contracting the shadows of the trees and bouncing off the hot bonnet of the Toyota. Just twelve years separated my last day at Selborne-Routledge in 1964 and Astonishment's at Matsvai in 1976, but the two schools existed in different eras, different countries even. The settled comfort of pre-war white Rhodesia felt a universe away from the disruption wrought by the conflict on the other side of the racial divide.

Astonishment picked up my thoughts. 'Ya, the war. I remember the night it came to our village. We were harvesting groundnuts when the *kraal* head, Mr Sabhuku Tizirai, approached across the field and signalled to Uncle Chengeta that he wanted to talk to him. Mr Tizirai was an important man, the person responsible for keeping the *kraal* records. Hence his title, *Sabhuku*, meaning 'one who keeps a book'. He took Uncle Chengeta aside and sat him down under a tree. They spoke earnestly with much wagging of heads. After a few minutes, Uncle Chengeta returned and explained to the rest of us that the war of liberation had started. That night there was going to be an all-night meeting, a *pungwe*, at Mr Tizirai's homestead. Everyone was ordered to attend.

'I didn't know what a *pungwe* was, but it sounded exciting if it meant being up all night. From the whispered conversations among the adults, I understood we were going to meet some very special people. They had to be special, because each family was ordered to bring a dish of *sadza* and chicken. Chicken! You didn't kill a chicken unless for very good reason.

'As night fell, we walked over to Mr Tizirai's homestead to find the whole village assembling – men, women and children seated on the ground, their clothes pulled tight against the evening chill and a buzz of expectation in the air. Waiting for us there were ten or twelve young men whom I hadn't seen before. They squatted on the ground next to Mr Tizirai's hut, their faces serious and impassive. One who seemed to be the leader was pulling on a cigarette and nursing a gun on his lap. I'd never seen a gun. It looked hard and brutal in the firelight.

'Once the stragglers were settled, the leader tossed away his cigarette and stood up. The talk subsided and all eyes turned to him. He was a powerfully built man, intense and energetic in his manner, but he addressed his audience politely.

'"*Manheru.* Good evening," he began. "I am Comrade Gabarinocheka." He gestured to his companions and listed their names. I remember some of them still – Comrades Mabhunu, Chinovava, Gambu, Toronga, Hondo, Chimurenga... and one called Shorty. These were *noms de guerre*, intended to instil fear and avoid identification.

Hondo means war. *Chimurenga* is revolution. As for Shorty – well, he was just Shorty, but he still looked fierce.

'Gabarinocheka continued. "There are many of us, the true sons of Zimbabwe, and we are everywhere. You will meet us when you go to your fields, when you search for firewood, when you graze your cattle. Do not run away when you see us. We are here to free you from the oppressor."

'He went on to tell the story of colonial rule and white exploitation in Zimbabwe. He told us of other countries where black people had thrown off their white masters and today had black rulers who treated them as equals. Now it was Zimbabwe's turn. "Digging your plots – that's hard work, hey? But when the liberation comes, you won't have to do that. Nor will you have to pay the hut tax, or any taxes." This was a lie and I'm sure people knew it, but the audience responded with murmurs of approval. Never had anyone so articulated their sense of subjugation and the suffering and indignities of colonial rule. It was heady stuff.

'Next came the practising of slogans.

'"*Pamberi nechimurenga!*" shouted Gabarinocheka. Forward with the war of revolution!

'"*Pamberi!*" replied the people raggedly. Forward! Gabarinocheka urged them on, then broke into song.' Astonishment beat time on the wheel and sang softly in Shona as if back at Mr Tizirai's all those years ago. 'Ya, the comrades did their job well. The words are still in my head.

'Nehondo nehondo, tichaitora nehondo.
Nehondo nehondo, nyika ndeyeropa.
Zimbabwe ndeyeropa.'

'Meaning?' I asked.

> 'Through this war, we'll rule our country.
> Through this war, we'll shed blood for the country.
> We'll shed blood for Zimbabwe.'

Under my breath, I hummed the tune from the other side of the divide, the anthem that Mrs Mackay had taught us back at Selborne-Routledge and which white children were still no doubt singing in the mid-1970s as their fathers and brothers went to war. This was our land, it declared – our Rhodesia, ours to keep and guard.

'The comrades began dancing and urged us all to dance too,' continued Astonishment. 'Feet were raised and pounded on the ground, thumping the earth like pile drivers while the voices of the comrades rose above the beat. The moon climbed and the stars wheeled across the sky and the comrades danced on, powered, it seemed, by a dark, fierce energy. It frightened and fascinated me at the same time. As for the people, though they were growing tired, the novelty of the *pungwe* kept them alert.

'Comrade Toronga stepped forward – *toronga* being the Shona for a sour, peppery fruit. Befitting his name, he was harsher, more abrasive than Gabarinocheka. Laying down the rules of warfare as they applied to the *povo*, the ordinary people, he ordered us to avoid all contact with Rhodesian soldiers. Any kind of cooperation or assistance was tantamount to selling out, and being a sell-out was the worst crime of all, punishable by death. Those whose sons were in town working for the whites – or worse still, serving in the Rhodesian army – should summon them back at once. The comrades had information on who these people were.

'Toronga swept his eye across the crowd and picked out an elderly gentleman called Mr Mutyairi. He called him to the front and made him face the people. He stood like a man already condemned, eyes to the ground and his hands fumbling with the hem of his jersey. "We know you have sons fighting for the oppressor," barked Toronga. "Bring them back to join the struggle and they'll be safe. That is an order. If they do not return, the comrades will kill them on sight as sell-outs."

'Still mute and swallowing nervously, Mr Mutyairi returned to his place. Toronga then kicked off a song about Dakotas, the aircraft used by the Rhodesians to parachute soldiers into the war zone once they'd had a tip-off of guerrillas in the area.'

Astonishment once more sang the words:

'Ukaona Dakota rauya,
Panenge paita mutengesi!

'When you see the Dakota coming,
You know there's been a sell-out!

'The third speaker, Chimurenga, was more conciliatory. He talked about recruitment and how it was an honour for families to send their sons to the struggle. He cited Chaminuka, Kaguvi and Nehanda, heroes who had fallen earlier in the struggle and thus become war spirits who would keep watch over the comrades and walk beside them in the conflict. And he listed further rules that we, the *povo*, were required to obey. Keep your eyes open. Report all strangers to the comrades. Make sure the *sabhuku* records all visitors along with origin and purpose of visit. Work with the comrades to overcome the oppressor.

'Raising his weapon above his head, Chimurenga led us in another chant.

'"*Muhondo...* " he shouted. In time of war...

'The *povo* responded: "*Iwe neni tine basa!*" You and I have a task in hand.

'"*Rei?*" To do what?

'"*Rekusunungura Zimbabwe!*" To liberate Zimbabwe!

'In this way, the comrades' programme of political education came to our village. As a nine-year-old, I found a lot of the talk beyond me. I didn't understand the politics, but I do remember exciting talk of AK47s, light machine guns and bazookas – and how the comrades feared the sophisticated armaments used by the Rhodesians. How could we, the *povo* of Zimbabwe, prevail against an enemy that could fly into battle in Dakotas? Answer – by the justice of our cause and the spirit of our people. *Pamberi nechimurenga!* Forward with the war of revolution! As we returned excitedly to our homes after that first session – a relatively early 3am finish on account of it being our first *pungwe* – most people believed the war would be over in a few weeks.

'Later sessions went on all night with no one allowed home until daybreak. Sometimes the comrades would reveal their tactics for the following day – where they intended to strike and when, so that civilians could keep out of the way. And sure enough, we'd hear the firing of guns or landmines going off in the distance and the women of the *kraal* would kick up the dust and ululate in celebration. In time, though, the prospect of yet another all-night session of political education began to pall. The war wasn't going to be over any time soon and people were growing weary of the same old slogans. The comrades took to filling buckets of water, ready to pour over anyone who fell asleep mid-*pungwe*.

'When the fighters were in the area, they lived off the local people. In the early days, most people in Chirimudombo willingly gave support and were prepared to donate their chickens and goats and cattle to the cause. Each night the women were required to cook *sadza* and take it to the comrades' encampment outside the village. And not just *sadza* with greens – it had to have meat. Those comrades ate like locusts! It was said they were so starved during their training in Mozambique that they had to spend the rest of the war making up for it.

'The demands on the *povo* became more onerous as the war dragged on. Many families ended up slaughtering every chicken they possessed, then their goats and finally their cattle in order to feed the ever-ravenous comrades.

'Being ten or eleven at the height of the war, I was more an observer than a participant. But children only slightly older than me had important roles to play. The boys became *mujibhas* or errand boys, sent to collect groceries or cigarettes from the village store when ordered by the fighters. They were also sources of intelligence, able to move about in the bush without attracting attention from the enemy. Rhodesian soldiers on patrol might not notice the small boy sitting on a rock, but the child would be taking note of their movements and passing the information back to the encampment. *Mujibhas* were often caught in the crossfire and died in large numbers in the course of the war.

'Girls, on the other hand, became *chimbwidos* – a name derived from *mbwido*, a kind of wild fruit. They were kept within the encampment, partly as hostages to deter their parents from betraying the comrades' location. Any attack on the base was likely to see their daughters killed. The job of *chimbwidos* was to wait on the comrades, serve the food and provide comfort in the night. Many became pregnant, so today there's a generation of young Zimbabweans who've never known which comrade was their father. Parents who refused to let their daughters become *chimbwidos* could be executed.

'When the comrades tortured someone, they usually did it out of sight in the bush, away from the village but often within earshot. Beating and stabbing were the usual methods. I've heard the victims groaning and screaming, pleading for their lives against a barrage of shouts and blows. It was horrible, but there was nothing we *povo* could do. That said, some punishments were carried out in full view. A sell-out, for example, could expect public execution. While I never witnessed that, I did see a man being hauled in front of the comrades for beating his wife. He was summoned to the front during a *pungwe* and made to stand facing the crowd like Mr Mutyairi on that first night. The basis of the charge was that an injured woman could not cook for the cause. "*Ukaremadza mai wauraya comrade nenzara.*" If you disable your wife, you starve a comrade. The man was felled with several blows and one of the comrades stamped on his head with both feet. He was then ordered to stay lying down and beaten with a heavy stick on his backside.

'The Rhodesians, meanwhile, were known to inflict collective punishment on any *kraal* whose inhabitants had helped the guerrillas or not reported their presence. Huts would be torched and cattle confiscated. We also heard of Rhodesian soldiers torturing prisoners and forcing country people into so-called protected villages – another term for prison camps. This was a war in which the loyalty or at least the acquiescence of local people was crucial. If Rhodesian troops were terrorising people to deter them from helping the freedom fighters, the freedom fighters had to inflict even greater terror to turn them back again.'

I pictured those ugly propaganda brochures put out by the Smith regime to show the cruelty of the terrorists against their own people. The pictures of African villagers shot, beaten and mutilated – innocent victims of Communist-inspired savages, claimed the government. So they might have been, but their deaths had a macabre logic in the race to out-terrorise the other side. Thinking of my Selborne-Routledge school friends, most of whom must have been called up, I asked Astonishment if he'd ever been near the fighting.

'Ya, ya,' he went on. 'Although my job was herding cattle rather than being a *mujibha*, I sometimes passed information to the comrades. The first time I saw Rhodesian forces close up, a group of soldiers had just come roaring into the village in a couple of Land Rovers and had seized my mother's half-sister and a few others to take away as hostages. Some of us kids saw them leaving as we were driving the cattle back home. We put the cows in the *kraal* and ran as fast as we could to the comrades' encampment to tell them what we'd seen. We thought they'd go and fight these guys and free our relatives.

'And you know what?' Astonishment threw back his head and laughed. 'They ran even faster than us – away from the soldiers!'

'And your relatives?'

'Oh, they got released, but only much later when they no longer served any use as hostages. But the one time I actually saw the action was when a patrol of black Rhodesian soldiers with white officers set up camp by the river near the Ndiya homestead. Now whatever the quarrels and conflicts at the homestead, it was known to be a place that made good beer. Granny Naomi's was particularly renowned. So when the soldiers arrived, they sent for some gourds of home-brew. Of course, the people delivering the beer were able to see the layout of the camp and how many soldiers there were, and they passed the information back to the comrades.

'A short time later, a group of ten to fifteen heavily armed comrades walked into the compound and said everyone should drop what they were doing and get out of there as fast as they could. There was going to be a firefight and they didn't want civilians getting hurt. As usual, I was herding cattle and was coming back towards the village when I saw these guys moving out to attack. They warned me away, keeping their voices low so they wouldn't carry towards the enemy.

'"Drive your cattle that way," hissed one of them. "Run! Stay out of the way."

'As I steered my cows around, I saw the comrades dropping on to all fours and crawling through the sorghum field towards the enemy encampment. I hadn't run far when I heard firing. The Rhodesians were taken by surprise as they drank their beer, and all but one were killed. But this lone survivor – he was a fighter. He chased the comrades as they retreated, firing as he went. Whether it was accidental or deliberate I don't know, but he shot one of my relatives who'd been drinking at the homestead and hadn't fled as quickly as he should. When we all returned to the homestead we found his body with a bullet wound in his back and the sand on which he lay turning black with flies and blood. His name was Mavhangira. I later went to his funeral.

'That evening, a Rhodesian helicopter landed by the river and collected the bodies. From up at the homestead, I saw it arrive and listened to the chop-chop of the blades as it dropped out of sight behind the trees. It was only a few minutes, the rotors running all the time, before it took off again with its cargo of corpses. It was shocking that day to see that war was not a game. For all the songs of triumph and liberation, it was bloody and violent and messy. Later in the conflict I saw corpses of guerrillas and each sighting made my stomach heave. Every time the fighting came near our village, there were many, many funerals to go to afterwards.'

Yes, I thought. *And more funerals of young reservists in all those places whose names no longer exist – Salisbury, Fort Victoria, Umtali, Enkeldoorn.*

'The fighting moved steadily westwards,' continued Astonishment. 'Month by month, the comrades took more swathes of countryside and declared them to be liberated zones. After we were liberated in Buhera, I never saw any further government activity. I think Ian Smith and the whites were too busy defending the cities to send more troops into country areas like ours. In fact, any movement across the line from non-liberated areas was strictly controlled by the comrades and the local leaders. If you had someone visiting you from one of those areas, you had to inform the *kraal* head that same evening, and the *kraal* head was obliged to take them to the comrades to be vetted. If they judged the person to be a spy or someone who'd been consorting with white people – well, probably they would not be seen again. Not alive, anyway.'

'So what about your family?' asked Lynda. 'How did they survive the war?'

'Ah, my family,' replied Astonishment. 'They were poor enough anyway, and the war made them even poorer. Whatever your political views, you still have to survive. For Uncle Chengeta, survival meant running the risks of crossing the demarcation line. To escape the grinding poverty of Chirimudombo, he left home, headed west towards Enkeldoorn and took up his old employment at Morrison Farm – not far from the Salisbury to Beitbridge road and so within the relative safety of the government-controlled zone. It was a one-way choice. Travelling out of a liberated area was a lot easier than travelling back in, so those of us left behind knew it could be a long time before we saw him again.

'Chengeta's departure left his wife, Bianca, with the obligation of looking after not just their own four children but Granny Naomi and me as well. In such a poor family, this was unsustainable. So next, partly to lighten the burden, my grandmother decided to make the long trek to Morrison. She said as she left that she'd try to persuade Chengeta to come home, perilous though the journey would have been. I pleaded to go with her, rather than be left alone in a family that saw me as superfluous. It wasn't possible. Travelling at the height of the war would be hard enough for an old lady, even without a child in tow. I had to stay. Like my mother five years earlier, she set off one day with her bundle on her head – though this time there was much turning around and waving and tears on her side as well as mine as she disappeared from view.

'The weeks and months went by and there was no word back. With the war intensifying, this wasn't surprising: communication across the line was almost nonexistent. All I could do was wait. Often, I would walk the bush footpath towards Buhera, scanning the flat horizon in the hope that I might see Granny and Uncle Chengeta coming the other way. I imagined their two figures shimmering in the heat haze and me running to greet them as they approached and morphed into solid people. It never happened and we never knew why – or even whether Granny had made it through.

'With Chengeta gone, and now Granny in an apparently failed attempt to bring him back, the one remaining extra mouth was mine. And the tensions were showing. One evening I was late bringing in the cattle. Bianca complained to a relative called Jacob who also lived in the *kraal*. The following day I was out again with the cows and Jacob came to find me. I greeted him as he approached. But instead of replying, he grabbed me and started beating me about the head with a tree branch he'd had concealed behind his back. "That's for being late with the cattle," he shouted. "Never do it again!" The beating was bad enough, but I also felt so vulnerable – not just that day with Jacob, but permanently. I knew I wasn't wanted. There was nobody interested in hearing my story. I just had to endure and hope that something would change.

'And change it did – for the worse. I was eleven and a good manual worker. In a move tantamount to selling a slave, the family decided to auction me.'

9

Into Slavery

The track from Morrison meandered through boulders and swaying grass and brought us to a pack of baboons, squatting in the sand along the verge. They stirred themselves and paced away, their mango-coloured buttocks waggling contemptuously and the little ones tumbling over themselves to keep up. The daddy of the family looked us straight in the eye and bared his fangs before slipping into the bush.

'Horrible, vicious creatures,' declared Astonishment. 'I dreaded meeting them as a child, especially if I had any food on me. They'd always try to grab it. Far scarier than anything in the war.'

Lynda interrupted. 'So what's this about being sold as a slave?'

'Ah yes. What happened was... the wealthiest people in the neighbourhood were the Mutyairi family who had their own farm and a good number of cows.'

The name had come up earlier. 'Mutyairi?'

'Yes, yes. The same Mr Mutyairi who was cautioned by the comrades at our very first *pungwe*. Their prosperity was relative – no one in Buhera was rich – but they had enough cash to build a sizeable compound. And one reason they were better off was the fact that the two Mutyairi boys were still serving in the Rhodesian army and sending money home to the family.'

'So the Mutyairis had ignored the comrades' warning?'

'It seems so.'

'And the sons could still send money home though the war zone? How did they do that?'

'It was difficult and dangerous,' replied Astonishment. 'Every few months, one of the boys would cross the lines under cover, walking long distances and always by night to avoid the comrades. Discovery would mean death, for sure. This guy would bring money for his parents and also for some of the other families who had sons in town. This was distributed secretly after he'd left, again by night to prevent the comrades finding out. So this way, some of the local people benefited from their sons' employment. They also got news of whether their sons were still alive.

'At the same time, this arrangement made for strained relations with the rest of the community when others were sending their sons to fight for the liberation. Theirs was an even greater sacrifice. The parents of freedom fighters spent years not knowing if their sons were alive or dead. The only news came from Radio Rhodesia, but that was government propaganda. All the reports were about how many "terrs" had been killed. For their part, the Mutyairis always maintained that they supported the struggle and had never wanted their sons to join up. After the warning from the comrades, they'd even travelled to find them and persuade them to desert. They'd failed. Knowing the fate that could have befallen their sons if they'd come home, let alone the loss of income from their wages, it's possible they didn't try too hard.

'I've no idea what the financial settlement was between the Mutyairis and the Ndiyas. All I know is that suddenly I was transferred from Chengeta's compound to the Mutyairis' farm some ten kilometres away, and put to work. I had no choice. Had Granny still been there, I know she'd have protected me from this kind of exploitation. But as it was, I had no one speaking up for me. I was totally alone.

'There were three children of about my age in the Mutyairi family – a daughter and the two children of one of the soldier sons. They were still being educated because for some reason their school was taking longer to close than my own ill-fated Matsvai Primary. But no one thought of educating me. Whatever money or cows had changed hands on my account, I was there to work.

'The Mutyairis installed me in one of their huts. Every morning I'd wake up early and herd their cattle, taking care to graze them away from people's fields so they didn't interfere with any crops. Letting your cows wander into people's fields was a serious matter.'

An image came to mind, one of those embedded in your childhood that only needs a nudge to rise to the surface. The family Ford Zephyr, parked at one of the clusters of tables and seats that offered shady picnic spots along the main routes in colonial times. I'd seen the same tables and seats travelling with Astonishment. All, though, were now derelict, their rusty metal reinforcement sticking out through crumbling concrete. Some had collapsed into the earth. None was ever being used. But back in Salisbury days, we used them often. The memory that rose was of a family picnic, interrupted by a shout – '*Hande!*' Let's go! – and the crack of a *sjambok*. A dozen skinny cows stumble out of the long grass and across the road, followed by a dusty, microscopic child, pot-bellied and near-naked, driving his herd with masterly precision. The bigness of the cows and the smallness of the boy are a source of wonder to the white family, distracted for a moment from its thermos flask and cheese sandwiches. And the tiny cowherd – well, what did he think as he looked back at us? We never knew. Until now, I'd never known one to talk to.

Astonishment went on. 'Ploughing season at the Mutyairis brought some variation to the work, even if it meant more toil. Each day I'd hitch up two of the oxen and go out ploughing on my own. Then I'd start herding cattle. The family gave me enough food to keep me working but no more, so my memory is of constantly being hungry. I never had any change of clothes. No shoes for my bare feet. The rags I arrived in were the ones I lived in for all the time I was there. At one point, I was very sick with measles. I remember being so weak I went several days without being able to open my eyes. And what did my owners do? Like a dog, they kept me quarantined in my hut for three weeks until I recovered. What they didn't do was tell anyone in the Ndiya homestead in case they came and took me away and I never came back. Not that they need have worried. The Ndiyas had got rid of me for being an extra mouth to feed, so it's unlikely they'd have reclaimed me – sick or otherwise. But eventually I recovered and went back to doing all the dirty and difficult tasks that no one else wanted to do.'

Lynda stepped in again. 'So did you think of yourself as being a slave?'

'Oh yes, that's what I was. I knew I was being exploited, but I thought that working hard would be a way to gain acceptance. The *murambiwa* name had been prophetic. Life to that point had mainly consisted of rejection, apart from the times with my grandmother and she had now gone. But something in me always thought of this time as being temporary. I don't know why, but I never lost hope that there was something better to come. Even an education, though that was hard to imagine at the time.

'In this way, a whole year went by. And in the end I got my payment. Do you know what it was?' Astonishment gave a hoot of laughter. 'A goat! Can you imagine? One little goat for a year's hard labour!'

After another pause to gather his thoughts, Astonishment resumed. 'After a year, my owners returned me to my family. Maybe that was the original agreement, I don't know. But as soon as I got home, the family decided to uproot. As I told you, Uncle Chengeta had returned to the commercial farming sector and everyone knew the risks of trying to get back across the line of liberation between Enkeldoorn and Buhera. My grandmother had followed and had not been heard from since. We didn't even know if she was still alive. My mother was in Mhari with her new husband and also out of contact. The Ndiya household had dwindled to Chengeta's wife, Bianca, and her four children, the oldest of whom, a boy called James, was just two years older than me.

'Bianca realised that life was not going to improve in poverty-stricken Buhera. She also knew there was little hope of seeing her husband again unless she followed him. So she made the decision to join the migration to Enkeldoorn and Morrison Farm. This time, I was to go too.

'Preparations were minimal. There was almost nothing to take. We left our few cows and goats with Angela and Sullivan, my own little goat included, and set off one morning across the veldt like a family of warthogs – Aunt Bianca with her few belongings in a bundle on her head, followed in line by her four children with me bringing up the rear. The rains had come, churning the roads and footpaths and slowing our progress as our bare feet slithered in the mud. For much of the journey we were drenched. We walked by day and slept at night under whatever shelter we could find. It took us three days to walk the fifty kilometres to the little town of Gutu, the nearest point from which, at that point in the war, it was possible to board a bus or a truck to Enkeldoorn.

'These were the summer rains of late 1979. Far away in London, representatives of the recently renamed Zimbabwe-Rhodesia led by Ian Smith and Bishop Abel Muzorewa had just signed the Lancaster House Agreement with Robert Mugabe and Joshua Nkomo whose joint delegation was known as the Patriotic Front. Back home, as our little procession trudged across the rain-swept landscape, the result was a nervous peace with rival armies moving to assembly points as a prelude to laying down their arms. If the rain made the going harder, the let-up in the fighting at least made for one less hazard on our journey.

'I don't know how much Aunt Bianca was aware of the country's changing politics. I certainly wasn't. After years of *pungwes* and the comrades' orientation programme, I knew for a fact that white people liked nothing better than killing black children – probably eating them, too. Having never seen a *murungu* up close apart from farm manager Kachasu and Dave and his family, who were more like black people in white skins, I had no reason to doubt that this was true. So when I saw white soldiers in uniform, toting their guns on the streets of Gutu, I was petrified. For the hour or so that we waited for transport to take us to Enkeldoorn, I pictured the hideous things I'd been told to expect if a white soldier caught me. I'd be bundled into a van and taken to prison. I'd be tortured and hanged as a "terr". With these terrors running through my head, it surprised me that the soldiers seemed oblivious to our presence.

'After a couple of hours' bumpy ride in the back of a truck, we disembarked in Enkeldoorn next to Vic's Tavern and walked the final ten kilometres to our old compound at Morrison Farm. The sun was going down as we arrived and the smoke of cooking fires was lifting into the still air, fragrant with the wet-dust smell of the afternoon rain. With a surge of joy I saw my grandmother, bending over her pot and preparing the evening meal. I shrieked and ran towards her, just as I'd often imagined doing back in Buhera. She looked up in surprise, then gathered up her skirt and rushed to greet me. I hadn't seen her for a year and a half. I didn't even know she was still alive. The tears flowed as she pressed me close and asked again and again how I was. Why was I so thin? What had I suffered? I scolded her for deserting me and not being there to stop me becoming a slave at the Mutyairis. She countered that because of the war, she'd never been able to return or even get a message through.

'Surprises followed. We learned that when my grandmother had got to Morrison to try to persuade Chengeta to return, she'd found he was living with a new, second wife, a lady called Silvia. Not only that, there was now a baby – another grandchild for Granny Naomi. Clearly Chengeta had no intention of coming home, so my grandmother, realising her mission was futile, had decided to stay. She'd made her home with him and Silvia and baby Lonia – named after my mother, though sadly she died while still an infant – and had settled in for a second time at Morrison Farm.

'The same shock now awaited Bianca. Expecting a joyful reunion with her long-absent husband, she found him married to wife number two whose existence came as a total surprise. Silvia was equally stunned. I think she knew about Bianca, but she never expected her to travel all this way in wartime – and not with Chengeta's four children, the oldest of whom was not much younger than she was. As introductions were made, Chengeta's two wives eyed each other like lionesses defending their place in the pride. Chengeta simply looked embarrassed, stuttering out his explanations to each wife in turn.

'After the initial tension, both wives realised there was little point objecting. Given that old Shadrach Ndiya had had six wives, his son's decision to take two was no great cause for complaint. Both Bianca and Silvia were entirely dependent on Chengeta economically, so had no choice but to make the best of the new arrangement and try to get along together. They tolerated each other, but never became close as far as I know.

'After the formalities, Silvia sealed the deal by cooking a massive meal of *sadza*, vegetables and that rarest of ingredients – meat! Having eaten very little on our trek from Buhera, we travellers fell on the meal like comrades in from the war, and gorged ourselves almost into oblivion.

'After four years away, it was good to be reunited with old friends like Kariba. And Dave, too. When Dave heard I was back in the compound, he pedalled down from the house to find me. When he saw me, he leaped off his bike and clasped me in a massive hug. It was an emotional moment. For a while we picked up on the old life, riding out on bikes and swimming in the dam or shooting at birds with Dave's pellet guns. But now we were both approaching our teens, it was clear we were moving in different worlds. Dave had started at boarding school in South Africa and was only home for the holidays. My schooling had consisted of three aborted weeks at Matsvai Primary. Beyond the messing about together, there wasn't much to link an educated white boy and the ragged, dirt-poor child of a migrant, farm-labouring family.

'In any case, it wasn't long before the next migration. That occurred when my mother came back on the scene.'

10

Sengwe Primary

The Toyota continued over tracts of sand, alternating with rutted, dried-out riverbeds in which we dipped and rose and picked our way around the boulders. The road straightened again and brought us to a wire gate, behind which was a small compound. Around the central area were two or three mud and thatched huts, a square, tin-roofed shack and a Datsun pick-up. A construction of lashed-together tree trunks supported a stack of maize stalks, drying in the sun. Goats grazed and chickens scratched. A dozen head of cattle stood like statues behind their tree-trunk stockade.

'The homestead of my mother's cousin, Nyasha,' explained Astonishment. 'Nowadays, when it's so hard to find meat in the shops, we have to rely on connections. Nyasha here has his own herd of cows. I've persuaded him to sell us a beast to feed the children at Matthew Rusike.'

People came out and greeted us. We were clearly expected. Someone produced a bowl of boiled potatoes and passed it round. As Lynda and I looked on, Astonishment drew a cluster of relatives around him for some kind of discussion. Among the group we noticed Tapiwa, Matthew Rusike's accountant and chief slaughterer. He waved. Discussion over, Astonishment and Tapiwa moved to the stockade. The branch across the entrance was pulled away and Tapiwa separated one of the cows from the herd. The doomed beast was led to a nearby tree and tethered. More discussion, from which it emerged that Tapiwa needed some assistance to carry out the slaughter and didn't trust the competence of the guys on the spot. But he did know some people locally who knew how to kill a cow and decided to go and find them. He jumped into the pick-up and roared away towards Chivhu.

So the cow won a short reprieve. I can't say how long, because Astonishment decided it was time to move on. Tapiwa would take care of the butchering and getting the carcass back to Matthew Rusike. Some of it might be frozen, subject to Zimbabwe's erratic power supply, but no one was setting much store on that. Chances were, the entire cow would need to be consumed by the end of the week. The killing itself must therefore remain undescribed, the only clue to the process being two murderous-looking knives as long as swords that Tapiwa removed from the pick-up before he sped away.

We drove on, the dust from the Toyota blanking out the *kraal* and the still-tethered cow as Nyasha's homestead shrank from sight in the rear-view mirror.

'So your mother appears on the scene,' I reminded Astonishment.

'Oh, yes. That was tied up with the politics. After the Lancaster House Agreement, the 1980 elections brought the war to an end and handed power to Comrade Robert Mugabe – our first black Prime Minister alongside our new black President, the Methodist minister, Canaan Banana. I was still only twelve, but even I understood that this was a significant day for Zimbabwe. The old enmities were put away. At his swearing-in, Mugabe spoke of his enemies as having become friends and of yesterday's hatred giving way to love that now bound old foes, one to another. It's incredible now to think that he spoke those words. Or that Ian Smith was allowed to live out his days on his farm.

'One result of the change of government was a drive for education to put right the discrimination of the past. Primary education would now be free. It didn't last long, I have to say. The government soon realised it couldn't afford to rebuild all the schools destroyed in the war and fees started creeping back in. But in those heady early days after independence, the prize of an education suddenly seemed available to all. Schools closed by the comrades began opening again. Poor people who'd never considered educating their children, or been able to do so even if they'd wanted to, started sending their sons and daughters to enrol.

'In that spirit, my mother made the journey from Mhari to collect me and take me home so that I, too, could have a proper schooling. Her arrival was unannounced. One day she simply turned up. Having not seen me for six years, I think she had trouble picking me out in the crowd of kids playing among the workers' shacks. But I knew at once who she was. I was surprised and pleased, but also shy if I remember rightly. After six years, this woman was a stranger and I'd never had the bond with her that I'd had with Granny Naomi. So my greeting was civil rather than excited. What was exciting, however, was the news that I would now be going to school. For my grandmother, this was a dream come true. Illiterate herself, she talked constantly about education as the way of escaping the grinding existence of the farm labourer. Though she hated to see me leave Morrison Farm, she knew it was for the best if it meant I could start school.

'So it was that my mother took me from my grandmother, from Uncle Chengeta and his two wives, from my friends – from Dave as well: I never saw him again – and brought me back to a new family. In the Mhari homestead I found myself living with my stepfather, Job Magondo, his two children from his previous marriage and three half-siblings I didn't know existed – Maudie, Richard and Esnath. The poverty here was as crushing as it ever was in Buhera. In the same way that the Ndiya family had resented the number of mouths that had to be fed at the homestead in Buhera, the Magondos weighed up scarce resources against increasing demand and decided that I was the scapegoat, the odd one out, the problem. From the start I was made to feel different. My presence at Mhari was an unwelcome reminder of my mother's previous relationship. Plus, I was another mouth. Once again I was Murambiwa, the rejected one, the object of hostility and abuse. My mother, who might have stood up for me, chose not to jeopardise her relationship with Job and the children they had in common, so stood by helplessly when the barbs and insults started flying in my direction.

'Clearly it got to me. I started wetting myself in the night. Every time I did so, Job would slap me about with his hand and sometimes beat me with a stick, yelling at me that I was a wicked and worthless child and he didn't know why he put up with me.'

'So did you blame your mother for not protecting you?' asked Lynda. 'For abandoning you for six years, then taking you away to something worse?'

'I could understand the situation she was in,' replied Astonishment generously. 'She had her other family to protect. Yes, she might have stood up for me, but actually I feel sorry for her. Remember, she herself was born into a polygamist family. Her father had six wives and she never had much attention from him. I was conceived by accident, so it's not surprising she didn't want me. My father was never around, so who can blame her for seizing the chance of a new life with Job?'

'So you've forgiven her for treating you like that?'

'Oh yes, I forgave her long ago. And also the Mukaratis for paying those three cows to wash their hands of me. I often think, if they'd kept me and we'd stayed together as a family, I wouldn't be the person I am now or have had the opportunities that came my way. Life has taken some surprising turns and now I'm grateful that things worked out as they did. I thank God that He's kept and guided me all through. The downside is that I'm still struggling to bond with my mother, even now. My grandmother was much more my mother than Lonia ever was, but I try to give my mother the unconditional love that I learned from her.

'In any case, there was a reason for being in Mhari and that was to go to school. For all the harsh treatment from the Magondos, that part of the deal held true. I remember the day Job took me to Sengwe Primary to enrol. From behind his desk, the headmaster, Mr Nzombe, peered over the top of his glasses and asked him how old I was.

'"Thirteen," said Job.

'"So you want him to go into Grade Six?"

'"Ah, no," said Job apologetically. "You see, my stepson has only done three weeks in primary. He doesn't even know his alphabet. He needs to go into Grade One."

'Mr Nzombe shook his head in amusement. "But this boy, he's almost as big as you. As big as a man. If I put him with the small children in Grade One, he's going to look ridiculous. Maybe he could start in Grade Five."

'"But Grade Five would be even worse because this boy knows nothing."

'I sat and listened, looking from one to the other as Job tried to convince this man of the true extent of my ignorance and bargain him down. Eventually they agreed that I should start in Grade Two with the seven-year-olds. On my first day, I hunkered down on one of the little chairs in the Grade Two classroom and tried to fold my teenage limbs under the miniature desk. They wouldn't fit, so I had to sit with my knees sticking above the table top. When the lessons began, I was totally baffled. The kids around me had had a year of school, so were well on with reading and writing. With no idea what I was doing, I tried to copy the meaningless squiggles I saw on the board into my exercise book. Some of the other children peeped over and sniggered – this gargantuan boy who couldn't write a single intelligible word! At break time, they snatched my book with its scrawls and ran down to the Grade One classroom to pass it around and laugh at my ineptitude.

'Every break time from then on, I attracted a tail of laughing children who followed me around and took delight in mocking me. Sometimes, like the Pied Piper, I led my swarm of tormentors to one or other of the teachers and pleaded to be allowed to go home because the day was becoming unbearable. Often they took pity on me and agreed to let me go.

'One day I decided I'd had enough of this torment. I hatched a plan to set off to school as normal, then hide in the long grass for the whole day and only emerge when the other children were coming home. Sengwe was four or five kilometres from home and I used to run – the normal thing to do after years of herding cattle. As I was jogging along on that particular morning, I became aware of one of the other pupils coming up behind. I picked up speed to try to shake him off. At the spot I'd chosen to hide in, I turned aside and crouched down. The day was already hot, so I stretched out and began basking in the sun. At last! No school. How wonderful. I felt my cares dropping away.

'Then to my alarm, peeping through the stalks of grass, I saw this guy stopping. He called out, "Astonishment! What are you doing? Hurry up! We're going to be late for school!"

'He knew where I was. Pretty soon he'd come looking for me. I had no choice but to come out, pretending I'd been having a pee. We carried on trotting to school together.

'By coincidence, that very day, a kindly teacher called Mr Muchenje was waiting to talk to me as we arrived. "Every lunch hour from now on," he said, "I want you to come to me in my classroom. I'm going to help you with reading and writing so you can catch up with the other children."

'Well, that was the end of my plans to abscond. If Mr Muchenje was expecting to see me every lunchtime, I could hardly go and hide in the bush. I said it was coincidence, but I see it now as God's good timing. If I'd managed to bunk off school for just one day, I would probably never have gone back and might have been herding cattle to this day. But lunchtime after lunchtime, Mr Muchenje took me through my numbers and the alphabet and the light started to dawn. In my second term, with his help, I came second in class. By the end of the year I was first and in Grade Three I became a prefect. Blossoming under Mr Muchenje's gentle encouragement, I started to enjoy being at school and now didn't want to go home.

'At one point during my second term, Granny Naomi came to visit us from Morrison. My mother told her I could now write and she burst into tears. "Asi," she cried, "show me how you do it! Write something and let me see." So I did, proudly cranking out a letter to Chengeta's son, James. *Dear James*, I scrawled in Shona in my wobbly, newly acquired handwriting. *How are you? I am well. I am going to school here in Mhari. How is everybody there?*

'She was ecstatic, gazing in wonderment at the hieroglyphics on the page. "My grandson can write!" she kept exclaiming. Scarcely believing my prowess, she asked if my talents extended to reading. To prove it, I read the letter back, sending poor Granny into paroxysms of delight. At the risk of inducing a heart attack, I rushed and fetched a Shona text book and spent the next half-hour reading it to her. This was almost too much for her to bear.

If she'd died then, she would, according to tradition, have gone to join her ancestors blissfully happy.

'As I made progress at Sengwe, life with the stepfamily became harder. Job Magondo's older children went to the same school. So did various Magondo nephews and nieces who shared the compound. None of them was doing particularly well and my late-flowering success increased the hostility.

'After two years at the Mhari homestead, two years of beatings and verbal abuse, my mother decided it wasn't safe for me to carry on living there. I'm sure she wanted to do more for me and be better able to protect me, but she remained torn between standing up for me and staying loyal to her Magondo children and stepchildren. She started making plans for me to go back to Morrison Farm and live with my grandmother once again.

'Though it was hard to leave the school I now loved, I couldn't wait to get back to Granny, the one person who had my interests totally at heart and who loved me as no one else did. I started counting down the days. Then, just two days before we were due to leave, a concerned-looking neighbour appeared at the door of the hut and asked to speak to my mother. She came with news passed on by the local bus driver. My beloved grandmother had died near Chivhu at the home of her sister, my great-aunt Faith.

'Squatting by the door, I overheard the conversation. I upped and ran blindly into the bush. There I hurled myself under a tree and howled at the sky with grief and disappointed hopes. I felt a light had gone out in my life. Yes, my grandmother was old and frail, but I never seriously thought that this one constant in my life, this sole source of unconditional love, would ever be gone. If circumstances had been different and she'd been with me in Buhera or Mhari, a lot of my misfortunes and mistreatment would never have happened. I'd never have been sent as a slave to the Mutyairis or been constantly beaten by Job Magondo. I'd have given anything to keep her with me a little while longer.'

Glancing from the passenger seat, I could see that Astonishment was affected, even now. He cleared the catch in his throat and went on. 'Taking the country bus, my mother travelled to the funeral at Faith's homestead a few kilometres from Morrison. But a Shona farewell is not simple. You know about Shona funerals?'

'Not really.'

'It's a two-stage process, and the burial is only the first part. Once the body is in the grave, the Shona traditionally believe that a person's spirit continues to hover a little way above the ground, round about tree level. It has not yet reached its final destination. Every spirit wants to join those of the same clan who have gone before. In Shona thinking, the dead live on in the spirit world in compounds of the same totem.'

'Totem?'

'Ah yes,' smiled Astonishment. 'All Zimbabweans have a totem, passed down from their fathers. For the Shona, these totems are mainly the names of animals. My grandmother was a *soko* – a monkey. Uncle Chengeta is a *shumba*, a lion, as is my mother.'

'And what are you?'

Astonishment threw up his hands and laughed. 'I am a mouse,' he declared with pride. 'In Shona, an *mbeva*. An *mbeva* married to a *shava*, an eland antelope! Can you imagine? So everyone who has the same totem as me is automatically my relative. And everyone who shares my wife's totem is also my relative. And if my mother is a lion, then every other lion is related to me. In the end, because the system is so interwoven, every Shona person ends up being connected to every other. Maybe that's why Africans are so aware of relationships. When strangers meet, after they've gone through the customary greetings, they'll start to establish their totems. "Ah, so you are a buffalo. Do you know ...? You must be related to ..." You feel a connection.'

I started to understand how Astonishment could claim kinship with almost every passing donkey-cart driver.

'And in this culture, the system persists after death,' Astonishment went on. 'When we die, so the Shona believe, we go to join our ancestors of the same totem. You go to your spirit clan and I go to mine. But you have to live well on earth in order to make it. The departed have the power to welcome or reject you, though they take their instructions from the highest spirit of all – God, if you will, the one the Shona call *Mwari*. If Mwari and your ancestors reject you, well that's when you come back and haunt the living.

'So the spirit has to be freed from its temporary abode in the trees and be sent to join the community of the departed. And that requires a memorial ceremony with much drinking of beer and an all-night vigil with drums and dancing. If you don't give your relative the right send-off, you risk terrible things happening. Complain to a tribal healer that you're getting bad luck and he'll very likely tell you that you failed to give some recently deceased relative the proper ceremony. "Your father is protesting because you haven't freed him from the trees. Give him the proper rites to help him depart and things will settle down."

'So in line with tribal belief, that's how it was for Granny Naomi. A year after the funeral, we held the memorial ceremony. This time my mother took me with her. She knew how deeply I mourned my grandmother and thought that being there would give me some kind of closure. As we were gathering with the rest of the family, my great-aunt Faith started talking to me about life with my stepfamily in Mhari. I told her honestly what it was like. She decided I couldn't be allowed to stay there and informed my mother that I should go and live with her.'

'Didn't your mother object?' asked Lynda.

'Not really.'

'Really?'

'Remember the tensions with the Magondo family. I was doing well at school. The younger Magondos were not, and that was stirring up jealousies. Plus, I was another mouth to feed. Maybe my mother saw this as a way out. She would have liked me to live with my grandmother, but now that Naomi was dead, my great-aunt Faith – Granny's sister – was the next best option. The arrangement was agreed and once again I was shipped off to another set of relatives.'

'Another set?' queried Lynda. 'Which were these?'

I was glad she asked. Astonishment's family tree looked about to become even more complicated.

'I'll explain,' smiled Astonishment. 'Round about the time of independence, Uncle Chengeta lost his job at

Morrison Farm and was turned out. The same thing happened to Nyasha, son of Great-Aunt Faith, the one whose compound we've just visited to kill the cow. Chengeta and Nyasha and their families left the farm with no more than the clothes on their backs and a few utensils and blankets. Also fired was Faith's son-in-law, Lovemore. This guy, though, had been quite senior at the farm – a foreman, what the whites would call a boss boy – and he got on well with farm manager Greg. In compensation, Lovemore was given a few head of cattle to help him set up somewhere else.

'These three, plus Chengeta's two wives and their children, my grandmother and Faith's daughter, Clotie, wife of Lovemore... I hope you're keeping up... all of these moved *en masse* into Faith's compound. Chengeta's son, James, was there. So was Amos, Faith's son by her fourth and current husband, Ezekiel.

'So this extended family became my family. Why did they agree to take me in? Not for any ties of blood, but because of my labour. I was fifteen, strong for my age and a good worker. Having escaped from slavery once, I was now back to something not dissimilar. I became the family workhorse.'

11

Hunger and Hard Labour

The track now ran flat and straight through brittle, knee-high grass, cresting a low ridge towards a line of blue-grey hills. Astonishment waved a hand across the landscape. 'All this,' he said, 'this is where I used to hunt.'

'Hunt?' I said. 'As a boy?'

'Ah yes. Rabbits, wild pigs, springbok, even bigger antelope like kudu.'

'But how does a young boy hunt a springbok or a kudu?'

'With dogs and a *knobkerrie*. We had a pack of dogs at Faith's place and we'd track through the bush with these dogs close by until they scented an animal and gave chase. So then it would be the animal running for its life, the dogs in pursuit and me at the back, sprinting as fast as I could in my bare feet to be there at the kill before the dogs had a chance to eat the prey. If I wasn't there quick, I'd find my supper already devoured! But assuming I could pick it up intact, I'd finish it off with the *knobkerrie* and carry it home to be skinned and prepared.

'We didn't have money to buy meat, and cows were too valuable to kill except for special occasions like funerals with lots of people to feed. When all you're eating is *sadza* and pumpkin leaves, a wild animal to eat is like manna from heaven. Whenever I arrived home with a buck across my shoulders, ya! I was popular. That was good eating!

'The only kudu I ever hunted was one that was exhausted. The dogs chased it into a river that ran past a village. Soon the river was full of people, beating and cutting the kudu until it died in the water. So of course we then had to share it out.

'There were dangers,' added Astonishment. 'One time I stumbled across a python that was half way through swallowing an antelope. I could see the back legs still sticking out with the coils of the python right there at my feet. I was already running, so all I could do was leap over it. Fortunately, this one was too busy trying to digest what it already had to be much interested in me.

'When I wasn't hunting, I'd go fishing. I'd find a hook and some twine and make a rod from a stick. As I herded my cattle sometimes, out all day with nothing to do except sit and think while the cows grazed, I'd fish for bream in the Nyazvidzi River and hope I wouldn't get attacked by crocodiles!'

We continued over rutted tracks to a shallow, saucer-shaped valley where tufts of tawny grass peppered the sand and a low *kopje* poked its knobbly head from a jumble of cactus and dry acacia trees. Astonishment stopped on a flat slab of granite and switched off the engine. For a few moments he sat in silence, eyes half-closed as if trying to summon a memory.

'Ya, ya. It was somewhere round about here.'

'What was?'

'One of the most terrifying days of my life. I would have been about sixteen, coming through here with a herd of forty cows and a flock of goats, just me and five or six dogs. I was standing right here when the sky grew dark and the air turned heavy, the way it does when there's a storm approaching. The birds stopped calling, I remember. It was like dusk, but this was midday. Then it began. The first sheet of lightning lit up the whole horizon and the thunder crack nearly knocked me off my feet. I had nowhere to shelter. If the next lightning strike was any closer, I knew I'd be dead. The cows hunched themselves against the storm, but the goats, I noticed, started streaming towards that *kopje* as the rain came lashing down. I ran after them and found a cave somewhere among those rocks. I've never been back since. I wonder if we could find it.'

We stepped out of the Toyota and scrunched across the brittle grass. The undergrowth around the *kopje* was rough and spiky, tearing at our leggings and scratching our bare arms. I went one way around the *kopje*, Astonishment the other. The rocks that had looked compact and neatly stacked from the car were chaotically strewn when seen up close. The cave, if there was one, could have been behind a hundred different boulders. Then Astonishment gave a shout. I continued round to rejoin him and found him peering into an overhang, pushing back the scrub that hid the entrance. Beneath the overhang, a sand and granite floor rose and receded, ending in a ledge a few metres in.

Astonishment gave a low whistle. 'This is it! This is where the goats came running. They crowded in and the dogs came too. Now normally, goats and dogs will never share the same space, but such was the force of the storm and the terror of the animals that they squeezed in here together – my goats, my dogs and me in this little space. For about an hour, the storm rolled around the landscape, more violent than any I've known, before or since.'

He squeezed through the bushes and hunkered down on the sloping floor, reliving the scene. 'I thank God,' he said. 'And I thank my goats. I'm told Zimbabwe has one of the highest rates of death from lightning in the world. Undoubtedly, this cave saved my life.'

We returned to the car and continued along sandy tracks, interspersed with dry riverbeds and crusts of granite.

'So there I am at Faith's,' continued Astonishment. 'Chengeta's son, James, and Faith's son, Amos, had their parents living in the compound. I was on my own, the outsider, the one there on sufferance whose only value was my ability to work. Then came a year of terrible drought when the compound had barely enough food to go round. James' parents and Amos' parents made sure that their sons got fed, but I was left to scratch what I could. We'd come home from school and the other two would disappear into their parents' huts for food – but no one thought to feed me. Or maybe they hoped that someone else would do it.

'One time I went into the hut where we kept the ropes for hitching to the cows for ploughing and I heard a scuffling in the darkness. I knew it wasn't James because I'd just seen him in the compound, so I assumed it was Amos.

'"Is it you in there?" I called.

'Amos' voice came back. He sounded startled, slightly guilty.

'As my eyes got used to the darkness, I could see why. Amos was crouched in a corner, guzzling a dish of *sadza* with vegetables – and not just vegetables, but juicy, chunky, mouth-watering meat. They must have slaughtered an animal, but no one had told me. The smell wafted towards me, delicious and tantalising. Amos tried to hide his plate, but when he realised he'd been discovered he held it out and invited me to join him. "Come and eat," he said.

'Hungry as I was, and I was hungry most of the time, I couldn't. The shock was too great – the shock that here was food, good food, but clearly I was not supposed to know about it. The others were eating in secret so I wouldn't find out, yet I was the one working harder than any of them. "No, you finish eating," I blurted. Then I rushed out of the hut and burst into tears at the injustice.

'At that time I didn't even have a blanket, so on winter nights there was cold to contend with as well as hunger. In the hut where James and I slept, James had a blanket just big enough for one person and I used to wait until he was asleep before sliding it carefully off and wrapping it around my own shivering body. Then of course he would do the same when he woke up. Eventually we came to an agreement that the one who was awake could have the blanket on the basis that if you're asleep you can't be feeling the cold.'

Astonishment remembered something and chuckled. 'You know how I got my own blanket in the end?'

'How?'

'I sold the only possession I had and bought one. And that possession was my little goat, the one I'd earned at the Mutyairis' for my year's labour. Sullivan drove it all the way from Buhera, on foot, plus the other animals we'd left behind with him and Angela for safekeeping. So finally it turned into something useful.

'If we did manage to sleep, we were woken at four o'clock every morning – and I mean *every* morning – by Amos' dad, Ezekiel. "Wake up, boys!" he would shout. "Time for work!" And always I would be the first to shoot out from the hut and be ready for duty. One thing you need to know is that I grew up easily terrified. Nowhere, except with my grandmother, did I ever feel secure. I lived with people who I knew had the power to harm me and against whom I had no protection, no one to stand up for me. My sleep was shallow. You know how an impala is constantly alert for danger? Well, that was me. I could never lower my guard. When people shouted, I jumped.

'Still in the dark, we made our way to the fields where always I was given the most difficult work. If we were ploughing, Amos would be in front leading the oxen. James had the easy job, flicking the whip, and I would be the one gripping the plough, pressing down to make sure it cut cleanly through the earth. Or if it wasn't the time of year for ploughing, we'd be out milking the cows before the sun was up. Whatever the task, we worked until about six o'clock when it was time to come home and get ready for school. And after school, we came straight back to work again.

'I say six o'clock, but none of us had a watch so we had to go by guesswork. There was one time we all three woke up before Ezekiel came calling. It was still dark, but the moon was full and we decided to make a start. We led the oxen to the field, yoked them up and started ploughing by moonlight. We ploughed and we ploughed, expecting the sky to start getting lighter to tell us it was time to go home. When we'd finished the area we intended to work, it was still dark. Only then did we realise what we'd done. When we got up, it must have been something like eleven o'clock. It was still the middle of the night. So we bedded down alongside the oxen and went back to sleep until the sun woke us up.'

I recalled the white Rhodesian despair at the African sense of time. 'African time', as everyone knew, could be hours either side of any agreed appointment. 'These people, hey? No idea how to run things. Can't even tell the time – and now they expect us to hand over the country.' But without watches, what do you do? As Astonishment pointed out, it's not easy to tell the time by moonlight. I asked him how he managed to get to school on time.

'Home-made sundials!' he laughed. 'We jogged to school, a distance of four kilometres, so it always took about the same length of time. Before we set off, we put a stick in the ground next to one of the huts and marked where the shadow fell on the hut wall. If we got to school before the bell rang, we knew we'd got it right. If not, we'd adjust the mark. A matter of trial and error. When you're as poor as we were, you have to use your ingenuity.

'Out of us three teenage boys, Amos was the least poor. His parents could afford paraffin, so Amos had a lamp that he could do his homework by in the evenings. But this is something I could never understand: if I went into the hut and tried to do my homework by the same light, I was told that the lamp was for Amos' exclusive use. As if my using the light would mean less for him! So instead I'd gather sticks from a type of tree that was known to give a good, long flame. I'd light one up like a torch and hold it over my book while I studied. You had to be careful of ash getting on the pages, or the book catching fire, but it worked to a point.'

'All that sounds like abuse,' remarked Lynda. 'Were you aware of it? Did you just accept it?'

'I accepted it in the sense that I had nowhere else to go. This was the family that had taken me in, even if there was very little care to go with it. When you're young, you can accept almost anything as being normal. This, for me, was the way life was. At least these people were my own kin, unlike the Magondo family. I could never have gone back there. It simply wasn't safe.

'One thing you need to know about my great-aunt Faith,' added Astonishment. 'She made very good beer, just like her sister, Naomi. Even in the hardest of times, she managed to grow enough of the drought-resistant grain we call rapoco to brew it in good quantities. People who didn't have rapoco could only make what was called one-day beer. This went off very quickly – hence the name – and was generally considered inferior. Faith's rapoco brew was a seven-day beer, which was much more highly regarded.

'When Faith had a batch ready, the word was spread by the simple method of people climbing to the top of *kopjes* and calling out, "*Ngoto! Ngoto pano!*" Beer! There's beer here! It carried across the countryside like a call to prayer. The news would spread and people would come long distances to sample Faith's latest brew. If supplies lasted, people would sleep at the homestead and resume drinking the next day. I remember being woken by one of the visitors – an old lady from Chibanda village who was too drunk to go home and who'd fallen asleep in the kitchen hut. She woke up in the small hours and started banging about and singing nonsense songs at the top of her voice. "Grass grows and nobody likes it!" I don't think we got any sleep before Ezekiel was hammering on the door of the hut and telling us to get up for work.'

Half an hour on from the cave, Astonishment came to a halt a few metres from a broken-down cement building – a door and two blank windows in a crumbling wall with a small tree protruding above the roofless façade. It sat alone like a long-abandoned hulk in a sea of waist-high, grey-brown grass. Over the door, a strip of faded, hand-painted lettering identified the place as a butcher's shop.

Astonishment switched off the engine and gazed at yet another ruin. 'My old workplace,' he said at last. 'I told you how Lovemore was given some cows by Dave's family. They made him a relatively wealthy man, the start of a herd, and he built this butchery for slaughtering and selling his animals. He employed one worker, but when that worker had to be off for any reason, he used to send for me instead. He never trusted James or Amos to count out the money and give customers the right change, only me. I used to enjoy that. It made a change from herding.

'This was when I didn't have a blanket to sleep under and was pulling James's off him when he went to sleep. I barely had any clothes, either. No shoes, just a ragged shirt and some cast-off trousers I'd had from Job when I started at Sengwe – now so tattered they looked like banana leaves and hardly covered anything. Lovemore realised this wasn't a good look for his shop assistant, but did he buy me new clothes? No, he didn't. He gave me a pair of his own long trousers, which were far too big. But they made a passable pair of shorts if you turned the bottoms of the legs inside and tied them above the knees with a piece of string. So that's what I did.

'But now… it's not far from here… I'll show you the school I went to when I lived at Great-Aunt Faith's.'

We drove on through the scrub, the track looping around granite *kopjes* and dipping into gullies. We levelled out onto white, prickle-covered sand and approached a line of gum trees behind which stood three or four whitewashed shacks half-covered with bougainvillea. Rows of stones marked out nonexistent flowerbeds. A cracked concrete bollard displayed the word IN with a faded, painted arrow pointing to the buildings.

'Welcome to my alma mater,' said Astonishment. 'Mutemachani Primary. Here's where I went with James and Amos, running to beat the sundial. It's nearly thirty years since I've seen it. Ya! These buildings were so big back in the eighties. How did they get so small?'

The school was deserted. The only sound was the sighing of the wind in the gum trees and the clattering of dry leaves and brittle, peeling bark. Astonishment pulled up at the door of one of the buildings and we stepped out. The door carried a sign with the unexpected message: *Abstinence. Say no to sex* – a reminder of the prevalence of

AIDS, even among schoolchildren. On the wall nearby was another instruction in Shona: *Marara Mugomba*.

'Put rubbish in the pit,' translated Astonishment. 'I'm glad to see they're keeping the place tidy.'

The school, Astonishment explained, was built in the first rush of development after independence. Along with the roads, bridges, clinics and hospitals bestowed on a grateful nation, it was represented as Mugabe's personal gift. 'The school choir used to sing songs – hymns more like – that extolled Mugabe as our saviour. The day the school was opened, the centrepiece of the ceremony was a song in praise of Mugabe.'

Astonishment strolled across the sand to where a length of railway track a metre long hung from a tree on a twist of wires. He picked up a metal bar from the ground, felt its heft in his hand and gave the rail three vigorous blows. 'Ah, that brings back memories. We could hear it half way to Faith's place.' I remembered it, too – the clanging of metal on rusty rail that had sounded from every country church and school I'd ever visited with my father.

'I can't believe it!' mused Astonishment. 'Apart from having shrunk, it all looks just the same. And over here – here is where I used to raise the flag.' He led us to a listing pole embedded in a crumbling concrete slab. 'I started here in Grade Four and I was head boy from Grade Five through to Grade Seven, so every morning at assembly I had to hoist the Zimbabwean flag as everyone sang the national anthem. But imagine my embarrassment. When I started, I was still wearing Job's banana-leaf trousers. And no underwear, of course. No one was wealthy at Mutemachani, but I was one of the most ragged. As I stood

167

with my back to the other children, raising the flag, I was always conscious of my practically bare behind.'

'So how long before you got any new clothes?' asked Lynda.

'Well, first I had the convertible trousers from Lovemore. At least they covered up my butt. They served as shorts at school, then turned back into long trousers when I went home. And by now, Chengeta had moved out from Faith's place and had a job at the Kango enamel factory in Bulawayo where he'd also found himself another wife by the name of Ma Moyo. So now he had three wives, Ma Moyo in town and Bianca and Silvia at Faith's. When he came home for Christmas, he'd bring me back a shirt or some trousers – one or the other – and that would last me the whole year until the next Christmas. So things were looking up!

'Also at Mutemachani, I had some wonderful teachers who really took an interest in this ragged, late-educated teenager and who encouraged me to do well. One of the best was Miss Mugariri, my teacher in Grade Six. She gave me food on the days when I came to school on an empty stomach. She also encouraged me to read. I remember her talking to the class about Booker T Washington's book, *Up from Slavery*, in which the author describes his life as a slave in America. She had just the one copy, but when she'd finished with it she gave it to me. "With the life you've had," she said, "I think this will help you." And it did. Having been a slave myself, I found it inspirational. At that time, I was just getting proficient in English, so was eager to read everything I could.

'The other teacher who inspired me was Mr Chimombe in Grade Seven. When things were tough at home, he'd also make sure I had food and would talk to me about my life and what I intended to do with it. When I moved on to secondary school, he was the one who bought me my pen and my books from his own meagre salary.'

We climbed into the Toyota and swung back onto the track. Astonishment now sprung another surprise. 'Did you know,' he said, 'that I am a twin?'

'Er… no.' Had we missed something?

'Oh yes. It says so on my birth certificate – where it also lists the wrong father and wrong mother. It's all Chengeta's doing, of course. Somewhere in the mid-1980s, he decided it was time to register the birth of his son, James, who was then approaching twenty years of age. A bit late, you might say, but in Zimbabwe there's no time limit for telling the authorities you exist. I was then eighteen, and Chengeta thought he'd get me registered at the same time. It's possible he didn't really distinguish between us: along with Amos, we were just those boys that hung around the compound, more or less interchangeable. So we went to the local registrar and Chengeta stated that both James and I were his sons by his first wife, Bianca. More than that, we were twins. Despite the two-year age difference, we looked enough alike for this to be just about believable.'

'But couldn't he just have said, "This is my son and this is my nephew"?'

'Ah, no. Unless you're an orphan, you have to be registered by your parents. But in my case, my parents were off the scene and not in contact with each other. So to keep life simple, Chengeta put me down as his twin son. That's how I am officially to this day – and that's why I carry his name, Mapurisa, the one he inherited from old Ngobho Mazvito, the policeman. I've sometimes thought I'd try to get the record corrected, but then I've said to myself, "What does it matter? It's only a name."'

I smiled at this latest twist in the story of Astonishment's name – the boy born Murambiwa, renamed by a fighter about to go to war, denied his father's family name on the whim of his uncle and now, for expediency, given the wrong parents and a fake twin. And all in a culture that places high value on knowing who your ancestors are and paying them proper respect. That should surely have messed with Astonishment's sense of who he was. Why it didn't was something we were still to discover.

12

Hopes Dashed

Lynda had a question from the back. 'So you're now in your late teens. All your life you've been rejected, passed from one relative to another, never really wanted by anyone except your grandmother, valued only for your labour. Even your name isn't your own. That must do terrible things to your sense of identity. So how come...? I mean...'

Astonishment laughed over his shoulder. 'You mean, how come I turned out so well?'

'Well, yes. You could have grown up really embittered, damaged, not knowing who you are. But what I see is not a damaged man.'

'Ya, it was a hard life, even by the standards of poor, subsistence farmers in Zimbabwe. And believe me, it got no better in the three years I lived at Faith's place – each day jogging the four kilometres to Mutemachani Primary, working in the fields before and after school, serving in Lovemore's butcher's shop in the holidays. And still I was Murambiwa, the outsider, the only kid in the *kraal* with no parents and no one to stand up for me. But something else was happening. I was starting to discover faith.'

'It began back in Buhera before Chengeta's family sold me to the Mutyairis. Chengeta had crossed the demarcation line to return to Morrison Farm. Granny Naomi had followed in her unsuccessful bid to bring him back. I was left with Chengeta's wife, Bianca, who didn't much care for me, to be honest, but she did do me the favour of taking me to church – the Apostolic Faith Church where a fiery old preacher called Jericho made a deep impression on my young mind.

'Now, going to church carried risks. This was still wartime. The comrades despised Christianity as the white man's religion, so we never knew if church services would be attacked. Fortunately, we in Buhera were spared, so Jericho continued preaching and we continued going. Each Sunday, after putting out the cattle to graze, I'd walk to church with Bianca. The building was like hundreds of other country churches – a rough, brick and tin construction with an earthen floor polished with cow dung to keep the dust down. Inside we sweltered in the harsh Buhera heat. The men sat on one side on benches, the women on the other side on the floor and we children crowded in at the back.

'Jericho, who was in fact my mother's uncle, the brother of old Shadrach, was just educated enough to read the Bible, but he spoke eloquently and with genuine love for God. Much of what he said was beyond my comprehension at the age of eight or nine, but I started to feel a connection with this person he talked about, the preacher called Jesus who lived in a faraway land and was a friend to the outcast and rejected – the *murambiwas* of his time. The conviction grew that this Jesus was more than just a good man in a book. When my relatives spoke of the great spirit, Mwari, the face that came to mind was that of Jesus in so far as I could picture him. As I listened to Jericho speaking with such passion from his old, battered Shona Bible, my understanding grew that Jesus was alive, even here in Buhera. I sensed Him standing in front of me, speaking to me, wanting to be part of my life. I knew my response had to be yes. I didn't fully understand what "yes" meant, but the call was irresistible.

'When I later moved to Faith's compound with James and Amos, the conviction remained. Faith was also a churchgoer. She had previously gone to the Anglican church, but there she'd been shunned by the congregation because she was Ezekiel's second wife and the Anglicans were anti-polygamy. The Methodists, though, were more relaxed on the subject, so she started going there. James and Amos weren't interested. "What's in it for us?" they said. "Those Methodists will only tell us we can't drink beer." That didn't worry me because I'd never felt any urge to drink since the days when Granny Naomi fed me beer-soaked *sadza* and peanut butter. So I took to going with Faith on a Sunday. The services were held in one of the classrooms at Mutemachani School, which meant a long walk each way. To earn the time off, I had to put in extra hours on Saturday, digging manure or whatever, in order to be free for church.

'As my faith grew, I discovered the strength that comes from praying. But time on my own for praying had to be snatched at night after all the work was done. James and Amos used to notice me creeping out of the hut and assumed I was going for a pee. They couldn't believe how regular I was! If I forgot, they'd say to me, "Ah! Astonishment. Tonight you are not relieving yourself?" And that would be my reminder.'

'So back to my question,' said Lynda. 'How come you're not embittered? You should be. Your life could so easily have fallen apart.'

'Sure, sure, sure. You talk about my name not being my own and how that affects my sense of identity. I say it doesn't matter if I have the wrong name and the wrong parents on my birth certificate. My true identity is in Christ. That's my security. And because of that, I can't hold anything against my relatives for the way they treated me. I know God has forgiven me, so I don't find it hard to forgive others. And without the challenges, my life would not have taken the course it has. Take James, who I grew up with. After he left home, he became a security guard in Bulawayo. He had three or four wives, wrecked his life with drinking and died of AIDS. That could so easily have been me, but somehow God used the hardships and rejections to set me on a different path. And at crucial moments, He gave me people to encourage me. Those teachers, for example – Mr Muchenje and Miss Mugariri. So despite everything, ya, I count myself a fortunate man. God has been good to me. Why should I be bitter?'

'But back to my story,' continued Astonishment. 'As the 1980s progressed, the new government launched a programme of resettlement to decongest the overcrowded areas in which many of the black population still lived. Faith and Ezekiel were among those who decided to take advantage of the scheme. In 1984 they moved from their *kraal* to a resettlement village poetically named Village Three on farmland adjacent to Coetzie Farm. But they needed labour, so they took me with them to help Ezekiel to clear the land of trees and build new huts so that Village Three could be established. Chengeta, his two country wives and the children they had between them all went too.

'But Chengeta was a restless man. A year later he was on the move again with his wives and children, buying three dilapidated huts a few kilometres from Village Three in Madamombe, a rundown *kraal* in an area of bad soil and poor crops. And having bought the huts, he had no money for repairs so they stayed semi-derelict. Why he settled on Madamombe, I shall never understand. It always looked a bad choice to me.

'Then, despite having James on the scene, he decided he needed a labourer. As a work-hardened nineteen-year-old, I was the obvious candidate and he insisted I move to Madamombe to help him. Faith refused to let me go: I was too useful at Village Three. There followed a stand-up row. As Faith and Chengeta haggled over who should have me, I stood like a cow, dumbly looking from one to the other to see what my fate was going to be. Had they asked me, I'd have stayed with Faith. At least at Village Three there was just about enough to eat and I was less confident of being fed adequately in Madamombe. But asking my opinion didn't occur to either of them. Eventually Chengeta was able to pull the family connection. "This boy is my sister's child," he declared. "What is he to you? Only your sister's grandchild." Nearness of kin was the clincher. Faith withdrew her case. I had no belongings, nothing to pack. I simply walked to Madamombe to start a new life there.

'My fears about not being fed were well founded. Chengeta had his first two wives and all their many children to support in Madamombe. There was also the third wife in Bulawayo where he worked and still spent most of his time. He liked to rotate his country wives, bringing them alternately to Bulawayo even if Ma Moyo, the Ndebele wife, never set foot in Shona-speaking Madamombe. With all these commitments and wives to be juggled, Chengeta was a man constantly pressed for money. The fields at Madamombe never yielded much and hunger was a constant fact of life.

'With Chengeta away in town, I was left with either Bianca or Silvia or both. I got on OK with Bianca, but for some reason Silvia turned against me and complained about me to Chengeta whenever he came home. She told him I was a nuisance, unmanageable, a pain to have around.

'The relationship with Chengeta, unstable at best, took a turn for the worse. My uncle believed everything Silvia told him and vented his anger on me. "I've given you a home and this is the way you treat my wife. You're a wicked, ungrateful boy! You're lucky to have a place at all."

'Despite being nineteen, I was still at Mutemachani Primary and facing a long walk to school. From Village Three to Mutemachani was eleven kilometres and the transfer to Madamombe added another three. So fourteen kilometres each way, every school day and again on Sundays for church.

'Now school, of course, costs money. Every Zimbabwean knows that. At this point, the system for primary school was that any number of children from the same household could be educated for a single fee as long as they had the same family name. Here's where Chengeta's whimsical decision to call me by his own name, Mapurisa, paid off. He could send me to school with James and all his other children at no extra cost. Had I been called Mukarati after my real father, the chances are I would never have gone to school at all. I see that now as God's providence at work.

'But the system changed for secondary school. There it was a separate payment per student. Uncle Chengeta was happy to pay for his own children to progress to secondary school, but he couldn't afford to send me. And why should he? Ultimately, I was not his responsibility.

'But now came an unexpected turn. The headmaster of the primary school, a kindly man called Ernest Warambwa, became aware of the situation and realised that this could spell the end of my education and condemn me to herding cattle for the rest of my life. He wrote a letter to the head of Mutemachani Secondary School, stating that Astonishment Mapurisa was a promising student and asking him to let me continue my studies without paying the fees – at least temporarily.

'It came to the first day of the new school year, a Tuesday. I arrived at the secondary school, just a short walk across the field from the primary school. In the start-of-year assembly, the head announced that fees for the term should be paid by Friday and that non-payers would not be allowed back to school the following Monday. I went through the week knowing full well that no money had come from Chengeta. Nor was it likely to, as he'd only just scraped together the thirty-Zimbabwe-dollar fee – equivalent at the time to about four US dollars – for his son, James, and was now back in Bulawayo.

'Monday came. It was a choice of herding cows or going back to school, and I chose to go to school just in case. The worst they could do would be to send me home. As assembly broke up, the head singled me out and told me to wait in his office. I sat there with a sinking feeling in my stomach, wondering if this was to be my last day of education. Through the window I could see other rejected students walking home in ones and twos. This wasn't looking good.

'When the last non-paying student had been sent away, the head called me over. "Mr Warambwa has told me your situation," he said. "We know you cannot pay the fees, but we want to help you as much as we can." How he managed to fix it, I don't know, but he allowed me to stay at school without paying for at least the first term.

'Welcome as it was, the reprieve only postponed the problem. My fees, eventually, would have to come from somewhere. Again, the kindly Mr Warambwa stepped in, giving me a letter to take to the Department of Social Welfare to see if they could help. This was situated at The Range, a cluster of government offices beneath a grove of gum trees on the road from Chivhu to Buhera. One Saturday, I walked the twenty-five kilometres from Madamombe to The Range and presented the letter to the social welfare officer on duty. She turned me down on the spot on the basis that my parents were both still alive and should be taking responsibility. Helping me out would be contrary to policies and procedures. Devastated, I took back the letter and slumped on a chair in the corridor, gathering strength for the long walk home.

'A lady who worked in Births and Deaths came by. "I heard you were applying for money for school fees," she said.

'"Yes, madam."

'"And they turned you down?"

'"Yes, madam."

'"How much do you need?"

'"For another term? Thirty Zim dollars."

'"I'll make you an offer," she said. "If you come and work for me, here at The Range, every weekend for a month, I'll give you the thirty dollars."

'My prayers, it seemed, were answered. For the next four weekends I did whatever work this woman wanted – clearing the yard, digging and weeding the garden, cutting grass, digging pits for compost. It was harsh, nonstop toil, but I consoled myself with the thought that I was working for another term at school. At nightfall on Saturday at the end of my day's work, I'd walk to a nearby homestead where one of my fellow church members allowed me to sleep. Then first thing on Sunday, it was back to The Range for another day's labour before walking the twenty-five kilometres back to Madamombe.

'At the end of my fourth weekend, I presented myself for payment. The lady surveyed my work and pronounced herself satisfied. "Unfortunately," she added, "I can't afford to give you a full term's fees. But here's something that might help."

'She pushed a note into my hand. I looked down and saw she'd given me five dollars.

'"But we agreed thirty!" I protested.

'She shrugged and raised her eyes in a mock-despairing look. "Ah yes. It is very regrettable. If only I could give you more. Unfortunately, that is all I can afford." With that, she disappeared into her office and shut the door.

'I couldn't believe it! Four weekends' work for five Zim dollars – less than one US dollar! I was used to injustice, but this was crushing. Without that thirty dollars, I could kiss goodbye to my education and any thought of escape from the poverty of being a cowherd. And there was nothing I could do about it. I couldn't force her to keep her word and there was no one I could appeal to. With my last hope extinguished, choking back the tears, I set off home to Madamombe. It was the most wretched journey of my life.'

13

The Warambwa Deal

'At the point of my greatest despair, who should intervene again but Ernest Warambwa? His suggestion was a bold one and it changed everything.

'It was 1987, my twentieth year, and Ernest was about to be transferred from Mutemachani Primary to another headship north of Buhera. This was bad news. Ernest was the only person in the world who cared whether I was educated or not. It was solely through him that I'd gained a foothold at secondary school, albeit a temporary one. If he left now, I'd be losing my only champion. Once again, a life of herding seemed to beckon.

'But Ernest had not given up. "Come with me to Masasa, to my rural home," he said. "There I have a house where my elderly parents live. They're frail and they need someone to look after them. Come and take care of them and look after the home. That way, I know they'll be with someone I trust. And in return I'll pay your school fees at Masasa High."

'This was miraculous. Finally, a chance to escape from my relatives and make a new start. I was still required to work, but Ernest, unlike the lady at The Range, was someone I could trust to keep a promise.

'When I told the family back at Madamombe, they were outraged. I knew for a fact that they wanted me to drop out of school so I could then become a full-time, unpaid labourer. Education has its place, but not when it gets in the way of ploughing fields and milking cows. The more precarious my school career became, the more I was in demand from relatives hustling to have me work for them. The folks at Madamombe objected bitterly, but Ernest stood firm and insisted that this was the best option for a promising student like me. This was, I think, the first time that anyone had ever made a decision with my best interests in mind.

'My relatives took it badly. "You're stealing our boy," they hissed back at Ernest. "If anything happens to him, if he gets sick or dies, then it's your fault. Don't expect any cooperation from us."

'I was not sorry to leave. On the weekend of my departure, Ernest told me to meet him at Mukanya bottle store, a business he owned near Mutemachani School and where he needed to collect some belongings. The plan was to leave on the Sunday morning. Rather than walk through the night from Madamombe, I got there on the Saturday evening and slept the night on the *stoep*. I must have been eager. Ernest swung by in the morning and collected me, driving me to Masasa in his Datsun pick-up. In my twenty-odd years, I'd travelled on country buses and in various vehicles at Morrison Farm, usually in the box-end of a *bakkie* where the labourers bumped and swayed on the metal base. But never had I travelled in such comfort or at such speed. I couldn't believe how quickly the countryside flashed by.

'We drove for an hour or so and came to a well-built, brick and concrete house with wide eaves and a chimney, standing alone on a large plot and set about with bougainvillea – the kind of house you could imagine white people living in. They were clearly a well-to-do family. There I met the ancient parents, Ernest Warambwa senior and his wife, Emilia. Both were in their eighties and getting frail, but they greeted me kindly and gave me my own room in a thatched rondavel next to the house. Most wondrous of all, my new lodgings contained a bed. This I could hardly believe. I'd seen beds at Dave's house many years before, but never had I slept in one. The dung floor of a hut was more what I was used to. I tested it cautiously, stretching out my limbs and leaning back on the pillow.'

'And how did you find it?' I asked Astonishment.

'Wonderful. Just wonderful – soft and billowy and s-o-o-o comfortable. I took to it at once.

'I was there to work, of course. I'd wake up early, tidy the house and the yard, prepare breakfast for the old people when they woke up and milk the cows so they had supplies for the day. Then I'd go to my new school, Masasa High. When I came back I'd work in the garden, tend to the goats and the chickens and then set off to round up the cattle. After that I'd prepare the evening meal, wash up and finally get round to doing my homework at 10.30 or 11pm.

'There was also work to be done on the house which was quite new and still needed completing. So I did the plastering and the flooring and the finishing off.

'Ernest Warambwa the younger, who I'll call Ernest Roger to distinguish him from his elderly father, was married to Marcie and together they had four children. Younger than me, they were all away at boarding school. In the holidays, my duties extended to coaching them for their exams.

'For all this there was no payment, of course. My reward was to have my school fees paid at the rate of thirty Zim dollars a term.

'So Ernest Roger got himself a good deal. I studied at Masasa High for three years from Form Two to Form Four. Over nine terms he laid out 270 Zim dollars or about thirty-six US dollars – a US dollar a month for an almost full-time labourer and carer. But that didn't matter. For the first time I was with people who appreciated my efforts and treated me with respect. I was being educated and getting regular meals. Also, Ernest Roger had a way of asking the kind of questions I'd never considered before. What were my ambitions? What did I want to do with my life? Until that point, the answer had been to survive another day and avoid getting hurt. The idea that there might be a future containing choices and possibilities was like a door opening. The interest and encouragement of the Warambwa family was all the motivation I needed to render the best service I could.

'Masasa High was about forty-five minutes' walk from the house. But whereas in the past I'd always gone barefoot to school, I now had my first-ever pair of shoes, bought for me in Chivhu by Ernest Roger. When he asked me what size I took, I had no idea. A barefoot cowherd doesn't need to know his shoe size. For some reason I said seven, but seven turned out to be too small. By then it was too late to change them, so I walked with a hobble until they stretched enough to be bearable. I was hugely proud of them – proper black school lace-ups that made me feel like a man of consequence rather than everybody's *murambiwa*. Ernest also bought me a school uniform, a pale-blue shirt and grey trousers. After Mutemachani where I'd always been conscious of my rags barely covering my backside, I could now swagger off to school as well-dressed as any of my classmates.

'I didn't totally blend in, however. For one thing, now in my early twenties, I was several years older than my classmates. Also, everyone knew I was having to work for my school fees and this was seen as a source of shame. In the playground I was *fudzamombe rekwa Warambwa*, the Warambwa's cattleherd. Either that or *mubhoyi wekwa Warambwa*, Warambwa's boy. That's a derogatory "boy", by the way – borrowed from the whites to mean a black working man of any age.'

Mubhoyi! Boy! I could hear in the word the call of the white madam, summoning the gardener across a suburban lawn. Or my Bulawayo driving instructor tut-tutting over a wobbly cyclist. Curious, I thought, that 'boy', this term of careless contempt, white to black, should have passed into Shona as an insult – one of those words where you can still hear the English underneath. Like Mapurisa... police.

'My other nickname,' continued Astonishment, 'was *Jamkoko* – Shona for "swarm" in reference to the herds of cattle that used to be driven to market and so another word for cowherd. I especially got these insults in the last assembly of term when we walked up to the front in order of achievement to collect our school reports. Invariably I was top in my year and so the first to go up, accompanied by cat-calls and mocking shouts of "Well done, *fudzamombe!*" Well done, the cattleherd!

'I was poor and people knew it. Some parents didn't want their children to associate with me. It's not that this was a wealthy community: nowhere in rural Zimbabwe was rich. But even in a poor community, the poorest can be looked down upon.'

We lurched down and up another gully and pulled up on a sandy plot in front of a one-roomed, whitewashed block – a door, one square window on either side like a child's drawing of a house and a verandah roofed with corrugated sheets resting on stick-like poles. Above the verandah in hand-painted lettering: *Mukanya General Dealer & Bottle Store.* In the deep shade of the tin roof, four or five men sat and chatted on the low verandah wall. They looked up curiously as we arrived.

'Where you could say my new life began,' said Astonishment, cutting the engine. 'Here's where Ernest Roger picked me up to take me to Masasa for the first time. He owned this place. When he was head of Mutemachani Primary, he used to come here and drink beer with the head of the secondary school. They were good friends, which is why he was able to swing the deal for my first year at Mutemachani Secondary. From Masasa, Ernest Roger used to send me here in the holidays when his shopkeeper was off. Ya, but it's a long time since I saw it. I don't remember it being so small! And look at those gum trees! I planted those. The last time I saw them they were no higher than my shoulder.'

We stepped down from the car. The men clustered round with greetings and three-stage African handshakes – shake, clasp the thumbs, shake again. Even after all these years, Astonishment was known. A slight, wiry man in black jeans, a cowboy shirt and a brown felt trilby slapped him on the shoulder.

'Ah! Ndiya. So you're still alive?'

'Yes, Mahamba, my brother. I'm alive. It's good to see you again.

'My friends from the UK,' said Astonishment, drawing Lynda and me into the group. More handshakes and murmurs of welcome. 'And this,' continued Astonishment, laughing and putting his arm round the shoulders of the cowboy, 'this is Mahamba. He was my friend at Mutemachani, a long, long time ago.'

'Ah, but I was the clever one,' grinned Mahamba, returning the shoulder slap.

'Yes, yes, yes. This man was way ahead of me in class. But we were two poor boys together. And still he calls me Ndiya, my mother's family name.'

We stooped inside to find a worn-shiny, black-painted, concrete counter behind which were ranged a few bottles of cooking oil, some packs of Marie biscuits and other sparse provisions, barely filling the shelf space. Astonishment surveyed the interior with a chuckle.

'The times I've been in this place! I used to stand right there behind the counter serving beer – African-style Chibuku brand that came in waxed cartons and you had to shake it before drinking. We called it Shake-Shake for that reason. In transit from the suppliers, a certain number would split and leak, so some of them would be only partly full. So I'd give a carton to a customer and he'd shake it and give it back saying, "No, my friend. This one is not full. Give me another." So I'd give him a fresh one. But by about 7pm when people had been drinking for a few hours, I changed my tactics. When a customer handed his Shake-Shake back and demanded a full one, I'd put it below the counter and produce the same one again. Invariably he'd give it another rattle. "Ya, this one is better!"'

Laughter from the men.

'You have to sell all the cartons to make a profit. That way I avoided waste and Ernest Roger was very pleased. But it was hard work. When I opened in the afternoon, people would come in all very orderly and polite to start drinking. But by the evening there was loud singing and people doing bump jive to the radio and yelling to me to turn up the volume. By 10pm when we were supposed to close, they would still be there, loud and happy and in no mood to go home. Sometimes this went on until 1am and beyond. But that was not economic for the bar. People were buying one Shake-Shake and making it last an hour. Meanwhile you were burning paraffin for the lamps and using up batteries in the radio, just to entertain the last few customers. But what could I do? I was just a schoolboy. There was no way I could physically throw them out.'

'So what did you do?' asked Lynda.

'I had to use my powers of persuasion. "Please sir, please madam, would you go now?" If that didn't work, I had to wait until they went out to the toilet and then quickly bolt the doors. They'd come back and hammer on the windows: "Ya! Bartender! What's happening here?"

'"I'm sorry, sir, we're closed!" Sometimes it was getting towards dawn before I managed to eject all the customers. Only then could I lock up and go to bed in the shack behind the store.'

Astonishment took a drawn-out leave of Mahamba and the gang and we climbed back into the Toyota. 'Now, let's retrace the route I took with Ernest Roger to Masasa,' he announced, pointing the car north towards the Chivhu-Buhera road. Where the dirt road met the tarmac, he turned east for a few dust-free kilometres – a welcome respite from the tortuous tracks around Mukanya. A fluttering in the back reminded us we still had supper in a loosely tied cardboard box and it wasn't happy.

'Settle down, chicken!' called Astonishment. 'Later, later. So where have we got to? Ya, I'm now at the Warambwas' where life was different to anything I'd ever known. In the intervention of Ernest Roger, I discerned the goodness of God in taking me from my family and giving me this new start. And my faith grew under the influence of old Warambwa who I soon discovered was a devout Christian. Often, late at night, he and I would sit and read our Bibles and discuss our experience of God – he from the perspective of old age, me as a young man for whom God had been my rock in the tribulations of my childhood. Despite the age difference, we became firm friends.

'Even so, there were family jealousies. A relative called Wilbur arrived at the door one day, kicking up a fuss and shouting for old Warambwa. His problem was the one endemic to Zimbabwe. "I have children's school fees to pay," he yelled. "Give me money."

'Ernest invited him in. "I'm sorry," he explained. "I don't have any money to spare."

'Wilbur turned to me. "But here you are, paying for this cowherd to go to school when I have children who may have to drop out. I am your own family and you're refusing to help me. You know what I'm going to do? I'm going to teach this *jamkoko* a lesson."

'He lunged forward to attack me. I braced to defend myself, only to find that Ernest had snatched a burning stick from the fireplace and was jabbing it at Wilbur to force him back. The old man was spritelier than he looked and ended up chasing Wilbur out of the house.

'But Wilbur hadn't finished. At that time, old Emilia Warambwa was seriously ill in hospital in Harare and everyone at the homestead set off that same evening to go to see her. The only ones left at home were me and a guy called Charles who used to help me look after the cattle. Knowing the others would be out, Wilbur returned with a big knife. He barged in through the door and made to attack me again. With lightning reaction, Charles grabbed a piece of firewood and cracked him over the head. Wilbur sank to the floor, bleeding from the wound. For a horrible moment I thought he was dead, but then we heard him groaning. We knew we had to tell the police, but the nearest station in Masasa was half an hour at a run. While Charles stood guard over the injured man, I sprinted across the field to our nearest neighbours, the Mutitis, to borrow a bicycle. In the end, Wilbur was taken to the clinic in Masasa for stitches to his head.'

'Was there any comeback?' I asked.

'No, fortunately. Under questioning, Wilbur admitted that he had been the aggressor and he didn't level any charges against us. And we had no wish to prosecute him, so the matter was closed.

'For Emilia, sad to say, that stay in hospital was her last illness and she died soon after, leaving me and old Warambwa alone at the homestead. But for me, things were about to change yet again.'

14

Seven Beautiful Mutiti Girls

The tarmac section of our journey was brief. After a few minutes we struck north again on a boulder-strewn track that wound through a landscape of abrupt *kopjes*. Signs of human habitation dropped away, almost the last trace being a hand-painted message on a whitewashed concrete stump. *Mashambamuto School*, it announced, pointing left into empty grassland. There was no road – a footpath, maybe, but nothing bigger. The music of the name appealed, like Zimbabwean words always have done. A glance at the map reveals Nyamatsanga, Chipwanya, Mupatsi and Chimumvuri on and around the road from Chivhu to Buhera – mellifluous names all.

Astonishment continued as we bumped along. 'I was three years at Masasa High, becoming head boy and passing seven O levels in 1989. On the day I went to collect my results, the headmaster said to me: "Astonishment! You need to be doing something new with your life. How would you feel about coming back to Masasa High as a teacher?"

'Me? A teacher! I couldn't believe what I was hearing. I said yes at once, so the headmaster picked up the phone and called the District Education Officer in Chivhu. I sat and listened to the conversation.

'"This is impossible," said the voice at the other end. "How can this boy be a teacher at the same school where he's just done his O levels? It's unheard of."

'"Ya, but I would ask you to make an exception. This fellow is twenty-two years old. He's my head boy. The way he helps the younger boys, he's a teacher already as far as I'm concerned."

'"OK, my friend. Send him to my office tomorrow and let me see him."

'The headmaster summed up the case for employing me in a letter and gave it to me to hand to the Education Officer. The following morning, I caught the pre-dawn bus from Masasa to Chivhu and presented myself at the Education Offices. On the strength of the head's recommendation and a short interview, I was taken on to teach Shona and geography to the younger pupils.

'I had a head start in that I knew many of these children already. I knew their families and their circumstances and the tough home lives that some of them came from. With my upbringing, I could empathise.

'One stifling day in October, the hottest month of the year, I heard one of my fellow teachers berating a small boy for wearing a woollen jersey. "You stupid boy!" he yelled. "It's far too hot for a jersey. Take it off."

'"But sir," said the boy, "I don't have a shirt."

'"I don't care. I'm telling you to take it off – now!"

'Reluctantly, the poor, sweating child peeled off his jersey. Underneath, all he had on was a frayed collar and a little scrap of shirt front – just enough to make it look like a shirt under his V-neck. My heart went out to him. I knew what it was like to come to school in rags.

'I couldn't believe it, but the teacher laughed. "So now we can all see what kind of person you are. A person so poor you can't even afford a shirt. You're a silly, foolish young man." The rest of the class joined in the laughter as the lad stood there with his pathetic piece of rag around his neck.

'I couldn't bear it. As soon as his lesson ended, I quietly asked him to come and see me before he went home. In the meantime, I went home myself and came back with three spare shirts of my own. When he knocked timidly on the staffroom door at the end of school, still sweltering in his jersey, I handed them over. I told him I knew how it felt to be humiliated for being poor.

'As a teacher, it was now no longer possible for me to devote all my spare time to old Warambwa as I had in the past. He was on his own and getting frail, so I called on Francis, one of my Ndiya relatives, to come and help with tasks such as herding cattle.

'Francis was unemployed at the time and spending a lot of time drinking beer, so I thought it might help him to have a job. In fact, he was more trouble than he was worth. One day, I remember, he was out drinking a pulverising form of beer called *mudzepete* with some of his friends. This *mudzepete* is made from an onion-like root and the effect, so I'm told, is similar to being head-butted by a hippo. A bit like its near relative, *kachasu*. After a lengthy drinking session, Francis saw an old man wobbling by on a bike and decided to give chase. The guys drinking with him abandoned their gourds and followed on behind, curious to see what he was up to. The man glanced back and saw Francis and his posse racing after him. Thinking he was about to be attacked, he pedalled faster and faster, wheezing and gasping until he fell off his bike with exhaustion.

'"It's OK, *Baba*," slurred Francis when he caught up. "I just need to check your air pressure." He pressed a thumb onto each tyre. "Ya. They're fine. You can carry on." With that, he fell over in the dust and had to be carried back to the Warambwas by his friends.

'Even that wasn't the end of it. When he was conscious again, Francis climbed through the Warambwas' window and ran away. His friends ran after him to try to bring him under control. In the end, they thought he must have a spirit in him and took him to a faith healer to be exorcised. The faith healer agreed he was probably bewitched and carried out the exorcism, only for Francis to admit, once he was sober, that the only demon was the *mudzepete*.

'Francis never shook off his beer habit. In 2009, after diamonds were discovered at Marange near Mutare, he joined thousands of other poor Zimbabweans flocking to the area to grab what they could. That was in the early days of the Marange diamond rush before the politicians took over and started lining their own pockets. Francis came away with a good quantity of gems which he sold in Buhera. And you know what he did with the money? He bought a cow for 150 dollars and he and his friends drank the rest. So he ended up with nothing. He could have looked after his family for life, but they're all still as poor as ever – including his widowed mother. That's why I help to support her to this day. There's no one else to look after her.'

'One day, soon after I'd become a teacher, we decided to dig a well in the school grounds. Before that, the only water came from a borehole at Masasa Clinic and teachers and pupils had to carry it half a kilometre in buckets every day. The well needed to be deep – about twenty-five metres – so we brought in some workers to do the digging. These were great guys and always up for a laugh.

'Digging in the hard earth with nothing but *badzas* and shovels is back-breaking work. And as the well gets deeper, you have to be careful of snakes that can slide in overnight and curl up in the bottom. Before you start a day's digging, it's advisable to take a mirror and reflect the sun's rays down into the hole to check for unwelcome visitors.

'One morning, the first digger of the day, a guy called Zvavahera, failed to check and shimmied down the ladder to start digging. Of course, this had to be the morning when a young python had decided to take up residence. It wasn't pleased to be disturbed and it wrapped itself around Zvavahera's legs. Why he didn't shout for help, I don't know. Maybe he was too terrified to speak. Anyway, he gathered his strength, grabbed the snake by the neck and squeezed its head against the wall of the well until it was dead – the python lashing and whipping about as he did so. It's a good thing it wasn't full grown or he wouldn't have stood a chance.

'The rest of us were up at the top, unaware that all this was happening and thinking only that Zvavahera was taking his time starting work. Eventually he called out, "Lower the bucket!" – the one we used for pulling up the soil. Joel, who was operating the rope, let it down and felt the weight going in.

'"OK, pull!" came the shout from down below.

'Joel hauled the load up. He was about to secure it when he saw the snake wrapped around the bucket, its head and tail swaying in a menacing way with the swinging of the rope. He screamed and let go. The rope rattled over the pulley and the bucket crashed to the bottom, narrowly missing Zvavahera's head. A second scream came from below as Zvavahera got his snake back again.

'We crowded to the edge and looked down. "Zvavahera! Are you OK? Are you alive down there?"

'The reply came back. "Ya, ya. Don't worry, guys. The snake is dead. I killed it."

'"But why didn't you warn us? We all nearly died of fright!"

'"Ya, and you nearly killed me, too!"

'From then on, until the well was complete, they never forgot the morning mirror test.'

Another half-hour's drive brought us to Masasa, consisting, as far as I could see, of a water tower, a police station with whitewashed stones marking out the drive and a line of shanty shops with cement *stoeps*, tin roofs and hand-painted lettering peeling away from sun-bleached façades. A beer hall, a butcher's shop and a grinding mill. Not much else. On the steps of the bottle store lounged three or four men in threadbare T-shirts, trousers ripped and stained and toes peeping through holes in torn trainers. They squatted in the shade and sipped on cartons of Chibuku to pass a torpid afternoon. Above their heads on a poster stuck to a tree, a smooth-faced ZANU-PF politician looked benignly down on the scene. Sharp-suited and displaying a dazzling set of teeth, he urged the people of Masasa to give him their votes while fiddling abstractedly with a lump of bling on his shirt cuff. The contrast with his ragged constituents was revealing.

Beyond the shops, we came to a faded sign set into a concrete gate post: *Masasa High Welcomes You*. Astonishment slowed and peered into the compound where biscuit-coloured lawns merged with pale sand and scorched flowerbeds and the multicoloured Zimbabwean flag hung listlessly from its pole. Behind were classrooms reminiscent of Selborne-Routledge – low, white-painted, rectangular blocks with corrugated roofs, shimmering in the afternoon heat. There seemed to be no one about.

'Ah,' sighed Astonishment, his elbow on the sill of the open car window and a faraway look on his face. 'Masasa High. For me, a place of torment as the penniless *jamkoko* – but also where I found a measure of respect.' He seemed about to turn in, but changed his mind. 'Let's move on. It's getting late and there's one more call I want to make.' He shifted into gear and in less than a minute we were through Masasa and out into open country. Astonishment stretched back in his seat and resumed his story.

'I mentioned our neighbours, the Mutitis, who lived a few hundred metres away and within sight of the Warambwas. These were another well-off family and they and the Warambwas were friends. When I arrived at Masasa, Mr Mutiti had just retired from his job in the marketing department of Harare's main newspaper, the *Herald*.'

The old *Rhodesia Herald*. Did it still carry letters welcoming newcomers to this wonderful country of ours? Probably not, I thought.

'As part of his retirement package, he was sent the *Herald* in the post every day. Whenever I could, I used to go over to the Mutitis and read it to catch up on current affairs. Mr Mutiti took a liking to me and always made me welcome, as did his wife who was amazed when I helped her with the cooking. An African man cooking is a rarity indeed, but for me it was no big deal. It was what I did every day for the Warambwas.

'But the newspaper and the welcome were not the only attractions. The Mutitis had seven beautiful daughters of whom the youngest three were still at Masasa High. The day I arrived, Emilia Warambwa was quick to tell me I'd have company on the way to school. So it was that I would wait for the Mutiti girls, or they would wait for me, and we'd walk to school together. The most beautiful of all, in my eyes, was the youngest, Bridget. We liked each other from the start, though I always felt conscious of being the poor *jamkoko*. In contrast, she was the daughter of an educated man who'd worked in an office in Harare. Her sister, Mercy, was in the same class as me and travelled frequently to Harare, coming back with tales I could hardly believe. Kitchens with every electric gadget. Air-conditioned supermarkets, stocked with exotic items like ice cream and chocolate. Eating pizza or chicken and chips instead of *sadza* and boiled foliage. With wonders such as these, Harare seemed like another planet while the gorgeous Mutiti girls struck me as impossibly sophisticated.

'While others at school scorned my lowly status, Bridget remained my friend. I liked her peacefulness, her serenity, the fact that she wasn't ashamed to be seen with me. I valued her friendship, and friendship grew into love.

'Then I became a teacher. No longer was I the cattleherd and an object of derision. I was suddenly a respected member of the community and parents who had previously refused to let their children associate with me began propelling their daughters in my direction. Bridget was then in Form Four. Fortunately, I was teaching Forms One and Two, so avoided the awkwardness of having to mark my girlfriend's homework. We worked hard to keep our relationship secret – at school, anyway. And even at home. I would still call at the Mutitis, ostensibly to read the *Herald* but really to see Bridget. Sometimes if Mr Mutiti was on the way out, he would slap me on the back and wave me inside. "Help yourself to the paper, my son. Your sister is in there. She'll keep you company."

'Sister! If only he knew!'

Astonishment slowed again at the edge of a field, scanning the beaten footpaths that veined the hard, dry soil to our left. 'From the Warambwas',' he murmured, 'I walked across these very fields with Bridget. I wonder if I can still find the way. Ya! This could be it.'

He turned off the dirt road onto no road at all and rattled the Toyota across the bare, rocky earth. A few hundred metres further on, we swung through a metal gate and pulled up in front of a brick house. I recognised it from Astonishment's description as the home of the old

Warambwas. It looked deserted. The crumbling chimney, the bougainvillea growing thick across the windows and the long grass licking at the threshold suggested it hadn't been lived in for a long time. But while the house was largely intact, the neighbouring rondavel, the little home where Astonishment had first slept in a bed, had lost its roof and had a tree growing through it. Astonishment gazed at the ruin, pensive at seeing the old place being reclaimed by the bush.

'Over there,' he said at last. 'Those are the graves of old Warambwa and his wife. And see those gum trees. I planted those.' He nodded to a grove of twenty or thirty eucalyptus behind the house. Although so many of the places in which he'd lived and worked were now derelict – the labourers' shacks at Morrison, Lovemore's butchery, the rondavel in front of us – Astonishment's legacy of newly planted gum trees appeared to be flourishing.

On the far boundary of the property, a barbed-wire fence and a gate constructed of wooden poles divided old Warambwa's house from a compound of thatched, cement huts. Astonishment made his way over. As he did so, an elderly lady appeared from one of the huts and came towards him with a cry of recognition.

'Mama, I am so happy to see you,' called Astonishment, dismantling the topmost bars of the gate and stepping over into the next-door compound. 'How are you? How are all your children?' He waved us over. 'These are my friends from the UK, and this, this my friends, is Marcie Warambwa, widow of Ernest Roger who saved me from my relatives and gave me my chance in life. Ya! If it were not for Ernest Roger, where would I be now?'

Marcie's wrinkled face creased into a smile. She answered his question in Shona, provoking a laugh from Astonishment. *Not arriving in a fancy car with a bunch of white folks* seemed to be the gist of it.

Having shaken hands, Lynda raised her camera and asked Marcie if she'd mind a picture. Marcie put her hands to her face and fled to her hut. We looked at each other in surprise. Was this some terrible mistake? Was Marcie offended? Astonishment offered no explanation, but two minutes later she was back. She'd changed into Sunday best – a skirt and a crisp, white jacket with a floppy, broad-brimmed hat of the kind you might see at an English summer wedding. Suitably prepared, she was happy to offer up her image for posterity.

I thought of Chief Siabuwa, similarly determined to dress for his photograph. A Zimbabwean thing, it seemed.

15

Lobola

Back in the car some twenty minutes later, I watched Marcie receding as Astonishment drove on. Frail beneath her big white hat, she continued to wave until she disappeared from view. In her sixty-something years, she'd have lived through the hardships and indignities of colonial rule and then the war of liberation, only to be subject to a new oppressor who treated Zimbabwe as his personal fiefdom and continued to inflict misery on his country. I marvelled at the graciousness of people like Marcie who had patiently suffered one malign government after another. So many stories of fortitude and suffering, of which Astonishment's was only one.

The chicken was restive again and the angle of the sun suggested that its end was near. Gripping the wheel against the juddering of the car, Astonishment retraced his route across the hard-baked fields and picked up the track that would take us towards Chivhu and the Mapurisa rural home.

'To tell you the truth,' he went on, 'I only got that teaching job in Masasa by accident. It so happened that another teacher called Shepherd had left to go and study at the School of Social Work at the University of Zimbabwe.

That created the vacancy that I was invited to fill. But once installed at the university, Shepherd thought the School of Social Work would be just the place for me. So unbeknown to me, he put in an application on my behalf. The first I knew was when a letter arrived from the university inviting me to submit an essay on why I wanted to be a social worker.

'*But I don't want to be a social worker*, I said to myself. Then I guessed that Shepherd might have had something to do with it. Reflecting further, I thought, *Why not?* Social work could be a worthwhile job. A lot of my work as a teacher was social work anyway, so why not make a career of it?

'I wrote the essay, sent it in and found myself invited for an interview.

'At almost the same time, an invitation came to be interviewed for a job at Zimbabwe Customs and Excise. This was one of many jobs I'd seen advertised in Mr Mutiti's *Herald* and I'd sent in an application. The date was a couple of weeks before the university interview. Scary as it was, I knew the time had come to face the big city. As cities go, I now know that Harare is tiny. Back then, when the biggest place I'd ever seen was Chivhu and most of my life had been spent in mud-hut homesteads, the city seemed an alien world indeed. There was no way I could face it unaided, so I asked my good friend, Elias, to come with me. Along with the Mutiti girls, Elias was among the few students at Masasa who didn't make fun of me for being a cowherd. And he also knew Harare. His father had a place there. By offering to pay his bus fare from Masasa,

I persuaded him to make the journey with me and guide me out to the government office in Newlands suburb.'

Astonishment slapped the wheel and chuckled. 'Harare! Ah! I couldn't believe it! I got off the bus at the terminal and stepped into this maelstrom. Such noise and shouting and honking of horns and people rushing about like stampeding cattle. I'd never seen anything like it! Here was I, a country boy, familiar with cows and goats and nothing more sophisticated than a wheelbarrow. Now I had to understand traffic lights. Traffic lights! I'd never seen such things – there were none in Chivhu. It's a miracle I wasn't killed in my first five minutes.

'Elias walked me to Shawasha Flats, a concrete block in the shanty part of town where his father and brother lived along with his brother's wife and their newborn baby. The four of them occupied one room, subdivided by a wardrobe and a flimsy curtain. This had been a hostel for bachelor workers in colonial times, but now whole families were living where one man had lived before. The noise and crush were incessant. Residents on each floor shared toilets and bathrooms and a kitchen with one big stove that everybody cooked on. You had to watch your pot or you'd find it removed and another in its place. Shawasha was a tense, edgy place with crime and violence simmering beneath the surface. But for Elias' family, it was all they had and they shared it with me.

'The following day, we caught another bus for Newlands. As we drove through the city centre, my jaw dropped at the size of the buildings. Some of them must have been ten, fifteen storeys high. So many people living on top of each other. I'd see a door open and twenty people walking in or walking out. Coming from the flat horizons of Masasa, I wondered how people could bear to be all piled up like this.

'Eventually Elias delivered me to the government office in Newlands. The interviews were going to take all day, so I couldn't ask Elias to hang around. I said if he went back to the city centre, I would get the bus when I'd finished and find my way back to Shawasha Flats.

'"Are you sure you'll be OK?" asked Elias.

'"Ya, ya, I'm sure," I replied. I think having made it from the bus terminal to Newlands, my confidence was running high. But when I came out at the end of the afternoon, my sense of direction deserted me. Disorientated by the buildings and the traffic, I found my south was my west and my north was my east! I joined a crowd at a bus stop which I thought was the right one. When I asked if a bus from here would take me into town, I was told, ah no, I had to cross the road and get a bus in the other direction. This seemed completely wrong, but all I could do was follow instructions.

'Eventually I found myself back in the city centre. But where were Shawasha Flats? Elias had told me it would be about a twenty-minute walk. This was before cellphones, so I had no way of making contact. By asking people, going wrong, asking again and walking around in circles for about an hour, I finally reached my destination. I was so relieved, and so was Elias. I was also exhausted. I could jog barefoot for twenty kilometres through the bush, no problem. But walking for an hour in rush-hour Harare – ah! I wondered people didn't go crazy!

'I failed the interview for Customs and Excise and Bridget gently teased me for being such an innocent in the big city. But it wasn't long before the next interview for the School of Social Work. My plan was to go back to Harare a couple of days beforehand so that Shepherd, who'd set me up for this whole thing, could coach me. This time, I thought, I'd show Bridget that I could find my way around. Well, it won't surprise you that I failed to locate where Shepherd lived. I had his address, but it didn't seem to make sense to anyone. Instead, I made my way to Shawasha Flats and stayed with Elias.

'The lack of coaching turned out not to matter. I did the interview at the university and got accepted in 1991 at the age of twenty-four to do a Diploma in Social Work. This was despite having no academic qualifications higher than O levels. I happened to hit the last year in which work experience could count instead of A levels, so my two years as a teacher got me in. Even so, after I started, it took me several weeks of carefully trailing my fellow students to find my way with confidence from the university hostel near the Holiday Inn to the School of Social Work in the middle of town.

'Because I was no longer a teacher, there was now no need for Bridget and me to keep our relationship a secret. I knew that this was the girl I wanted to spend my life with and I wrote her a letter from Harare asking her to marry me. I'm pleased to say she accepted.'

'Did you have to ask the family?' queried Lynda.

'Of course. But in Shona tradition it's not so simple. You see, if your intended says yes, you need a go-between. So in this case we went to see Bridget's aunt, Mrs Mashiri, who lives near Mhari. The go-between's role is to talk to the couple about their intentions and to make sure they're serious. If she's satisfied, she sets a date to present their case to the girl's parents. The suitor takes a relative as well. But because I had no relatives – or none that were available – I asked old Mr Warambwa to come with us.

'Well, given that old Warambwa and Bridget's father were such good friends, there was not much doubt about the outcome.

'"Can this be true?" exclaimed Mr Mutiti when he realised why we were there. "Astonishment is like my son. And now he's becoming... my son!" So we had his blessing.'

'But you still have to pay something to the parents?' I added, thinking back to that housemaid of the Kynastons whose employment with the white *mufundisi* enhanced her bride price – her *lobola*. 'Did *lobola* come into play?'

'Ah yes, *lobola*,' replied Astonishment. 'A blessing and a curse. Traditionally, when you pay *lobola*, you're buying a womb and the wife becomes a child-bearing machine, duty-bound to produce as many children as the husband wants. So if she turns out to be barren, the husband can demand a refund. When husbands and wives quarrel, you'll often hear the husband saying, "Remember, I paid your parents many cows to buy you." *Lobola* can also make for trouble between a man and his in-laws. I heard about a guy who was so incensed when his in-laws-to-be demanded twelve cows that he put them in a truck, took them round to his in-laws' modern house in a smart suburb of Harare and released them onto the front lawn! I don't think he was the favourite son-in-law after that.

'But *lobola* is good if it cements the relationship. In my case, obviously, I didn't have much money. On the other hand, you don't want a wife for free and the parents don't want to give away their daughter too cheaply. She's worth what she's worth. And you want the parents to value you as well. If you don't pay much, you don't have their respect. They'll wonder if you're really able to look after their daughter. It's a matter of pride to be able to pay a decent price.'

'So how much?' asked Lynda. 'How much did you pay for Bridget?'

'Well, there was some bargaining between old Warambwa and Mr Mutiti. But they were such good friends and the Mutitis liked me anyway, so they let her go on generous terms.'

'But how much?'

'A down-payment of 1,000 Zim dollars.'

'Ha!' I retorted. 'Back home I have a note for 50 billion Zim dollars.'

'Yes, yes, yes!' laughed Astonishment. 'That would buy many wives! But remember, this was pre-inflation when a wife typically cost around 5,000. My 1,000 was just the first instalment to allow the marriage to go ahead. I wanted to show that I respected and appreciated my in-laws by paying more. Eventually I handed over 10,000 plus eight head of cattle.'

'A bargain!' said Lynda.

'The best deal of my life,' agreed Astonishment. 'We married in December 1993, just after I'd completed my social work diploma. The wedding took place at the Methodist church in Chitungwiza, just outside Harare, where I was now a lay preacher and a church leader. I wore a cream suit and a black bow tie and Bridget looked stunning in a lacy white dress. A small group of relatives turned up. I paid the bus fare for my mother and stepfather, Job, to come in from Mhari. We also invited my aunt Martha and uncle Elison who happened to be living in Chitungwiza. And Uncle Chengeta was there. But we didn't have James or Faith or Ezekiel. Over time the ties had loosened. For many of my relatives, our Western-style white wedding must have seemed a world away from the culture they were used to.

'In another sign of the gulf between my old life and my new, my social work studies gave me two separate meetings with Robert Mugabe. The first was in 1992 on the death of his first wife, Sally. The bond between Mugabe and Sally was very close – or it had been until the later years when Mugabe's attention started wandering. Early in their marriage, she'd campaigned for his release when the Smith government locked him up for ten years in Salisbury jail and refused to let him out, even for the funeral of their three-year-old son. As First Lady after 1987, Sally was popular in the country and her death was greatly mourned. I was in a delegation from the School of Social Work that went to give our condolences at State House. We each shook hands with the President and chatted briefly, and then we left.'

I thought back to that motorcade screaming through Harare and wondered what Astonishment had made of the bloodstained tyrant of popular imagination, this pantomime baddie of the international media. 'Did you think of yourself as shaking hands with the devil?'

'Not at all,' replied Astonishment. 'My first thought was… Isn't education a wonderful thing if it means a herd boy like me gets to shake hands with the President? Whatever the killings and torture that he might have sanctioned, there's no doubting that face-to-face he can charm an audience. The man has charisma. Maybe that makes him even more dangerous. At the time I met him he was still highly regarded, both in Zimbabwe and outside – despite the *Gukurahundi* rumours.'

'*Gukurahundi*?'

'Shona for "the early rain that washes away the chaff". Mugabe's name for Zimbabwe's notorious Fifth Brigade, trained in killing by the North Koreans and let loose on the Ndebele down in Matabeleland after Joshua Nkomo fell from grace in the 1980s. This was Mugabe's attempt to crush Nkomo's ZAPU and create a one-party state. There were some terrible massacres with people being forced to dig their own mass graves and bodies being thrown down mineshafts, but the news and the evidence didn't get out until much later. Even when it was known about, Mugabe denied responsibility. There's a view that Sally reined him in. While she was alive, Mugabe was not the man we know today. There was no talk of private palaces, or lavish shopping holidays, or the looting of Zimbabwe's diamond wealth. It was only after her death that the tyrant emerged from behind the mask.'

'And the second time you met him?'

'That was in 1997 at the end of my Bachelor's Degree in Social Studies – the qualification I went on to take after my diploma. This was still a few years before the farm takeovers that stained Mugabe's name and again it was just a handshake. Beyond that I've had no direct contact with him – nor any wish to meet him again.'

I gazed at the passing landscape and reflected on the enigma that is Robert Mugabe. The man who charmed his enemies at independence and sent Korean-trained troops to slaughter the Ndebele. Father of the nation, or bogeyman embodying the worst nightmares of the settlers? Murderous from the start, or did something change to make him want to cling to power at whatever cost to his people? Now in his dotage, was he still President by choice or was he held prisoner by the snake-pit politics of ZANU-PF and an inner circle with too much to lose if he went?

Astonishment was moving on. 'As I was finishing my diploma course, we had a guy come to speak at the university from the UN's refugee agency, the UNHCR. This was at the end of the long civil war in Mozambique between the Marxist ruling party, FRELIMO,[4] and the resistance movement, RENAMO[5] – both struggling for control in the vacuum left by the Portuguese when they pulled out in 1975. About a million Mozambicans died from fighting and starvation. Landmines took a terrible toll and about 5 million civilians were driven from their homes. A lot of them came across the border into Zimbabwe and ended up in refugee camps.

'That's what the UNHCR guy had come to talk about. Now that there was peace, the agency was starting the work of repatriation and needed people to help process the

---

[4] Frente de Libertação de Moçambique.
[5] Resistência Nacional Moçambicana.

returning refugees. Did anyone at the School of Social Work want a job?

'I decided I did. I put my name forward, had an interview and found myself on a bus to Mazoe Bridge Camp at Mount Darwin, about 130 kilometres north of Harare. What I discovered when we got there was a shanty town of 40,000 refugees – an ugly, desolate place on the bare veldt where people lived in tin and cardboard huts, under plastic sheets or in tents provided by the UNHCR. Heat and mosquitoes added to the misery. So did the rats and litter and lack of sanitation. Pit toilets were built eventually, but until then these thousands of people used the open bush.

'Almost as distressing as the squalor was the disruption to family life and the breaking of social ties as thousands of Mozambicans fled their homeland, not knowing when the war would end or how long it would be until they returned. Families had been torn apart, with different members fleeing in different directions and arriving at the camp at different times – or finding their way to the other camps in eastern Zimbabwe. Many had left husbands and wives behind, or didn't know where they were or whether they were still alive, and had struck up new, transient relationships. If the original partners turned up, as they sometimes did, the feuding could lead to violence and even murder. These were people torn from their roots. The sense of community and belonging that's so important in Africa had been lost.

'Home for me was a wooden cabin in the staff compound alongside the main camp. As part of a team of social workers, psychologists, educators, nurses and police, I helped to distribute essentials like food, soap and cooking equipment and to trace and reunite fragmented families. I spent long hours checking records with the other camps at Nyanga, Chipinge and Chiredzi and arbitrating disputes as new arrivals found husbands or wives shacked up with someone else.

'I quickly found it wasn't just the refugees living disrupted lives. The camp officers had come from all over Zimbabwe, many, again, leaving family and spouses and using the anonymity of a new place to cast off their inhibitions and live as fast and loose as they liked. The officers' compound was a place of heavy drinking and hard partying. It was easy to claim to be single and to take up with whoever you liked under the notion that what happened in Mazoe Bridge stayed in Mazoe Bridge. There was unspoken agreement that this was no place for families. Officers could go home from time to time, but no one wanted husbands or wives turning up and seeing what was going on.

'The bed-hopping was to be expected, but it bred a mood of unhappiness and distrust that poisoned the atmosphere and put people on edge. You could sense the rootlessness and dissatisfaction in the way the officers carried out their jobs and dealt with each other. Processing 40,000 displaced people was difficult enough without the tensions and angry outbursts that accompanied the work. The officers' compound was not a happy place.

'This disturbed me, both as a Christian and as an African. Traditional society has many faults – don't I know it? – but one of them is not the naked individualism and erosion of community that I saw at Mazoe Bridge.

'I pondered what to do, feeling very much alone in my views. Then a couple of weeks after I arrived, I met up with a camp clerk called Moses Mutendi. Also newly arrived, he turned out to be a Methodist like me and equally uneasy at the environment in which he found himself. We started spending time together, often staying up late at night discussing the problems of the camp. We'd both expected to be going to church during our UNHCR employment. A naïve hope. There was no church to go to. So we did the next best thing and met for a Bible study each evening in one or other of our homes.

'We then agreed to ask our wives to come and live in the compound. It was a provocative thing to do, a gesture of defiance against the prevailing culture, but we felt the need to uphold a different code of conduct. When we raised the idea with the camp administrator, he was not exactly encouraging. A bad decision, he told us. "This is not a good place for married couples," he said. "Trust me. I know."

'He was right, but we went ahead anyway. Bridget, then pregnant with our first child, came up from Harare along with Moses' wife and their one-year-old son. And sure enough, it wasn't easy. Some people shunned us completely. Others paid too much attention. Bridget could rarely walk out alone without some colleague sidling up and making lewd suggestions. But we persisted with our Bible studies, the four of us, singing hymns at the top of our voices each time we met.

'One day a lady officer said to us, "I heard you singing. You must be Christians. Can I come and join you tonight?" And we said yes, please do.

'So she came, and the following day she was back with someone else. While the rest of us sang, these two women sat on the sofa in tears. We asked what the problem was and they started pouring it all out. "We hate it here. Life is terrible. So many of us have lost the faith that we had back home. Please can you help us?" they pleaded.

'"I have a husband in Bulawayo and the man I'm living with now is not my husband," the second woman sobbed. "I don't understand what has happened to me. How has it come to this?"

'The next evening their partners came as well. The numbers continued to grow, such that we had to transfer out of our homes and into one of the classrooms at the neighbouring school. From evening Bible studies, we progressed to holding church services on a Sunday, enlisting the help of the Methodist minister in the local area. More officers started attending – not all of them, by any means, and there were still some who hated us, but a high proportion were there on a Sunday. Then some of the Mozambican refugees who understood Shona began to filter in.'

'So lives were changed?'

'Oh, certainly. We found increasingly that these were not people with no experience of church. It was simply that the anonymity of Mazoe Bridge persuaded many to abandon their faith and their principles and join in the fun. Except they then found it wasn't so much fun. When someone reminded them of what they'd lost, they were desperate to reconnect. And also, as our church community grew, there was less anonymity. We started to know each other and each other's backgrounds. People began acknowledging the husbands and wives they'd left at home and behaving differently.

'And you know what? The atmosphere started to lighten. We noticed people applying themselves to their work with greater enthusiasm – even pleasure, if that's not an odd thing to say in the context of a squalid refugee camp. I see that now as God's transformative work. All it took was someone to make a stand. By the time my contract ended in September 1994, we'd built up a real community. I was sorry to leave.'

16

Murambiwa Goes to London

We bounced off the track from Masasa and onto the tarmac of the Chivhu-Buhera road. For a few kilometres, the juddering eased and conversation became possible at less than a shout. Astonishment took advantage of the lull to press on with his story.

'While I was a student at the School of Social Work, I'd joined an organisation called ZACRO – the Zimbabwe Association for Crime Prevention and the Rehabilitation of Offenders. As a member, I got involved in the training and rehabilitation of prisoners and in lobbying on their behalf. For my fieldwork placement, I worked at a ZACRO centre in Mbare township in Harare where former prisoners were trained in soap-making and tailoring to help them reintegrate into society. Here I counselled ex-offenders, went into prisons to pray with inmates and helped meet the needs of prisoners' wives and children. We also lobbied the government for more rights for offenders, especially women prisoners with babies who badly needed childcare and early learning services.

'All of this became relevant in 1994 when the repatriation of refugees from Mazoe Bridge was nearing its end and I faced the prospect of being out of work.

'To that point in the history of Zimbabwe's penal system, there was no such thing as community service. The options available were a fine, a suspended sentence or prison – and prison in Zimbabwe was a terrible place to end up. In a country struggling to provide for its law-abiding citizens, there was little money to spare to make prison anything more than a place of incarceration. Food was scarce and corruption and violence were endemic. The only rehabilitation was fear. If life in prison was grim enough, you might hope that no one would ever want to return. But things don't work that way.

'In 1992, in a bid to keep less serious offenders out of Zimbabwe's jails, the Minister of Justice with support from a London-based NGO[6] called Penal Reform International – PRI for short – launched a study on whether community service could work as an alternative. If some offenders could be kept out of prison, would it stop them becoming corrupted and sliding into worse criminality?

'Well, the study was carried out, the findings were positive and an act was passed in Parliament to allow a pilot project to go ahead. By 1994 the programme was operating, but with little supervision of offenders and inadequate screening as to who should be given this option. What was needed was officers on the ground to get the thing running smoothly.

'All of which resulted in a call from the Under Secretary at the Ministry of Justice, asking on the basis of my ZACRO work if I'd like to be one of three community service officers funded by PRI. I agreed at once, took my oath

---

[6] Non-governmental organisation.

before the Commissioner of Prisons and found myself employed in Harare by the Ministry of Justice on behalf of PRI. The work involved assessing offenders to see if they were suitable candidates – would they serve a community placement without absconding? – then organising somewhere for them to go and making sure they were properly supervised. I found myself dealing with police, prison officials, court officers, MPs, judges and even heads of government departments. Imagine it – the ragged, uneducated *jamkoko* from Buhera mixing with the high-ups in the Ministry of Justice. It seemed surreal.'

I remarked that Astonishment must have seen some interesting cases.

'Oh, ya. In one case, a girl of sixteen was raped by her father – a polygamist with two wives and nine other children. She reported the assault to the police, but all they did was send the child to hospital to get a medical report. No one went with her, which meant that two of her aunts were able to intercept her and persuade her to drop the charges. "Think what will happen to your brothers and sisters if your father gets arrested," they said to her. "You wouldn't want him sent to prison, would you?" This frightened her so much that she went back to the police to withdraw the charge.

'Next, the police arrested the girl for making a false report and she ended up in my office for me to decide if community service would be suitable. I believed it would be. When the court found her guilty and passed sentence, I then had the task of finding a placement. At that point I didn't know of the aunts' involvement and had no hard evidence that this was a miscarriage of justice. All the same, something made me uneasy. From what I'd seen of her, I couldn't believe that this sixteen-year-old child was capable of cooking up such a serious allegation against her father.

'The community service was due to begin two weeks after the sentencing and I used the time to investigate further. I talked to the girl and discovered that her aunts had persuaded her not to press charges – at her father's instigation, she thought. She'd been so intimidated, she'd even pleaded guilty at the trial. So I sought out the aunts and challenged them about it. Sure enough, they both admitted that they were trying to get their brother off the hook, even if it meant an innocent child being prosecuted. I wrote a report to the High Court and succeeded in getting the sentence quashed. The father by then had fled to South Africa, but we still couldn't guarantee the girl's safety if she stayed at home. In the end we had to place her in a children's home.

'Such sad cases we came across. One young officer I worked with was discovered taking bribes to let people off their community service. Knowing he was going to be arrested and sent to jail, he swallowed poison, got on his motorbike and set off at top speed down the Bindura Road. When the poison took effect, he fell off and died of his injuries on the highway.

'The pilot project funded by PRI ran for six years. After that it was deemed to be established and able to operate without external support. The NGO withdrew and the whole operation was transferred to the Prisons Department within the Ministry of Justice. This meant that all community service officers were now Prisons

Department employees. As such, we had to undergo the training course for prison officers.

'This was like basic military training, the aim of which was to crush your individuality and all traces of civilian mentality, then to instil the discipline and endurance required by the Zimbabwe security service. I reported to Chikurubi training depot in Harare and found myself in the tender care of Senior Prison Officer Kuda, an angry, bristling man in his late forties, bullet-headed and built like a baobab tree. SPO Kuda regarded social work professionals like me as namby-pamby office boys and his mission in life – one he took to with a passion – was to make proper men of us. At four o'clock every morning, without fail, we'd be woken by his elephantine bellow: "Fa-a-a-all in!" We bounced out of bed as if the building were on fire, knowing we had three minutes to get dressed, make our beds immaculately and be out on parade for physical training.

'Kuda would survey us with contempt, then begin the routine. "Up! Up! Up! Mark time! Higher! Higher!" On the command, we bounced up and down like grasshoppers before embarking on the morning jog that lengthened over time from five to thirty kilometres. For once I was grateful for the cattle herder's life that had hardened me for running that kind of distance. Back at the depot we had twenty minutes to wash, dress and be back on parade for marching drill. Yes, there was some classroom training, but my main memories are of jogging in formation down the still-dark roads of Harare in the early morning, of endless marching drills and obsessive rules about keeping your bed and your kit in the regulation order. By the time we went to bed, we felt we'd been hit by a train – only for the whole thing to start again before the sun was up.

'Kuda, who it turned out had left school after Form Two and had never taken O levels, reserved his greatest scorn for those with fancy degrees. It was part of his mind games that we had to accept, without questioning, that our academic qualifications were not our own but Kuda's.

'"Your degrees are all fake!" he would bawl at us on the parade ground. "You're all worthless. You have nothing. Repeat after me: 'I am a stupid goat. I have no education. My degree belongs to Mr Kuda.' Now jump and sing it. 'I'm a goat with no degree!' Run! Keep singing!"

'So we'd canter round the parade ground, extolling Mr Kuda's nonexistent academic achievements. All of this might have had a point for young recruits to the army, but for men being trained to make sensitive decisions on how to deal with vulnerable prisoners, it was ludicrous – an accidental outcome of a structure that placed community sentencing under the prison service and made the prison service a branch of state security.

'One day Kuda had us digging a pit with shovels in the bare earth. When he decided it was big enough, he ordered us to fill it with water from a tap, racing to and fro with buckets to counter the seepage. By running fast enough, we finally managed to raise the level until the pit became a slimy brown mudbath.

'"Now jump in!" screamed Kuda.

'We hesitated. Did he mean it?

'"I said jump in! Now! In your clothes. Now roll! Everybody roll."

'We did, squelching from side to side like warthogs at a watering hole. Kuda waited until we were well-coated in slime. "Right!" he yelled again. "Fall in! Back to barracks at the double. I want you all clean and on parade in thirty minutes!"'

'In 2000, after I'd been in the job for six years, PRI created an award for the world's best non-custodial programmes. They sent evaluators to the various countries that were being funded and mentored to implement such programmes, and I met some of them when they came to Zimbabwe. They submitted their reports... and what do you know? Zimbabwe came out on top. One Zimbabwean judge and one regional community service officer were to go to London to collect the award from none other than Princess Anne. The designated judge was asked to choose an officer with a heavy hint from the PRI evaluators that Astonishment Mapurisa might be the man. When the call came through that I'd been selected, I nearly fell off my chair.

'As a kid in the bush I'd seen aeroplanes in the sky and imagined them as no bigger than flying ploughs. It was inconceivable then that I'd ever end up sitting in one and looking down on the landscape of my childhood. Now the *jamkoko* was taking his seat in Business Class for the British Airways flight from Harare to London Gatwick in the company of a high court judge! As I buckled myself into this metal tube and we lifted into the sky above Harare, the noisy, churning city, green from the summer rains, was transformed into tranquil, abstract patterns on the earth. It's what every flyer sees as they rise from take-off, but I found it spell-binding. I still do. My home city, familiar but strange. Looking down as the plane banked, I felt as if I were soaring like an eagle. Through the window, I followed Domboshawa Road as it threaded past Borrowdale racecourse and up through the northern suburbs. Then the ribbon of tarmac lost itself in the bush, the rainy season clouds came whipping past the window and Harare was gone. I sat back and wondered what to say to the learned judge for the next eleven hours.

'The first challenge arose when the stewardess handed out the menu cards for dinner and asked us to make our selection. The list was a minefield. What were these things called prawns? We never had those in Madamombe. Foolishly, I ordered some. When the meal arrived, it looked like a dish of pink *chongololos*, those fat Zimbabwean millipedes that come out in the rainy season. How were you supposed to eat them? I glanced sideways at the judge, but he was tucking into something different. Nervously, I started popping them into my mouth. They were definitely crunchy. I swallowed as much of the shell as I could and surreptitiously disposed of the rest, spitting out the bits into my starched napkin. If the judge noticed that his regional community service officer had no idea you took the shells off first, he tactfully didn't show it.

'I'd been told that London in January could be cold, so I'd packed an extra jersey. Nothing, however, could have prepared me for the blast of freezing air as we emerged from the airport into a grey English winter. And if Masasa to Harare had been a jarring exposure to noise and traffic, London was a frenzy. Not a patch of earth to be seen – just tarmac, pavement, buildings; things hard, resistant and impervious. Nowhere to sit and idle and pass the time, as you would in Africa. No umbrella trees to squat under. Instead, the rumble of pounding feet and people with intent, purposeful faces fixed on the middle distance. In Africa you stop and greet. In London, clearly not. And the Underground! Imagine! For the boy from Chivhu, dropping down into that thundering, subterranean world took me right back to the cattle dip at Morrison Farm. In the rush and crush, all the animals would merge into one – a beast with a hundred heads and a blur of legs. Add sunshine and a *baas* with a *sjambok*, and the stampede of underground commuters could have been that beast.

'A shock it might have been, but England was endlessly fascinating. The judge and I stayed at the extremely grand Rubens hotel, just a short step from Buckingham Palace. I'd seen some nice hotels in Harare, but this was in a different league, with its massive chandeliers and carpets the size of football fields and flunkeys in uniform at the door – and after Harare, how odd to have the door opened for me by white people! After the prawns episode on the plane, I tried to keep to the familiar whenever a waiter placed a menu in my hands. Anything with chips was usually safe.

'Our hosts from PRI took us to see community service projects in and around the capital, then brought us back for the awards presentation in Westminster Abbey. The Abbey was mesmerising. So famous. So old and dark and cavernous. So many kings and queens and poets and statesmen slumbering under its ancient stones. And so much gold, winking in the gloom. There was a short ceremony which I only half took in while gawping at the surroundings. The Home Secretary, Jack Straw, gave a speech. Next to him was his deputy, Paul Boateng, later to become British High Commissioner to South Africa. Awkward in my unaccustomed suit, I shook hands with both and then with Princess Anne who presented us with the award. She and I exchanged a few words. I can't remember what was said, but I do recall her genuine interest in our work and my own astonishment at the gulf fleetingly bridged by that brief handshake.

'Murambiwa meets British royalty. I guess if you're royal, you're used to meeting people from all stations in life. For my part, I thought how proud Ernest Warambwa would have been to see what he'd made possible.'

17

The Billion-dollar Tomato

We were now off the tarmac, back on the dirt corrugations that had Astonishment shouting to be heard above the vibration. I moved my recorder closer to catch the details.

'My career as a civil servant shaped up well,' he went on. 'By 2001, I'd completed a Bachelor's Degree to add to my diploma and had just enrolled for a Master's Degree in policy studies. I knew all the processes and procedures of the community service system and was now number two to the national coordinator. Further promotion looked a certainty. I had a lovely wife and we now had two small children – a son, Tatenda, born in 1994, and a daughter, Vimbai, who came along in 2000.

'The only thing to cloud this sunny outlook was Zimbabwe's descent from the bright, new hope of Southern Africa to political lunacy. Partly this was the result of unrealistic promises made during the war of liberation. When the fighting is over, the comrades constantly told the people, you won't have to dig your plot any more. You won't have to pay the white man's hut tax. You can go and live in town in a big house. You'll drive a car. The life the white man is living now, that will be your life.

'Many people believed it. Why else would they be making such sacrifices for the struggle? And once we had our freedom and people could live anywhere, they flocked to the towns in search of the good life they'd been promised. So the towns became overcrowded and services and amenities started buckling under the strain. And still – surprise, surprise – people had to pay taxes, though now the money had a way of disappearing into politicians' pockets so that not enough was invested in roads and hospitals and schools.

'All this meant growing discontent with the government. The fruits that people expected from independence were not coming through. People were waiting for the former comrades – those now in government, those who'd wooed them with honeyed words and AK47s – to deliver the good life. But it wasn't happening. Poverty increased rather than diminished. Workers' pay wasn't keeping pace with inflation. Jobs were less and less secure.

'What happened next was perfectly foreseeable. Out of the labour movement emerged a new opposition party, the MDC, under its trade unionist leader, Morgan Tsvangirai.

'The government might not have worried too much about the MDC, except for one thing. It united workers with those who owned the means of production, namely companies and white commercial farmers. In other words, it brought together workers and bosses. These groups usually sit on opposite sides of any confrontation and it's very unusual for a government to find itself opposed by both. But that's what was happening. To the government's alarm, Morgan Tsvangirai was garnering support among the farmers.

'To destroy this alliance, the ruling party knew it had to disempower those white farmers who not only supported the opposition but had the means to finance it. This was a new kind of threat, more serious than the one from Joshua Nkomo whose ZAPU party was simply swallowed up into ZANU-PF in the 1980s. Tsvangirai refused to buckle in the same way, so a different strategy was needed – one that targeted his white backers. Hence the farm takeovers in the early 2000s. Don't believe the line about the takeovers being to transfer land to the deserving poor. It was all about smashing the opposition. What happened to the land after it was taken was secondary. Grabbing the land was the key thing.

'At one point, ZANU-PF put out a video of white farmers signing cheques for the MDC. We saw it on TV, with pictures in the papers as well. It's widely suspected that clerks working in the banks were in the pay of the party, so were able to tell the authorities which farmers were involved. And as we know, quite a few of them paid for it with their lives. It wasn't indiscriminate killing. It tended to be one farmer from each branch of the Commercial Farmers' Union, especially if he was known to be an MDC supporter. This was to intimidate the maximum number of people. They wanted people to see what had happened to their neighbours and surrender without a fight.

'I knew some of the farmers who were killed. Some I even worked with when I sent offenders to do community service on their property. Such senseless murders, every one. And under the pressure, some farmers went the other way, cosying up to ZANU-PF and informing the government as to who was supporting the MDC. Even those who've been thrown out have sometimes remained supportive of the government. It's said that one expelled farmer formed a construction company and supplied bulldozers for the government to flatten people's houses in Operation *Murambatsvina*.'

I remembered the name, *Murambatsvina*, from news reports at the time and from two of its victims – the little Matthew Rusike girls, Marigold and Enid, who'd been left helpless in the open with their AIDS-stricken mother after their home was bulldozed.

'Ya, ya,' continued Astonishment. 'The farmers suffered from the takeovers, but so did the workers who lost their homes and employment and mainly fled to the towns. The result was a sprawl of shanty houses on the edges of the cities. That left the government with a double problem – shanty towns in the urban areas, likely to be fertile ground for the MDC, and no one in the country to work the farms for the new, fat-cat owners. Both, of course, caused by its own policies.

'Now Mugabe's first resort is always to impose his will by force. As with *Gukurahundi* in the 1980s, the undesirables had to be smashed. So he sent in the bulldozers in 2005 in what he described as an "urban renewal campaign". One senior policeman was more direct. He said Operation *Murambatsvina* was to cleanse the country of the crawling mass of maggots bent on destroying the economy. Either way, over half a million people lost their homes or livelihoods or both. Some inhabitants of the shanty towns were forced at gunpoint to pull down their own homes. At the time, the 2004 tsunami in the Indian Ocean was still very vivid in people's minds. *Murambatsvina* came to be called Zimbabwe's tsunami after the devastation it caused.'

I thought of Marigold and Enid, helpless victims of their own government's malice and economic ineptitude. And also of the sinister appropriation of two lovely Shona words that sound like thunder over distant African hills. *Gukurahundi*, 'the early rain that washes away the chaff', twisted to mean 'Kill the opposition'. And *Murambatsvina* – 'clear out the rubbish'. Into my mind came the well-meaning sign at Mutemachani Primary: *Marara Mugomba* – 'rubbish in the pit'. I hoped it would never become a ZANU-PF slogan.

'Through the early 2000s,' continued Astonishment, 'life grew steadily worse as the economy crumbled and inflation went hyper. Eventually you needed a bag full of cash to get half a bag of groceries – the only kind of shopping where the load on the way to the shops was heavier than the load coming back! In the supermarkets, you could pick something off the shelf at one price and find it had gone up by the time you reached the checkout. If you then went home to scoop up some more money, you'd find another hike in prices by the time you got back.

'In January 2008, Bridget and I spent a few days out of Harare at our rural home. When we left, you could get a few tomatoes for about a billion dollars. When we came back to town, we were shocked to discover they now cost a billion each. Just one tomato!

'And buses. Every day the fare going home was more than you paid in the morning on the way in. And the next day would be different again. By around 2008, a typical one-way bus fare to work could cost over 3 billion Zim dollars, which was more than most people's wages for the week.'

'Surely,' I interrupted, 'life must have come to a standstill as everyone spent hours a day counting out notes?'

'Ah. In the end, people didn't bother. No one had time for counting those bundles of rubbish. When you bought your ticket for the Kombi bus, you just handed over a stash of paper and if the weight was about right you could get on. People literally went about with satchels full of cash. But at least we didn't have to worry about muggings. Nobody wanted your money because it was worthless.

'At around that time, one US dollar was equivalent to 5 quadrillion Zimbabwe dollars, or five quad as we called it – five with fifteen zeros after it. The quad became the unit of currency. The Reserve Bank kept introducing bigger and bigger notes – 50 billion, then 100 billion dollars – to help you make up your quad, but it didn't do much to keep down the weight of paper you had to carry around with you. The last banknote to be printed in 2008 was for 100 trillion, but even that wasn't enough for a week's bus fare to work.

'Bridget was teaching at the time and found herself doing maths with the children with pre-inflation text books. They found it very confusing to have a problem worded something like: "You have five dollars to buy eggs… " Five dollars for eggs! This was incomprehensible, like something from another world. Which, in a way, it was.'

By now the shadows were lengthening and our captive chicken was attempting another breakout. Clear of the corrugations, we sloughed along sandy tracks for a few more kilometres and came to a wire-fenced compound set back from the road. Behind the gate were two or three thatched huts, a square, tin-roofed dwelling, a maize rack and a stockade enclosing half-a-dozen languid cows. A ridgeback lay prone and panting at the threshold of one of the huts. Strewn across the sand were a couple of carved, wooden, upright chairs, a bicycle and a plastic, ten-gallon water container resting on a wheelbarrow. Behind the huts by an outcrop of cacti was a metal frame piled high with enamel bowls and iron cooking pots. The air was luminous with the warm, golden stillness that infuses an African sky in the minutes before the sun drops and turns fiery. In the late sunlight, a pair of flat-topped umbrella trees cast dappled shadows across the sandy concourse. The air was fragrant with woodsmoke.

We drove in through the gate and stopped. Astonishment switched off the engine and sat back with a sigh of satisfaction.

'Welcome to my rural home,' he said.

18

A Blood-soaked Election

A figure emerged from one of the huts – a slow-moving, solidly built lady in her sixties in a headscarf and a patterned skirt wound loosely around her waist. She shaded her eyes against the low sun with one hand and waved with the other.

'My mother,' smiled Astonishment.

He strode across the sand and hugged her and exchanged a few words in Shona. Then he led her to Lynda and me to be introduced. Lonia Magondo, long widowed from Job, had little English, but she smiled and greeted us with the cupped-hand gesture traditional among Shona women. Beneath the cracked and weathered face, I tried to picture the spirited sixteen-year-old who had borne her baby out of wedlock and called him Murambiwa. Despite everything, Astonishment's affection was obvious and she looked pleased at his return.

There were others to be introduced. Lonia's sister, Elizabeth – a large, jolly woman in a hooped rugby shirt – and a younger lady called Blessing. 'Blessing is related to the husband of one of my Magondo half-sisters,' explained Astonishment. 'And here is Gillian who is still at school, daughter of another half-sister, Esnath. But Esnath is late.'

Late? Late for what?

Then it clicked. In Zimbabwean English, if someone is late, they're dead. That's what the street child, Zondiwe, was trying to tell us about his parents in Victoria Falls.

Gillian – barefoot, early teens, denim-skirted – came shyly forward and shook hands with a curtsy. Astonishment went on: 'Bridget and I have given Gillian a home here ever since she was born. Her mother died soon after delivery, so Bridget and I looked after Gillian from birth. Also her brother, Thomas, who's three years older. Their father had abandoned them, but he turned up again just this year and reclaimed Thomas. Gillian he didn't want, so here she is still. We pay her school fees and we pay Blessing to help around the compound to make life easier for my mother and my aunt Elizabeth.'

I looked at Gillian, motherless and rejected by her father, another *murambiwa* were it not for Astonishment picking up the family obligation at considerable expense to himself.

Astonishment pulled the irritated chicken from the back of the Toyota and handed it to Blessing. You could almost see the thought bubble floating above its head. 'About time! Outrageous treatment. A proud fowl should be free to roam… Hello?'

Whatever Blessing did, it was so quick it passed in a blur. The chicken was on the ground, a knife flashed and the scrawny head was off. In a few minutes the carcass was plucked, dismembered and simmering in an iron pot over a fire that burned in the centre of one of the huts. Blessing and Lonia squatted alongside, working on the evening meal.

Later, tin coffee mugs in hand, we sat out on those heavy, msasa-wood chairs, carved with reliefs of buffalo and lion. A bloated sun had sunk into the veldt, silhouetting the acacia trees along the flat horizon. The short African sunset flared and faded and the stars began to twinkle, first in ones and twos and then in clusters until the Milky Way arched over our heads in a shimmering, silver cascade. The night was soft and benign in that fragrant African way I'd completely forgotten in all my years in the northern hemisphere. It caressed like velvet. It lent itself to staring at the stars and talking softly. I remember feeling entirely secure. For all Zimbabwe's sufferings and insecurity, Astonishment's homestead embraced us with something older and deeper, something African, something to do with the primacy of relationships and taking care of family and friends. Our tourist stash of US dollars lay in a holdall in the hut behind us. Elsewhere we'd have locked it away. Here, who was going to take it? In Astonishment's little kingdom, bounded by its rickety wire fence, peace reigned. I understood why every Zimbabwean yearns to be buried in his rural home.

The cows in the stockade shifted and snorted. A dog yawned and scratched and Astonishment continued his story.

'So inflation has gone stratospheric. People are becoming poorer by the day and the government has been cracking down with farm takeovers and Operation *Murambatsvina*. And so we come to the 2008 presidential election – Robert Mugabe of ZANU-PF versus Morgan Tsvangirai of the MDC.'

To me, this was familiar territory – the election I'd followed obsessively from the UK, having booked to take the family to Victoria Falls that same year. The one I'd so worried about on my hike through the Yorkshire Dales. I'd seized on every scrap of news of the first round in March, knowing that Zimbabwean elections could be violent but hoping, like the timid tourist I was, that the dust would have settled by August. Not so. It was more than a month before any official results were announced, prompting speculation of a ZANU-PF power-struggle behind the scenes. The rumour was that the party knew the result within days of the poll and that Mugabe had lost. The old man was ready to stand down, but some of his inner circle – fearful of being called to account for their crimes by a new government – allegedly persuaded him to stay and face a second round.

That was the start of weeks of violence against the MDC. Observers filed reports of opposition supporters being tortured, both as punishment and to make sure they voted correctly the next time around. The MDC reported further attacks and a rising number of murders – more than thirty by mid-May. A police raid on the MDC headquarters in Harare piled on the pressure. Faced with this onslaught, Tsvangirai withdrew a week before the run-off vote in June, calling it a 'violent sham' and saying he didn't want any more of his supporters killed.[7] The vote went ahead regardless. Not surprisingly, Mugabe won.

This was the outline of events as I'd picked them up in the UK media. But I wanted to know what 2008 had felt

---

[7] www.seattletimes.com/nation-world/zimbabwe-opposition-leader-pulling-out-of-election/ (accessed 31st January 2019).

like on the ground to citizens like Astonishment. As a voter, had he been exposed to the violence?

'Fortunately, not directly,' he answered. 'After the first round, I sometimes came across roadblocks set up by ZANU-PF youth to stop the MDC campaigning in certain areas. On one occasion my car was stopped and a young man shouted through the window, "27th June!" – this being the date of the run-off. I was supposed to respond, *"Mugabe muoffice zvachose!"* – Mugabe in office forever! Ducking the issue, I told him I worked for the government and had no time to attend rallies of any sort. Thinking I must be a senior civil servant, he let me pass.

'When it came to 27th June, every voter in my ward in Harare was obliged to pass through the house of a local ZANU-PF official. Names were recorded and each of us was given a slip on which to write the number of our ballot paper. We were told to hand these back before we left. There was no attempt to disguise the reason. "Should ZANU-PF lose at this polling station," the agents told us, "we'll be able to see who voted for the opposition." This was all very intimidating. As we saw from the result, it was hard for MDC supporters to hold their nerve.'

Even though Mugabe remained President, the 2008 election at least ushered in a shaky, power-sharing government (an ungainly beast appropriately known as the GNU, the Government of National Unity) with Tsvangirai as Prime Minister. Now in charge of the Ministry of Finance, the MDC was able to bring some economic sanity back into the system. Parts of the country, notably tourist areas like Victoria Falls, had been using the US dollar for some time. The Ministry of Finance now ditched the worthless Zimbabwean dollar and adopted the US dollar as the national currency. The move almost immediately killed off inflation, averting total collapse and even producing a spurt of economic growth.

As Astonishment traced the events that had pulled Zimbabwe back from the brink, I tried to picture how a country changes its currency in the midst of rampant inflation. Did it happen overnight?

'Oh yes. We woke up one morning in February 2009 to find our bank accounts wiped clean. The government just said, whatever you have in Zim dollars is no more. There was no conversion from one to the other. If you had 20 million in the bank, you lost it. If 20 trillion, you lost it equally. In reality, there wasn't much difference between the two amounts. Numbers had lost all meaning, so everything you had in the bank evaporated overnight. On the first day of the new currency, everyone started from zero. Prices that had been in Zimbabwe dollars in the shops were now in US dollars, but with no conversion rates the shopkeepers more or less had to think of a number. What is a loaf worth in US dollars? What price a shirt in the new currency?'

'And where did the dollars come from on that first morning?'

'You know, trading in US dollars had unofficially become the norm and people had supplies stashed away for such time as it became legal to use them. South African rand, too, sent back by migrant workers to their families in Zimbabwe. But I'm running ahead of myself. Let's pick up at the Ministry of Justice where I'd been since 1994. Out of the blue, in September 2001, I had a call from the Methodist Bishop of Zimbabwe. He asked to see me at his office.

'I knew the bishop as a wise and saintly man, so was interested to hear what he had to say. It wasn't what I expected. He started to talk about Matthew Rusike Children's Home at Epworth, a Methodist institution that needed a new superintendent. The job had been advertised twice, but no suitable candidate had been found and the post was still vacant. The right person, the bishop explained, had to be a social worker and a Methodist in good standing with the church.

'"You happen to fit both those criteria," he said. "Would you be interested in taking the job?"

'Overcoming my surprise, my first thought was to say no. I was doing well at the Ministry. I'd just enrolled for a Master's Degree to enhance my prospects. Promotion was on the cards. Why would I want to give all that up to go and look after seventy-five children in Epworth, especially as the expectations for the home were pretty low? All that was required of the superintendent, it seemed to me, was to maintain the place and make sure the children were fed and went to school.

'I demurred, but the bishop came back at me. "I know the life you've led, my friend. I know the struggles you've had, how you were abandoned and abused and had to make your own way in life. Don't you think a man with this kind of life experience is just the person to identify with these children and help change their lives? It's not so much the qualifications, it's the struggles you've been through that lead me to believe you're the right person for the job."

'My resistance crumbled. I felt ashamed of my reaction – mortified that my first instinct had been to hang on to my security. What had I become? I remember tears stinging my eyes as I realised I'd spent the last few years turning my back on my own childhood – trying to forget it, even – in my quest to get on in life. It hit me at that moment that I had a calling. This was the reason I'd trained in social work. It wasn't to work with prisoners. Yes, I was doing a useful job in making sure the wrong people didn't go to jail, but all this experience with people on the fringes of society was now to be directed to those even more vulnerable and in even greater need. The conviction was sudden and certain. I had to accept.

'Looking back, it's curious to think that whenever I applied for a job on my own initiative – the Zimbabwe Customs job, for example – I didn't get it. Every job I did end up getting, from Masasa High to the refugee camp to the Ministry of Justice and now Matthew Rusike, came at somebody else's initiative with no application from me. Doors have closed and opened in unexpected ways. I'm convinced that God has been in it.'

19

Matthew Rusike Children's Home

'When I joined Matthew Rusike Children's Home – MRCH – in October 2001, the place was barely subsisting and almost bankrupt. A few days into the job, I asked my predecessor, "What exactly is my role here at Epworth?" He replied very much as the bishop had done: "Keep the place ticking over. Make sure the children have food and go to school. Oh, and pay the salaries of your staff."

'With what, I wondered. For one thing, there was hardly any money to do any of those things: my secretary had just handed me a cheque book and told me there were 300 Zim dollars in the bank. Secondly, I was then working for my Master's Degree in Policy Studies and concluded it didn't need someone with a Master's to meet such an undemanding brief. It was clear to me that MRCH would either develop or die. I wasn't going to let it die, so it had to be development.

'I called my staff together for some serious strategic planning.

'One of our first moves was to deinstitutionalise the children. With the help of the UK charity, Action for

Children,[8] we ended the system of children sleeping in dormitories and built individual houses in which they could live in family units of ten or twelve under the care of a house mother. For children who often had no experience of family life – or at best, a very bad experience – I wanted us to provide the nearest thing we could to a stable, loving environment in which every child could feel cherished and special.'

'So the bishop was right about drawing on your own experience,' suggested Lynda.

'Oh yes. That kind of security was something I had craved throughout my childhood. But I also wanted to integrate the home into the surrounding community. Instead of shutting ourselves off, I thought we should use our resources to empower the people of Epworth township, one of the poorest areas of Harare. So we opened up our gardens for people to have a plot of their own and to grow and sell their own vegetables. Others would be given a few chicks along with seed for food and be sent off to rear and sell their own poultry. The little tailoring shop we had on-site for making clothes for the children began to provide training in dressmaking so that local people could supplement their income sewing uniforms for schools and overalls for companies.

'As things developed, so various international agencies took an interest. The Australian charity, Uniting World,[9] agreed to sponsor some of the work and invited me to travel to Australia to raise the profile of the organisation. A little earlier we'd been taken up by the Qantas cabin crew

[8] See www.actionforchildren.org.uk.

[9] See www.unitingworld.org.au.

as one of their causes. You know how some airlines make a collection during the flight for a specified charity? Well, we became one of those charities, thanks to one of their stewardesses, a lady called Susy James, who flew into Harare with Qantas, got to know us on her stopovers and became a good friend.

'Other support came from the Friends of Matthew Rusike Children's Home[10] in the UK. In 2003 they funded a visit to Britain in order to look at best childcare practice over there. Out of that experience came individual development plans for every child along with discharge and aftercare plans for when they came to leave.

'Looking beyond the home, we started to encourage local churches to be aware of the needs in their own vicinity and to take responsibility for them. With a whole generation decimated by AIDS, the greatest need often lay in households where grandparents were looking after young children or where orphaned children had been left on their own to take care of younger siblings. We began training childcare coordinators in local churches – people able to identify those needs, be it child heads of households, or children who were malnourished or chronically ill, or those missing school because their parents couldn't afford the fees. And out of MRCH funds, we started providing practical support – food, blankets, medicines, school fees.

'My thinking here was that residential care – although essential for some children – can only benefit a limited number. If deprived children can be helped at home by

---

[10] See www.friendsofmatthewrusike.org.

members of their own community, then every dollar goes further and it's better for the child anyway. So in the same way that we tried to support the community in Epworth, we looked to develop the communities in and around the participating churches. We replicated the poultry project. We put in boreholes to help create market gardens so people could get some income. Zimbabwe is a family-orientated society. If your relatives can't look after their children, you have to do it. However grudgingly and badly my own relatives looked after me, at least they acknowledged their responsibility and made sure I didn't die. But if resources are stretched, people will naturally send their own children to school and allow any orphans in their care to drop out. So small-scale community development leads directly to more children going to school.

'It was all about decentralising the work of MRCH – not so much asking supporters to send money to look after children in Harare, but empowering them to take care of their own orphans nearer to hand. Getting more done by having the church network participating in childcare, rather than us being the specialists.

'Across the country I think we trained around 500 caregivers and now we're helping about 7,000 children out in the community compared to the 150 in the home at Epworth. That's more children who we hope will grow up to become good citizens and make a useful contribution to their country.'

My short time at Epworth had given me some idea of Astonishment's impact. I knew that in the years following his appointment, Matthew Rusike had developed from a children's home into a national childcare organisation, a model of good practice with a growing reputation in Zimbabwe and across Southern Africa. It was therefore inevitable that Zimbabwe's politicians would want to become involved, both to keep watch on the home's activities and to feed off its good name. I wondered how this had affected its work.

'Zimbabwe under ZANU-PF has parallels with Communist East Germany,' replied Astonishment. 'One in every so many citizens is an agent of the CIO, the Central Intelligence Organisation. From Kombi drivers to prostitutes, they're paid by the government to watch what's going on and report anything that could threaten the party. At any public gathering, like a funeral, there'll be CIO informers keeping an eye on things. But it's all a badly kept secret. Most people are aware of who these agents are. There's a relative of Blessing's who collects a monthly allowance for doing no discernable work and it's commonly accepted that she's an agent. And children, too. Where we once lived in Harare, the neighbour's young son was a ZANU-PF spy.

'Being ex-Ministry of Justice, I can usually recognise someone else who's been through government training and is likely to be a CIO agent. We've had them trying to infiltrate MRCH. Once, for example, we had a student intern who was obvious from the start. One way you can tell is they come in bad-mouthing ZANU-PF and encouraging you to do the same. My response was not to be drawn, to be completely transparent and to let her go about her business. If her brief was to find out if MRCH was a front for the opposition, well, *good luck to her*, I thought. There was nothing for her to discover.'

I put it to Astonishment that someone running a high-profile organisation like Matthew Rusike could hardly avoid getting embroiled in Zimbabwean politics.

'Ya, it's not easy. I'm always careful to tread a neutral path between the government and the opposition. My priority is the children, not which political party is in the ascendancy. If either side wants to donate to the home, whether genuinely or just to burnish their own image, well, that's fine by me. Morgan Tsvangirai gave money once. I said I was happy to receive it as long as it didn't put me under any obligation to be a conduit for money back to the MDC. ZANU-PF is paranoid about foreign money coming in and funding the opposition, so any suspicion that we at MRCH are channelling money to the MDC from our overseas supporters would get us into serious trouble. I used to get calls from the bank – or purporting to be from the bank: it was really guys from state security – demanding to know where our donations were coming from and what purpose we were putting them to. So again, my strategy was to be transparent and let them know that every cent was to help the children. Which was true.

'It isn't easy, all this attention from the politicians. But I have to stay impartial to protect our credibility and independence. That's why, when the MDC asked me to help formulate their strategy before the 2008 election, I had to decline. And the same with ZANU-PF. The First Lady, Grace Mugabe, has given quite generously to our work. In the days of inflation and food shortages and empty supermarket shelves, she sometimes sent us food hampers and bags of mealie-meal which she, as a member of the ruling party, could always get hold of. I wouldn't presume to say what her motivation was. Maybe simple charity, maybe good publicity for her. Either way it was welcome. But when her agents tried to headhunt me to help run a children's home that she wanted to set up in her own name in Mazoe – again I said no. I didn't want to be aligned with any one political party.

'It's the children that matter. I will never play politics if it jeopardises the well-being of the children in my care.'

One of Astonishment's ridgebacks came padding into the circle from the darkness beyond and flopped at his feet. He ruffled its ears and spoke to it softly in Shona. It yawned and nuzzled his hand. The bond between Astonishment and his dogs was obviously a strong one, derived, I guessed, from his hunting days as a boy.

'I've been at Matthew Rusike now for nine years,' he went on. 'But my time there very nearly ended after two.' Stroking the dog's wiry coat, he told us what had happened one Saturday evening in 2003.

'I was driving from Harare to Chitungwiza. It was getting dark. The rain was coming on and I was travelling quite fast because I wanted to arrive before nightfall. On the outskirts of Harare, I heard a bang and the car swerved. I knew I'd blown a tyre and I jammed on the brakes. After that, the memories are confused. The car left the road and overturned, I think several times, before coming to rest on its wheels, totally smashed up with me still strapped inside. I had an impression of people crowding round.

Somebody reached in and touched me on the shoulder. "Ah, he's dead," I heard him say.

'The next thing I remember was waking up in The Avenues Clinic in Harare with Bridget at my bedside. She burst into tears as I opened my eyes and gave me the nearest she could to a hug through all the paraphernalia of the hospital bed. It turned out I had nine broken ribs, a broken collarbone and shoulder blade and two fractures to my skull, along with multiple lacerations. My head felt as big as a watermelon. Possibly it was. Behind me I became aware of a couple of doctors discussing the fractures in my skull in low voices. They sounded concerned.

'This was now Sunday evening, twenty-four hours after the accident. When I'd first been admitted, the clinic had demanded payment upfront. These were the inflation years, remember. The fee was 3.2 million Zim dollars and it had to be paid in cash. If the money was not forthcoming, Bridget was told, she'd have to take me to the government hospital at Parirenyaywa – where, as it happened, the doctors were all on strike.

'Though desperate to stay at my bedside in case I died, Bridget had had to spend all of that Sunday trying to raise the cash. She did so in the end by borrowing from friends, and was back with a suitcase full of notes by 4pm. Only then could the treatment start. Except it wasn't treatment as such, it was what they called being on trial. Before investing precious time and resources, the doctors give a critically injured patient a period of time to see if he dies. Being still alive, it was obvious I had passed the test and the treatment could begin.

'It was several days before the doctors could be certain I'd survive. Others were less optimistic. When the elders from our church came to see me, they clustered round the bed, shaking their heads sadly and murmuring to each other that I was unlikely to live. The fact that I had just vomited blood over the sheets maybe confirmed that opinion. Even when I started to improve, the question was how disabled I'd end up being. "Yes, you'll continue to function," said one of the doctors a few days later. "We'll be pleased if you end up 80 per cent functioning and 20 per cent disabled." The view seemed to be that I'd come out disabled, or a vegetable, or some combination of both. When my children came to see me, they told me they'd rather have a disabled dad than no dad at all. Certainly no one expected me to walk.

'Almost as moving as seeing my family were the letters I had from the children at Matthew Rusike. They told me how special I was, that I was like their father and that God was never going to let me die because that would make them orphans twice over. I read the letters again and again with tears running down my cheeks.

'Miraculously, I was out of hospital in two weeks. And when I went back for my check-up a week later, my broken bones had almost fully knitted. This was amazing in medical terms and the doctors were astounded. I'm convinced that God intervened and hastened the healing so I could get back to working for the children. In fact, my first night back at home, a group of Matthew Rusike children came to the house to pray with me and thank God for bringing me back from the brink of death. After that, I felt I couldn't let them down. So even though Bridget and

251

the medical staff urged me to convalesce, I went straight back to Matthew Rusike, driving with one hand because the other arm was still in a sling.

'So I don't even know how I'm still alive. For months after the accident, I'd be replaying the sound of the car crashing and rolling over. I became very sensitive to noise. Even something like a spoon dropping on the floor would send me into spasms. But I'm over it now. I'm not disabled. And the only long-term effect has been to lose my sense of smell. But even that is now coming back, seven years after the accident.

'Oh, and as for the hospital fees, the Friends of Matthew Rusike put out an appeal to their supporters, many of whom I'd met on my trip to the UK earlier that same year. Thanks to their generosity, we were able to repay our friends the 3.2 million Zim dollars, index linked. I'm a fortunate man and I thank God for keeping me alive.'

A slender, nail-clipping moon was now glinting over the homestead and stars I'd watched earlier as they crested the horizon were lifting towards the zenith: a sense of the world turning as the night deepened and Astonishment reminisced. Although it was getting late, neither Lynda nor I wished to break the spell of that starlit conversation, the feeling of connectedness in the soft darkness. We drained our coffee mugs and Astonishment offered one last story.

'Shortly after my accident and return to work, MRCH had word of a family in which the father had abandoned his wife and remarried. The old *gogo*, the man's mother, was fully behind this decision and took it into her head to make life a misery for the rejected wife. Not long afterwards, the wife died. Whether Gogo was directly involved, I can't say. But after that, bizarre things started happening in the house that Gogo shared with her son and grandchildren. Stones were thrown out of nowhere into the house, zigzagging and changing direction. The same stone would break one window, then hurtle back and break another and another. Sometimes when the old lady was trying to cook, the pot would be lifted off the fire by unseen hands, tipped out and returned to its place. On one occasion, Gogo herself was picked up bodily and dropped some distance away. Next, an audible voice came to Gogo out of thin air. "I haven't finished with you yet," it said.

'These events seemed only to occur when the children were present, so the father and Gogo sent them to stay with relatives in a different house. But exactly the same thing happened there. Once again the children were moved, but the disturbances continued. Eventually, we at Matthew Rusike were called in to try to find a home for the children. We arranged for some foster parents to take them, but a few days later we had a call from this couple begging us to take the children away. The same things were occurring and they couldn't stand it a day longer. I called to see them and they showed me the broken windows, explaining how the same rock had broken this one and that one and that one. They spoke of spirits at work. It was clear they were petrified.'

I glanced around the compound. The huts were inky cut-outs against the brilliance of the stars. A few metres away, a faint glow seeped from the embers in the kitchen hut. Otherwise, the night was a deep, impenetrable black. The dark was strangely soothing, reducing the world to a smear of starlit sand and the murmuring of voices. All the same, it wasn't hard to believe that witchcraft could be brewing in the void.

'So how did it end?' asked Lynda.

'In Shona culture, events like this usually indicate some injustice that needs to be corrected. In this instance, the father paid restitution to his ex-wife's family and Gogo herself went to them to beg forgiveness. After that, things settled down and the children were able to return home.'

'And all this really happened?' I asked.

'Oh yes. I saw the terror of the foster parents and I saw the damage. They were certainly not responsible and no child could have thrown an object with that ferocity. But you know, these things are not so unusual in Africa. Maybe in the West you find it hard to credit, but here in Zimbabwe where witchdoctors still wield power and magic is closer to the surface – well, perhaps it's no surprise if the forces we face are more than simply human.'

The stars had swung another few degrees and the embers in the kitchen hut were fading. Astonishment glanced at the shimmering infinity above us, tipped out the dregs of his coffee and declared it time for bed.

20

How to Negotiate Roadblocks

We woke in one of Astonishment's huts. As the sleep cleared, the first thing that shimmied into focus was the tracery of poles against the thatch above our heads. Next, the sunlight dancing on the foliage outside the window. There was birdsong. Somewhere a goat bleated. Otherwise silence apart from somebody – Blessing, I guessed – rhythmically sweeping the ground outside the hut with a bundle of twigs. I couldn't see her, but I could picture the stance – straight legged, sharply bent, elbows close to the ground as she swept. I absorbed the early morning stillness and began to understand Astonishment's deep connection with his rural home. This was where he and Bridget would want to end their days. This was where the funeral rituals would be performed, the graves be dug and the relatives be summoned to pay their respects. Coming from restless, rootless Europe, I'd never known such a powerful, spiritual tie to one small patch of earth. I felt a peace I hadn't known for a long, long time.

I clambered out of bed, pulled on some shorts and pushed open the rough-boarded door into the sunlight. One of the ridgebacks came sniffing at my heels and the wonderful Blessing approached silently with a bowl of warm water. In the little cement toilet block, I shaved in a fragment of mirror balanced on a nail and thought of Beauty, the child rescued from the hellish depths of just such a long drop.

The compound was stirring. A sliced loaf, a tub of margarine, a jar of peanut butter, a bowl of boiled eggs and an old enamel teapot appeared on the table outside the kitchen hut. Astonishment greeted us from the door of his house. '*Mangwanani!* Good morning! How are you?'

'I am fine. How are you?'

'I am fine, too. So today we drive to Bulawayo. Maybe we will find your old home. Are you fine with that?'

We threw our bags into the Toyota (more space now the chicken was gone), waved goodbye to Blessing and Lonia and Aunt Elizabeth and followed the previous day's tyre marks past Morrison Farm and the derelict workers' shacks, past the spot where Astonishment had stopped to greet his uncle on the donkey cart and where he'd been arrested in the war and so to the strip of tarmac that took us into Chivhu and the main route towards Beitbridge. The highway south of the town was rutted with potholes; the edge of the tarmac eroded into deep, jagged fjords. A wheel dropping into one of those at speed could tip a vehicle over. Frowning in concentration, Astonishment switched from the middle to the edge and back again to avoid the gullies. We passed a burned-out bus, a lattice of rust-coloured ribs crumbling into the soil. Further on, a freshly overturned tanker lay on the verge, its undercarriage shockingly exposed and its wheels pointing uselessly at the sky. There was no sign of the driver.

'You know, potholes are not the only hazards,' said Astonishment, slowing to circumnavigate a long-horned cow that stood on the carriageway and seemed unable to decide whether to cross. 'The people that took over this farm here – and that one on the other side – they never bothered to maintain their fences. So now you find cattle wandering onto the road.' He cautiously skirted the cow while the animal followed our movement with a slow swing of its head. On the ruler-straight road, we could see it in the mirror for at least the next kilometre. When a truck piled high with mattresses and furniture groaned by in the opposite direction, I feared for both cow and truck. We were over the next rise before we could witness the encounter.

Almost the only private cars were 4x4s and high-end BMWs, invariably black and shiny-new and driven, I guessed, by politician-businessmen. Otherwise it was buses for the *povo* and trucks lumbering up from Beitbridge to supply a country that now made almost nothing for itself. Somewhere, Ruwadzano-Manyano must have been holding a convention. I remembered them from childhood – the Methodist women's organisation whose name means 'Fellowship' in Shona and Ndebele respectively. At every country church I'd ever visited with my father, I'd watched them swaying and kicking up the dust in their black skirts, poinsettia-red blouses and white mob-caps. You couldn't miss them then and you couldn't miss them now. Every few kilometres, another convention bus rattled by with big, bold texts pinned against the windows. 'Be strong in the Lord … God is my refuge.'

But most startling was when Astonishment pulled out to overtake a minibus. As we drew alongside, I glanced up at the faces looking down on us. *Varungu!* White people. We hadn't seen one of them since, oh, when? Harare airport? The travel company logo on the side marked them out as tourists. I was glad to see them for Zimbabwe's sake, if a little possessive that this was my country they were gawping at through their picture windows. *My country?* I was as much a visitor as they were. But in contrast to my race-restricted childhood, I realised I was starting to feel at home in this beautiful, tragic, maddening but strangely happy land. Perhaps it was the tranquillity of Astonishment's rural home – to this day, one of my favourite places on earth. Something was changing. Maybe this was my country after all.

Just beyond the town of Gweru, we happened on one of Zimbabwe's less attractive features. Parked at an angle up ahead was a police Land Rover with three or four uniformed officers standing at the side of the road. One of them waved us to the side.

'Another hazard of the road,' explained Astonishment, with a wry smile. 'These are traffic cops. They like to check you have everything correct in terms of documentation and a fire extinguisher and reflective jackets and what-not. And also that your lights and wipers are working. Of course, they're really after bribes. If they can find some trivial offence to fine you for, well, you might be persuaded to pay a bribe and save a bit of money.'

He wound down his window as one of the officers approached. The policeman nodded pleasantly at Lynda and me. There was a short exchange in Shona. 'OK. You are fine,' said the officer and waved us on.

'Well, that seemed painless,' remarked Lynda. 'Didn't he want to check?'

'Ah, let me tell you what happened there. You remember my military training long ago with the Ministry of Justice?'

'With the wonderful Officer Kuda? Yes, I do.'

'Well, part of that training was learning how to salute if you're driving a government vehicle and you pass one of your seniors. Without removing your hand from the wheel, you give a flex of your wrist, like so.' He demonstrated. 'And if a junior officer salutes you, you brace in the same way. That's not just in the prison service, it's also in the police and the army. And it works equally in Zimbabwe and South Africa.

'Once people see the sign, they know you're a military man or a government official or maybe state security. They may not know exactly who you are, but they know you're someone with influence. That's how I get through roadblocks. This thing with the wrist effectively says, "Don't mess with me. I could be your superior."'

'Does it work every time?' I asked.

'Mostly, but not always. Sometimes the constable thinks, "Hey, this guy could be important. We'd better show we're doing our job and really search him."' He threw back his head and laughed. 'And of course, you have to get it right! Don't try it until you've got it perfect!'

The next roadblock was less good-natured. Again the parked Land Rover and the waving arm. This time, as Astonishment wound down his window, a uniformed policewoman poked a gadget into his face – a digital speed reader with a number blinking on its screen. She barked something in Shona. With an apologetic look at Lynda and me, Astonishment opened his door and got out. He accompanied the woman to the rear of the car and the other constables gathered round. We watched in the mirror as some kind of debate went on – what old-time Rhodesians, borrowing from the Ndebele, would despairingly call an *indaba*, the thing 'these people' did endlessly as a substitute for action. At first it looked heated. The woman, in particular, was gesturing in Astonishment's face and pointing back at us. Then the body language relaxed. Eventually there was laughter. After ten minutes, Astonishment broke away with handshakes and slaps on the back and rejoined us.

'So?'

'Ah, ah,' grinned Astonishment. 'I was five kilometres over the speed limit just back there. I couldn't deny it, so I insisted they fine me in the correct manner. But they weren't interested. They wanted a bribe, but I refused. So that policewoman – she kept pointing at you and saying, "Get your white friends to pay it. They can afford it." In the end, though, I persuaded them to let me off.'

We continued towards Bulawayo. The place names as we approached spoke of its history as a railway town and centre of industry. Heany Junction. Cement. Northolt. Then, before I knew it, a billboard was wishing us a pleasant stay in Bulawayo. The sun was sinking and we needed somewhere to stay. The first hotel we tried was a mock-Tudor, half-timbered edifice with a portrait of Winston Churchill behind the reception desk – a design clearly calculated to make the English tourist think of Warwick or Stratford-upon-Avon. They were full. As we left, Lynda and I lost sight of Astonishment. We heard him before we saw him, laughing uproariously by the other exit. He waved us over.

'My cousin!' he exclaimed, introducing an equally jocular gentleman who pumped our hands and continued laughing as he explained a complicated connection to Astonishment. We laughed too. It was impossible not to. Laughter comes naturally in Zimbabwe, despite the country's afflictions – or perhaps because of them. And how could we expect Astonishment not to meet a cousin down in Matabeleland on a chance visit to a local hotel?

We continued our search and ended up in what appeared to be a Scottish chateau, recreated in deepest Matabeleland. Approaching through the gardens, our first view was of crenellated turrets and a stone gatehouse guarded by carved griffin. Inside, an echoing baronial hall continued the theme, except that on the wall, in place of the traditional stag's antlers, there glowered an elephant's head with tusks and splayed ears and a look of being about to charge if only it could work itself free. That and the stuffed crocodile at our feet at least confirmed we were still in Africa.

Astonishment left us and drove away to spend the night, far more cheaply, at the township home of yet another cousin. At bedtime, Lynda and I made our way to our chamber down spiral steps and gothic stone corridors to find the bed turned down, sweets on the pillows and hot-water bottles under the covers. And right next door, a voluminous, roll-top, lion's-claw bath with running hot water. After two weeks of washing from a bucket at Matthew Rusike, this was luxury in the extreme. But though the comforts were welcome, we missed the tranquillity we'd experienced twenty-four hours earlier under the stars at the Mapurisa rural home. This was Disneyland, Bulawayo. Reassuringly, Africa reasserted itself when we found in the morning that the bowl of fruit had been attacked by something with long teeth and a cockroach crawled out from under the pillow. We should have taken more notice of the can of cockroach killer by the bedside.

Breakfast was served at a long, polished, wooden table, Lynda and I at one end and a middle-aged, sun-burnished white couple at the other. Their accents marked them out as local. Waiters in starched uniforms came and went and then stopped appearing. Someone seemed to have forgotten the coffee.

'What do these guys think they doing?' demanded the husband, at the far end of the table. He cocked his head and listened to the chatter going on in the kitchen. 'All we want is coffee and they got some great *indaba* going on.'

He strode to the kitchen door and said something in Ndebele – or it could have been Chilapalapa, that pidgin blend of English, Shona, Ndebele and Afrikaans with which white masters and madams used to instruct their servants. Wrex Tarr – he of the wartime comic songs – made ample use of it in his act. 'Would you believe it?' the man announced to his wife. 'They think coffee's supposed to come at the end. They don't get that it's breakfast, not dinner. Honestly, these people!'

Embarrassed in our liberal English way, we made a point of being exceptionally nice to the waiters when the coffee finally appeared.

Astonishment was back mid-morning and drove us to the town centre. After the screaming pace of Harare, Bulawayo felt sedate and relaxed. The colonial streets, lined with jacaranda and wide enough for parking down the centre, had, at first glance, changed little since I'd last cycled them in 1969. The cars were different, of course – Toyotas and Mitsubishis instead of the finned and chromed Austin Westminsters and Ford Zodiacs of my memories. And Cecil Rhodes no longer gazed out from his plinth at the junction of Main Street and Eighth Avenue. Even as we passed, the site was being prepared for a statue of Joshua Nkomo. (Researching it later, I read that the statue, once erected, was almost immediately taken down. The problem wasn't the subject: Nkomo is revered in Matabeleland as 'Father Zimbabwe'. It was more the fact that the three-metre bronze had been cast in North Korea, famous for its kitsch political effigies and infamous for having helped to train Mugabe's Fifth Brigade who'd unleashed havoc on Nkomo's fellow Ndebele in the 1980s. This diplomatic blunder on somebody's part, plus its dodgy likeness, forced the statue's removal to a Bulawayo museum – the same one, apparently, where Cecil Rhodes had ended up after independence. Possibly, to this day, Rhodes and Nkomo stand toe to toe in some neglected corner of the museum grounds.)

I wanted to find the old house on Abercorn Street. My city map told me Abercorn Street was now Jason Moyo

Street, but I hoped the house would still be there on the corner of Second Avenue. Astonishment took a right off Main Street and pulled up on the bare-earth verge at the next junction. The crossroads stirred a memory, but where there'd been a straggly thorn hedge and a gate on whitewashed posts, there was now a blank, brick wall higher than our heads. A sign identified the place as a clinic specialising in natural remedies. It seemed we'd got the wrong junction. Then I glanced above the wall and saw the old, familiar corrugated roof, now no longer even pink but sun-scorched to bare tin. A few paces sideways brought me to a pair of industrial-style gates, opening onto a crazy-paved path to the verandah and the front door of my memories.

'Shall we go in?' asked Astonishment.

We walked up and rang the bell. I'd like to say that forty years fell away as we waited, but the place was a little too alien for the full back-in-time effect. A parapet now enclosed the verandah, replacing the elegant wooden balustrade that had probably, long ago, succumbed to termites. The coarse, prickly lawn where Christine and I had splashed in our tin tub under the poinsettia tree was now bare earth, bounded by that utilitarian brick wall. And on the precise spot where I'd built my diving board, there now stood a monster satellite dish on a five-metre-high gantry – there to pick up TV channels other than the state-owned Zimbabwe Broadcasting Corporation.

But through the four decades of accretions – the stuck-on stone cladding, the French window punched into the wall of Dad's study – the house seemed to smile at me like an old friend in disguise. Little details did it. The same burglar bars at the windows. The same ox-blood verandah that Elsie used to polish to a shine. And the same step on which I'd been sitting when the stampeding cow galloped by. Part of me was back while another part conceded that the past is indeed a different country.[11] You can get near, but you can never re-enter. As with my return to Selborne-Routledge, trying to transport myself to the same spot half a lifetime ago was like pushing together a pair of resisting magnets. There wasn't the full and satisfying connection I hoped might happen. Maybe I shouldn't have been surprised.

The door was opened by a smartly dressed lady who could have been a secretary or a natural remedies clinician. Feeling like a tourist interloper with my camera in hand, I explained my connection to the house and asked if I could take some pictures. Astonishment chipped in with something in Ndebele that made her laugh and she said of course I could. Asking to come inside was, I felt, pushing it, so I contented myself with a glance down the corridor to the door of my old bedroom.

For twenty minutes, I paced the garden and the back yard where I used to toast my knees in school holidays. The orange tree and Mum's brick-bordered marigold beds had been uprooted, leaving the yard as smooth and bare as a basketball court. Also gone were the *kaya* and the wobbly, wrought-iron gates onto Second Avenue, replaced by a sliding metal oblong like the entrance to a distribution depot. I was sad to see the place industrialised and made

---

[11] To adapt L P Hartley, *The Go-Between* (London: Penguin Classics, 2004).

ugly, but glad that it was still there with enough of the old to strike a small pang of nostalgia.

The last call before returning to Harare was the Matopos Hills, scene of many a family trip out from Bulawayo. Despite frequent calls to have him dug up and his bones either thrown away or returned to England, Cecil Rhodes still slumbers among the lichen-yellow boulders on the dome of rock known as World's View, his grave marked simply: 'Here lie the remains of Cecil John Rhodes'. For old time's sake, we stopped in the car park and climbed the rocky ascent to the graveside. It's a place of ethereal beauty with granite-topped hills rolling away on every side, the landscape studded with fantastical outcrops of balancing rocks, and not a sound to be heard other than the breeze and your own voices. Amazingly, Rhodes has not only been left undisturbed, he's undefaced. His grave plate was as pristine as I knew it in the 1960s.

A few metres away stands the Shangani Memorial, inscribed 'To Brave Men' and commemorating our Selborne-Routledge heroes – the thirty-four members of Allan Wilson's Shangani Patrol massacred by King Lobengula's Matabele warriors in 1893. Each of its four sides bears a bronze-relief panel depicting the patrol in a style reminiscent of a Roman procession. Erected in 1904 at the height of Edwardian imperialism (no word here of the several hundred Matabele who died), the memorial and the story it tells became part of the mythology of white Rhodesia, its potency still felt decades later when my own contemporaries went to war against overwhelming numbers.

We fell in with a couple of elderly Zimbabweans, scholarly in manner, who we found circling the memorial and discussing the events of the time. As we chatted, they showed no anti-colonial resentment nor any feeling that Allan Wilson, symbol of the white oppressor, should not be commemorated here in granite. While Rhodes and his ilk are demonised in Britain, he's a fact of life in Zimbabwe and you can't understand the country without him. Not all Zimbabweans are as sanguine as these two were (Comrade Bob, for one), but again and again I've been moved and inspired by the capacity of ordinary Zimbabweans to forgive if not forget. I'm grateful that that's the case.

And so back to Harare. Night had fallen as we pulled off Chiremba Road and into Epworth township. Reassuringly, the shacks along the main strip had their lights on: we at least had electricity for our homecoming. As we drove further in, however, we started to hear the clatter and chug of diesel generators, a sure sign that the power was off – again. Once through the gates of Matthew Rusike, the darkness was total. We unloaded by starlight and groped our way back into Shamie's house while Astonishment drove away to rejoin Bridget in town.

We had one full day left before our departure. On our last evening, Lynda and I sat on what had become our favourite rock, a low, scrambly-up dome as smooth as an egg beneath the flamboyant trees that shaded the playing field. The last time we'd sat there, we'd watched four Matthew Rusike children gambolling like lambs in the dusk. Now, as then, the flamboyant pods were snapping in the evening cool and a smelting-furnace sunset was going on behind the gum trees along the far edge of the compound. No children this time, but from one of the classrooms behind us came the sound of children's voices practising the old hymn, 'God Be With You Till We Meet Again'.[12] From time to time the singing stopped and we heard the voice of Wilbert, the choirmaster, correcting and demonstrating how to do it. The practice went on for nearly an hour until Wilbert was satisfied. We guessed it was something to do with us.

And so it was. At staff devotions the following morning, some twenty of the children filed in on Wilbert's signal, stood in two rows and sang the hymn unaccompanied from words hand-copied into school exercise books. Watching those eager faces giving their all for the visitors from England, and knowing some of their stories and the uncertain future that faced them in Mugabe's Zimbabwe, it was hard not to be moved. There may just have been a tear, wiped away on pretence of adjusting my glasses. I thought of Zondiwe, the Victoria Falls street child who'd unwittingly brought us here, and hoped someone was taking care of him as Astonishment and his colleagues were doing for these children against such odds. Of the shining faces in front of us, we knew only half a dozen at all well. Before the road trip with Astonishment, we'd been at the home for just two weeks. Our contribution was negligible. And yet we were seen off like royalty, first with singing and then with every available vehicle stuffed with staff and children for the motorcade to Harare airport. In Departures, there were bear hugs from Astonishment and

---

[12] Jeremiah Rankin, 1828-1904, 'God Be With You Till We Meet Again'.

Tapiwa and clasping of hands and embraces from Bridget and Shamie and Beatrice the teacher and Charity the nurse and a long line of others we wished we could have got to know better.

'We can't bear to go,' said Lynda to Margaret the chaplain, the home's wise and respected *mufundisi*.

'Oh, don't be sad,' replied Margaret. 'God goes with you. If we don't see you in this life, we'll meet again in heaven.'

With heavy hearts (though, to be honest, dreaming of the moment the British Airways stewardess would come down the aisle enquiring if we wanted the beef or the chicken), we made our exit.

We next met Margaret not in heaven but in Kent when she came to the UK on a visit funded by the Friends of Matthew Rusike Children's Home. She stayed at our home and Lynda took her to buy a pair of shoes in genteel Tunbridge Wells.

'It's so hard to find comfortable shoes in Zimbabwe,' Margaret explained. 'When I'm preaching, ah! Sometimes it's agony.'

She bought herself a pair of sensible flatties and Lynda treated her to a second pair, a little more elegant. The youth who was fitting her pointed out that with two pairs you got a third pair free. Margaret clapped her hands and broke into a jig in the middle of the store. I don't think she hugged the guy, but she must have come close.

'Ah! God is so good,' she announced to the startled, middle-England customers dispersed around the shop.

'Thank You, Lord! I came for one pair and I'm going home with three! I cannot believe it!'

By then, Lynda and I were feeling the pull of another visit to Zimbabwe. We contacted Astonishment to see when it might be possible.

Part 3

2013
Reconnection

21

Across the Limpopo

Astonishment had left Matthew Rusike – indeed, left Zimbabwe – by the time Lynda and I saw him again. In June 2012 he handed the directorship to Margaret and transferred to a sister organisation taking care of neglected children in Germiston on the eastern edge of Johannesburg. Confusingly, it shares its name with the Harare township that encircles Matthew Rusike. Epworth Children's Village is another legacy of Methodist missionaries naming places after John Wesley's home village in Lincolnshire, much as imperial explorers named most things after Queen Victoria if they couldn't think of anything better.

We flew to Johannesburg in September 2013 and Astonishment came to meet us at the airport with his now grown-up son, Tatenda. Just as he'd done at Harare airport in 2010, he greeted us with a shout of delight and leaped from the crowd to wrap us in a bear-hug welcome. After three years, it was good to see him again. Then, as last time, a drive into the suburbs – this time not on potholed and litter-strewn Harare streets but on multi-lane highways that swept us towards the glittering Johannesburg skyline.

'Ya, you see I have a different car,' chuckled Astonishment, deftly changing lanes in his silver Daihatsu Terios. 'When we came south, I sold three of my cows from the rural home – turned them into US dollars. With the state of the South African rand, that was enough to buy a car.'

Three cows. Like a recurring motif, they'd been there at the start of Astonishment's story. Three cows from the Mukaratis to rid themselves of Lonia's *murambiwa*. Three cows to acquire a smart Japanese car in Johannesburg. Astonishment had come a long way in the intervening forty-six years.

Off the highway, we glided through the neat grid of streets that was Germiston. Bungalows with tidy gardens sat behind high, gated walls topped with razor wire. 'GUARD DOGS ... ARMED INSTANT RESPONSE ... DANGER OF DEATH', snarled the signs on every property. I wondered what would happen to a child innocently kicking a football into a neighbour's garden. No chance of trotting round to the front door to ask for it back. Even if they made it over the wall and survived the spikes and the electric fence, it seemed they'd either be shot or eaten by an Alsatian. Such was the fear of intruders in this middlingly prosperous neighbourhood. What the sense of siege must be like in Johannesburg's wealthy suburbs I could only imagine. Gazing out on the empty streets, I couldn't help thinking of Astonishment's rural home – open to all comers and protected by no more than a crooked wire fence, yet an island of tranquillity and welcome. The new home in Germiston seemed a long way from Chivhu.

Astonishment pulled up at a heavy steel gate, though the wall in this case was low enough to see over and was free of aggressive signage. Tatenda opened up and we drove in to find Bridget and her three other children, Vimbai, Rutendo and Tanatswa, waiting to greet us.

Epworth Children's Village lay directly behind the house, a compound of low-roofed buildings not unlike Matthew Rusike. The atmosphere, though, was very different. This place was more sophisticated: computers hummed (the electricity worked) and newish cars filled the car park. But almost the first thing we noticed as Tatenda showed us around that first afternoon was a run of smashed windows, the work of an angry child who didn't want to be there. The previous evening, so Tatenda told us,

Astonishment had been up into the small hours liaising with the police as they tried to trace two girls who'd bunked off for a night in downtown Germiston. This was far from the childhood innocence we'd seen at Matthew Rusike. The facilities may have been better, but the children seemed tougher, more cynical, perhaps more damaged. No chance here of a choir of shining faces singing 'God Be With You Till We Meet Again' when the time came to leave.

As we toured, a little boy of three or four caught our attention. He was standing alone in the car park and in obvious distress. In another contrast to Matthew Rusike, he was white. The cause of his tears seemed to be a car that was turning and about to leave. The driver, we later learned, was the boy's father. Next to him was a woman who had recently become his partner. The woman's daughter was in the back.

The scene tore at our hearts. A tearful boy, seemingly abandoned by a father who made perfunctory visits, couldn't wait to get away and had transferred his affections to his partner's daughter, the favoured child who was now going home with the couple while the boy stayed behind. The boy's brother, we also learned later, was the one responsible for the broken windows.

As the car paused in its three-point turn, Astonishment stepped out of his office and knocked on the passenger window. The woman wound it down. There was a short exchange. We didn't catch it all, but we heard Astonishment saying to the woman: 'Lady, if you truly love this man, then let him be free to love his children.'

Who knows what hurts and damaged relationships lay beneath that briefly observed scene? Clearly, there was more going on than we had any right to know. But Astonishment knew. And as always, his thoughts were for the child. At heart he was still Murambiwa, wrenched with compassion for every other *murambiwa*, black or white, who crossed his path.

The plan was to spend a week at Epworth Children's Village before driving together to Zimbabwe to revisit Matthew Rusike and the rural home. But the evening after we arrived, Astonishment took a phone call. We could only hear one end of it and that was in Shona, but it sounded serious. Eventually, Astonishment put the phone down and turned to Bridget.

'That was my mother, calling from Zimbabwe,' he said. 'It's Uncle Chengeta. He died yesterday at Driefontein Hospital at Mvuma.'

Bridget laid a hand on his arm. 'I am so sorry. When is the funeral?'

'This weekend. Saturday and Sunday at Madamombe *kraal*.'

'So you'll want to go?' added Lynda, as she and I adjusted to a change of plan. Though we'd never met Uncle Chengeta, we knew the part he'd played in Astonishment's story and we understood the sadness.

'Ya. And not only go. I have to organise the whole event.'

'Why's that?' answered Lynda. 'Shouldn't it be his sons?'

'In normal times, yes. But James, the one I grew up with, he died from AIDS some years ago. And his younger brother, Muzorodzi – he's on the run for theft and the police are looking for him even now. So Chengeta effectively has no son to oversee his funeral. That's why it falls to me as nephew.'

'So we'll see you when you get back?'

'Not at all, not at all. You must come as well. And we need to leave first thing in the morning.'

And leave we did, weaving through the sprawl of greater Johannesburg in the early morning traffic, past the slag mountains thrown up by the gold mines where stick figures in ragged clothing scavenged in the spoil, and out eventually onto the long, straight N1, the Great North Road, that would take us to the Limpopo and the Zimbabwe border. Along with Astonishment, Lynda and me, the little Terios contained Bridget and five-year-old Tanatswa – his older brother and sisters left behind for a few days to get themselves to and from school.

'From here to the rural home, about a thousand kilometres,' said Astonishment.

'So ten, twelve hours?' I guessed, glancing at the speedometer.

'Ah, that would be excellent. Unfortunately, we have Beitbridge in the way. Sometimes it can take five hours to get through Zimbabwe immigration. But let's hope we're quicker than that today. The trick is to get there before the daily buses from Johannesburg. If the buses beat you to it – ah! – you can wait forever.'

The flat, wide landscape rolled by and the talk turned to the reason for our trip – Astonishment's late uncle.

'You know,' said Astonishment, 'for all his powerful physique and his skills as a boxer, Chengeta was not a healthy man. Back in the 1990s, he had to leave his job at the Kango enamel factory with an illness that rendered him almost paralysed. He went back to his rundown hut in Madamombe and stayed there for a month with no medication and his illness undiagnosed. It was only then that I heard about it and decided we could not leave him in that state. I brought him to our home in Harare and Bridget and I took him to hospital. That's when he was diagnosed as having TB of the spine. Well, after that, he stayed with us for six months until he recovered. I still remember the joy on his face the day he could stand on his own for the first time.'

'That sounds to me to be very selfless,' said Lynda, 'considering the way he treated you. Giving you the wrong parents and a fake twin and all that.'

'Ya, ya, he had his faults – the drink, the chaotic family life, the quickness to take offence. This was a man who could nurse a grudge for years. It was well known that he couldn't stand his uncle Jericho, the preacher who'd had such an effect on me as a child. And also his half-brother Gabriel, the son of old Shadrach's fifth wife. But no one can remember why. I don't think he could, either. But for all that, there was much goodness in him. He at least made sure I didn't starve as a child. Taking him into our home was a chance to repay his kindness to someone who wasn't even his own son. And the same in his final illness. After he was diagnosed with the heart condition that killed him, we made sure he got the right treatment and we helped to support him financially.'

The goodness of the man, I thought – meaning Astonishment. I wondered aloud if Chengeta's many family feuds would sour the funeral.

'A few years ago, yes, you might have said so,' replied Astonishment. 'But quite recently, since your last visit, in fact, he was reconciled to the family members he'd fallen out with.'

'You should tell them how it happened,' prompted Bridget, from the back.

Astonishment chuckled and stretched back in his seat, the way he did when collecting his thoughts. 'Indeed, it wasn't just Chengeta who harboured grudges. My whole family has been riven with feuds. Think of the animosity that simmered for years between the Ndiyas and the Mukaratis. And just like Chengeta, my aunt Angela took against Gabriel and old Jericho. Another feud existed between Angela and the wife of her younger brother, Elison. You're keeping up, yes?'

Listening to Astonishment picking his way through family connections was sometimes like trying to follow a Russian novel. I got the point, however.

'Then there was Julia, the wife of Faith's son, Nyasha – she had a quarrel with Nyasha's sister, Clotie, the wife of Lovemore. My mother was close to Clotie, which meant she had to keep her distance from Julia. Everywhere you looked, this was a family seething with hostility.

'Bridget and I saw all this and it pained us. Life's too short to waste time feuding. The time God gives is for loving and enjoying good relationships. So we started thinking what we could do.

'At the time, we'd just bought a diesel-powered grinding mill for the rural home. We use it to grind maize for our neighbours to bring in a bit of income. Well, we decided to get the whole family together to celebrate our new acquisition.

'To make sure they came, I went and collected as many as I could in the Matthew Rusike minibus. After I picked up Angela and her husband, Sullivan, I drove on to Gabriel's house. I could sense Angela and Sullivan tensing up as they saw where we were headed. When I went to the door to collect Gabriel, they sat in the car and refused to come and greet him. With Gabriel in the back, the atmosphere was like a thunderstorm about to break. Worse, we then called at old Jericho's. Now Angela, Sullivan and Gabriel, all three, clammed up completely. Our last passengers on that trip were Uncle Elison's widow and her two teenage daughters, noted for their feud with Angela and also, as it happens, with Jericho. So now we had a busload in which practically everyone detested everyone else. As you can imagine, the conversation was stilted.

'Back at the rural home, we'd killed two goats and many chickens. On the day itself, we slaughtered one of our cows, which is not something you do lightly in rural Zimbabwe. In the end we had more than a hundred people, sleeping in all our huts and on the ground and even in our chicken run – now empty of chickens, of course. Chengeta was there, too, looking very uncomfortable with all these people he didn't like. Bridget and I did the rounds to try to put people at their ease and to make a start on mending relationships.

'The main event was not the demonstration of the grinding mill – though we did show it off a bit. Rather, it was to stand up and speak to all the family members together. In the morning, after they'd slept, we spoke to them for about an hour and a half. Our inspiration came from the Bible, from 1 John 4:20. Here it says, "Whoever claims to love God yet hates a brother or sister" – these words we translated as 'relative' – "is a liar. For whoever does not love their brother and sister, whom they have seen, cannot love God, whom they have not seen." We told them that we loved them all and would never side with one against the others.'

A brave move, I thought. Not the kind of thing you'd easily do with warring relatives in Britain. This had to be testament to the naturalness of Christianity in Zimbabwe, a place where faith does not embarrass and is talked about as English people discuss the weather. Either that or the famous Zimbabwean tolerance of long speeches. I wondered what the reaction had been.

'It was amazing. Even as we were talking, we could see God at work. People started sobbing and those with grudges were standing up and hugging one another. It became very emotional. At one point, old Jericho stood up with his arm around Chengeta, the two old foes, and said something like: "I have grown to be very old and never have I seen anyone who was so determined to restore good relationships. Here are people who would even lose a cow for the sake of bringing family back together."

'I tell you, the cow was a small price to pay. There were lots of tears and many relationships were healed, which I can only describe as a miracle.'

This sounded like Mazoe Bridge refugee camp all over again. It occurred to me that such miracles tend to happen when Astonishment and Bridget get to work to repair broken relationships. We didn't know it at the time, but Astonishment the reconciler had in mind a further mending of relationships at our journey's end.

He went on. 'When we took our relatives home the following day, Angela, Jericho and Gabriel sat in the minibus and trilled away like birds on a wire. When we passed some shops with a business centre, they asked me to stop and went inside to have a photo taken of the three of them together. I have a copy myself – my three smiling relatives, their arms around each other's shoulders as if there'd never been a harsh word between them.

'Old Jericho died soon after. But by then he'd sought forgiveness from his relatives, and in turn forgiven them, right across the family. You could tell that it was so because hundreds of people turned out for his funeral. I'm hoping it'll be the same for Uncle Chengeta.'

On all sides stretched the arid flatlands of Limpopo Province. As the city of Polokwane slid away to our left, Astonishment pointed to the steel and concrete stadium built for the 2010 football World Cup. 'I always get a little nervous on this part of the road,' he remarked.

'Why's that?'

'It's where I was car-jacked in 2009. I used to come down from Zimbabwe for meetings and I always took the opportunity to buy food for Matthew Rusike. Coming back one time, I had a carload donated by the home in Germiston. As I was passing Polokwane, I got spotted by car-jackers who came alongside and threatened me with a gun. I pulled in and they swerved in front of me, blocking the way. These two guys got out and ran back towards me. I tried to press the door lock, but couldn't get it down quickly enough. I realised, in any case, that they'd probably smash the windows if they couldn't get in. They flung the door open and pulled me out. The first punch laid me flat on the ground. Once I was down, they started kicking me and stamping on my head. Knowing they had a gun, I decided not to resist. Instead I rolled over and tried to shield myself. The blows kept coming. If the pain hadn't told me otherwise, I'd have thought I was dreaming. The whole thing was surreal.

'Once they were satisfied I wasn't going to get up, one of the men jumped into my car and the two sped off together, back the way they'd come. I saw them zigzagging across the road, tyres smoking as they accelerated. They disappeared with a month's worth of food and a couple of thousand in cash donated by the Friends of Matthew Rusike. I tried to stand, but my legs gave way and I collapsed.

'I don't know how long I lay there at the side of the road. I was aware only of the pain all over my body – that and my own helplessness, and wishing this wasn't happening. When I did manage to stand, I tried flagging down the next few cars. I don't know how long it took, but someone eventually pulled in. A white man got out and came and looked at me.

'"Are you OK?" he said.

'All I could do was croak at him to say I'd been attacked and ask him to help. He put an arm around me and helped me back to his car where he eased me into the passenger seat. Then he drove me into Polokwane and left me at the police station. After giving my statement, I slept the night in one of the cells. The following morning, I used all the money I had in my wallet to get the bus to Harare.'

'Still injured?' I said.

'Still injured. That was a terrible journey, still shaking and nursing my bruises on the long ride north. When I got to Harare, I phoned a friend in town to ask him to take me to hospital. And that was the first treatment I had.'

'Thank goodness somebody stopped,' put in Lynda.

'Ya. And a white man, too. I never found out his name, but if this story ever becomes a book and my good Samaritan happens to read it – well, I hope he'll recognise himself and understand how grateful I am.'

On from the sleepy town of Louis Trichardt, the road lifts and winds through the green of the Soutpansberg mountains before dropping to the dry Limpopo plain. Somewhere near the border settlement of Musina, we fell in behind a small saloon car towing a trailer to which was lashed a crude wooden coffin. I watched with interest as the box rattled on the metal base, pulling at the frayed ropes that held it in place. It seemed it wouldn't take much to bounce it off the trailer and into our path.

'Is that what I think it is?' I asked Astonishment.

'Oh, ya.'

'Occupied?'

'Yes, yes. You know how every Zimbabwean, wherever they die, wants to be buried at their own rural home? Well, when you think that there are 2 to 3 million Zimbabwean exiles in South Africa, that must equate to hundreds of corpses crossing the border every week.'

'And in this heat?'

'Exactly. You can see why this guy's in a hurry. He must be hoping for a quick transit through Beitbridge.'

'Surely the dead would get fast-tracked at immigration.'

'Well, you'd think so. Quite recently, though, we heard of a coffin going through, just like this one, with all the relatives crying and wailing at the border post and begging to be allowed to get on their way and bury the body. Well, one of the inspectors opened the box – and what do you think was in there?'

'A stinking corpse?'

'Ah, ah,' laughed Astonishment. 'No corpse at all. Instead, the coffin was full of contraband for selling in Zimbabwe. The grieving relatives were just part of the show. So now these border guards are much stricter.'

Did that mean every coffin was opened? I didn't like to ask, simply hoping we wouldn't end up in the queue behind this particular deceased Zimbabwean. In the event, we overtook the coffin and lost it in our wake. What happened when it reached the border will have to be left to the imagination.

On the banks of the crocodile-infested Limpopo that forms the border with Zimbabwe, the lady in South African emigration was charm itself as she stamped our passports and wished us God bless.

'Well, that was easy,' I said to Astonishment, as we regrouped at the car.

'Ha! That was just leaving South Africa. Now the real problem begins – how long to make it into Zimbabwe. You know, a few months back at holiday time, people were waiting literally for days. Maybe today won't be so bad.'

We rattled over the bridge that I'd crossed many times in the past on family holidays Darn Sarth. Back then, so my mother tells me, you barely stopped in either direction: a wave of a passport was enough and a friendly official nodded you through (if you were white, that is: black travellers no doubt had a harder time of it). Today, Beitbridge is one of the busiest border crossings in Africa, the crush of numbers compounded on the Zimbabwean side by a chaotic and corrupt system that seems determined to make it as difficult as possible to gain entry.

Once over the bridge, we joined a queue of cars – though 'queue' is hardly the word. It was more a logjam that shifted only occasionally as a car popped out at the far end, a hundred metres or more in the distance. There we stopped. Clearly, we were not going anywhere. A young man, part of a gang working the queue to left and right, knocked on the window.

'Ya, let me help you. Give me your documents.'

Astonishment waved him away. The guy scowled and moved to the car behind. 'These marauders,' said Astonishment. 'If you hand over several hundred dollars, they'll do the queuing for you and get you preferential treatment, splitting the proceeds with the immigration officials. You see, this way, there's no incentive to speed things up. The longer you think you'll have to wait, the more you'll be willing to pay to extract yourself.'

With bribery not an option, we gathered our documents and followed the flow of people to the immigration hall – a cavernous, dimly lit warehouse full of queues snaking in many directions and thrumming with a kind of subdued roar. The sound was like waves on distant pebbles, the aggregate effect of hundreds of voices and the shuffling of a corresponding number of feet. Astonishment peeled off to deal with the tortuous bureaucracy of bringing a car in. Bridget and Tanatswa and Lynda and I found other queues to join, inching our way towards a bank of windows behind which sat the guardians of Zimbabwe's borders. I scanned their faces, hoping to avoid the scowly one who looked like Mugabe's less jovial cousin. From time to time, a cross-looking woman behind the end window banged on the glass with her pen and shouted directions to the next in line.

Lynda and I got the grouchy one. Picture a face as inexpressive as an Easter Island stone head with outsized Mugabe spectacles and that's what we found staring back at us from behind the glass.

'Hello, how are you?' breezed Lynda, remembering that conversations in Zimbabwe traditionally begin with mutual enquiries as to the other's health. The man's scowl simply deepened. As we'd taken the precaution of buying our visas in London, we hoped the process of getting them stamped would be quick. Not so. Features hardly moving, he handed us each a form and grunted at us to fill it in and rejoin the end of the queue. Second time around (same official), the stamp was finally poised above our visas when a hand slid in from behind and dropped a dog-eared Zimbabwean passport on the counter. There followed a bad-tempered exchange in Shona, the gist of which seemed to be that Easter Island Man thought the passport was a forgery while the old man next to us indignantly insisted it wasn't. He eventually got shooed away as you might shoo a dog. Only then did the stamp come down and we were free to return to the car.

Bridget and Tanatswa were already there. Astonishment wasn't. Still crowded in by other vehicles, we wound down the windows against the heat and we waited. To our left where the sun fell blisteringly on hot, cracked paving stones, hundreds of passengers decanted from their buses sat on the ground in long, ragged lines, their belongings unpacked and spread out for inspection. They'd been sitting there before we went in. Nothing had changed when we came back. Their patience was monumental.

Eventually, a movement in the line of cars. The logjam seemed to be breaking with an almost imperceptible current in the direction of the searching bays. Bridget phoned Astonishment with the news. Astonishment, still queuing, suggested I leap into the driver's seat and take advantage of this new development. Bumper nudging bumper, I manoevered the Daihatsu to catch the flow. I progressed a metre or two and stopped again.

Someone tapped on the window. 'Excuse me, sir,' said a pleasant-faced young man. 'Could you move forward just a little?'

I did my best. The car behind then swung out, negotiated an impossibly small gap and ended up two spaces ahead. An old Beitbridge hand, obviously.

After half an hour and a few more metres, Astonishment rejoined us. As well as having his personal documentation processed, he'd had to go through a vehicle importation process involving the payment of a road access fee, an application for a temporary import permit and the stamping of a gate pass. He sighed as he took over the wheel. 'It all means different queues. And the thing was, every time I got near the front, one of these touts would barge in with documentation from ten or twenty drivers who'd paid the bribe. So all of that had to be processed before the queue could move on.'

Eventually we made it to the searching bays. Astonishment parked and opened up the boot and we settled down to wait for some kind of inspection. There was one lady officer on duty, tugging behind her a little knot of youths who now and then would point out which cars to inspect next according to whether their owners had paid. As non-payers, we clearly weren't going to get processed for some time. Astonishment and Bridget walked over and joined the group, following her from car to car and grabbing a word when they could. Whatever they said, it worked. Muttering about being overworked, she brought her clipboard over to the Daihatsu and glanced at the contents of the boot. Then that most welcome of sounds, the thud of a stamp on Astonishment's gate pass.

Three hours after crossing the Limpopo, we approached the final barrier. Just short of our escape, a man motioned us to stop and leaned into the open window.

'I need your car keys,' he said.

Astonishment was taken aback. 'What are you talking about? I have my gate pass stamped. I'm free to proceed.'

'Ah, no, my friend. I really need your car keys. And all your money. This is a robbery.'

'What?'

'Ha! Only joking. Have a nice day. Welcome to Zimbabwe.'

The barrier lifted and we were through.

22

The Mugabe Legacy

'So three hours. That's not so bad,' said Astonishment. But we still had 500 kilometres to drive and the afternoon was wearing on. We exited unlovely Beitbridge town, skirting a half-eaten donkey carcass on one side of the road and a burned-out bus on the other. We'd seen other such buses on our earlier travels and we passed at least two more in varying stages of disintegration before we reached Chivhu. One explanation, surmised Astonishment, was that buses in Zimbabwe run and run until they can run no more, and are then torched. It sounded feasible.

After South Africa's smooth highways, it was a shock to be back to Zimbabwe's lethally potholed trunk roads. We passed a lorry driver mending a puncture next to a hole that could have swallowed the Daihatsu entirely had Astonishment not slalomed around it. He chuckled as he overtook a van emblazoned: HIGHWAY MAINTENANCE.

'Ah! There is no highway maintenance in Zimbabwe! The only work being done nowadays is the building of shiny new toll booths, so that when it rains the road tolls can still be collected. How else can ZANU-PF keep paying its informers and buying the allegiance of members of the MDC?'

As Astonishment continued to zigzag around the potholes, the talk turned inevitably to politics. With our talent for visiting Zimbabwe in election years, we'd done it again. The election two months earlier in July 2013 had brought an end to the fractious Government of National Unity, the GNU, and handed undiluted power back to Mugabe at the age of eighty-nine. His defeated rival, the long-suffering Morgan Tsvangirai of the MDC, protested foul play. His party, he said, had been bounced into the election with little time to prepare. When the MDC finally got to see the electoral roll on the day before voting, it found evidence of tampering including more than 100,000 centenarian voters in a country where average life expectancy is a mere fifty-one.

Election day itself brought more abuses. Western observers were banned and polling stations were heavily policed. People were caught on video being bussed into key constituencies, hiding their faces as they disembarked. Voters in MDC-supporting urban areas were turned away on grounds such as turning up at the wrong station or their names not appearing on the roll. And in rural areas, large numbers of voters – even teachers – were persuaded to declare themselves illiterate in order to qualify for 'assistance' in the polling booth.[13]

In the event, Mugabe won comfortably. Tsvangirai mounted a brief legal challenge but succeeded only in

---

[13] www.bbc.co.uk/news/world-africa-23591941 and mg.co.za/article/2013-08-16-00-morgan-sets-out-case-for-zimbabwe-poll-fraud (accessed 14th April 2019).

delaying the old man's inauguration for yet another term in office.

'So what do you think?' I asked Astonishment. 'Was it rigged?'

'Certainly there is evidence,' he answered, diplomatically. 'But you know, the MDC had lost a lot of support during five years of power-sharing, so maybe it didn't take too much tampering to tip the result.'

This surprised me. 'You think so?'

'I think they were naïve. During the period of unity government after the 2008 election, ZANU-PF ran rings around the MDC. They gave their so-called partners the most contentious ministries which absorbed all their time and distracted them from planning for the next election. In the process, the MDC lost touch with ordinary Zimbabweans. Being in government and driving Mercedes and living in official residences, they forgot who had put them into power. It was also very easy for ZANU-PF with its well-funded security apparatus to infiltrate the MDC and learn all its secrets. So although they deserve credit for killing inflation and stabilising the economy, they failed to push for any substantial change. They were so busy in government, and deliberately kept busy by ZANU-PF, that they forgot the mission inherent in their name – democratic change. As a result, Mugabe has regained total control and they won't get another chance.'

By now the soft African night was coming on and the first stars were winking through the filigree tops of the lowland baobabs. After the heat of the day, it was good to catch the cool, evening air through the open window, even if dusk made the potholes harder to see.

On a bend south of Masvingo, the headlamps of the Daihatsu picked out a bus at an odd angle on the roadside. As the fuzzy blotch of light swept across the scene, we saw the cab of a lorry that had shed its load on the highway. There were people standing, burst-open cases on the road, gashed metal, a police Land Rover. The impressions were brief and fragmentary, conveying nothing more than the aftermath of an accident.

'Oh, dear God,' gasped Astonishment. 'Let us hope this is not too serious. I've seen so many crashes on this road, including some on this very same spot.'

He picked slowly past. As you do after passing such a scene, we stayed silent for the next few kilometres. But now I had Astonishment's attention in the dark cocoon of the car with only the dashboard lights for distraction, I wanted to understand what an educated, articulate Zimbabwean really made of Robert Mugabe. 'How will history see him?' I asked. 'A blood-soaked tyrant, or a man who actually did some good?'

Astonishment took a long time answering as he gathered his thoughts. 'Sure, this man did some good things in carrying out the liberation struggle and adopting a policy of reconciliation at the end of the war. Early on you might have called him the great African liberator: that's certainly how he wanted to be seen. But that was before Mandela stole the title and outshone Mugabe on the international stage. Mugabe resented that. It probably made him all the more determined to keep the party and himself in power. And the longer ZANU-PF stays in power, the greater the vested interest in keeping it that way. Being toppled is now unthinkable. There's too much to lose. The survival of the party has become the ultimate good, greater even than to feed, educate and employ Zimbabwe's people. That's why ZANU-PF had to win the last election, come what may.

'But I wonder if, even now, Mugabe still wants his legacy to be one of peace rather than killings and corruption. Unlike 2008, this year's election was largely peaceful with Tsvangirai free to address huge rallies in a way that wouldn't have been permitted previously. This time, the party's strategy for staying in power was electoral manipulation rather than violence.'

'So… history's verdict?'

'A good beginning and a sad end. However much Mugabe might long for a clean legacy, I fear it is now too late. All is tarnished by death and brutality and a mindset that cannot think otherwise than imposing his will by force. I think this will haunt him to his grave.'

I thought back to the presidential convoy screaming through Harare on our last visit. The man himself had been invisible behind the blacked-out windows of his stretch Mercedes, but I wondered what we'd have seen if we could have peeked inside. I conjured a picture of a crumpled, birdlike figure in a Savile Row suit with comedy glasses and pipe-cleaner moustache, lost and diminished like an African Wizard of Oz in the back of that big car. Did he still nurse illusions of being the saviour of the nation and going to his grave amid outpourings of grief from his devoted people? Or, as he blinked out at his countrymen forced to cower at the side of the road, was he stung by the realisation that he'd wrecked his inheritance and inflicted so many decades of suffering on his country?

Were there times, I wondered, when he longed to shed the burden and end his days in the tranquillity of a rural home like the poorest of his people, only to find he couldn't? Was he now trapped, pinned like a butterfly in a box by generals and ministers who refused to let him go because their own political survival depended on his: imprisoned, too, by a personality incapable of change after so many years of imposing his will on others?

A man who had so much and threw it away. The tragedy is almost Shakespearean.

The Daihatsu buzzed on beneath an arching black canvas blasted with diamond dust and studded with a zillion stars. Astonishment fought his fatigue and dodged the potholes and counted down the kilometres while Tanatswa slumped asleep against his mother. Sixteen hours from Germiston, we turned east at Vic's Tavern for the final ten kilometres to the rural home.

23

Return to Madamombe

Saturday 14th September 2013, the first day of Uncle Chengeta's two-day funeral. Leaving Tanatswa at the rural home with Blessing, the four of us – Astonishment and Bridget and Lynda and I – drive the twenty kilometres to Madamombe village. It's slow travelling, the car pitching and rolling as the dirt track threads over riverbeds and gullies, meanders through dry grass and now and then disappears into tracts of white sand. Though we'd skirted Madamombe on our earlier travels with Astonishment, we'd never made the detour to see it. Perhaps the memories it held, those of struggling for survival and tensions with Chengeta's wives, were not ones he'd wanted to reawaken.

As we drive, I recall Astonishment's account of a rundown *kraal* in an area of bad soil and poor crops. The desiccated landscape fits the description as we make our approach. An hour from the rural home, we bounce along a strip of bare earth and come to a stop on the edge of a cluster of scruffy huts, six or seven in all, where there's already activity going on. Most of it centres on a fire and a large drum in which something – *sadza*, I guess – is being cooked. Teams of women are vigorously stirring. Bridget smiles and says it takes strong arms to stir *sadza* for so many people.

Five or six men gather round to greet Astonishment with three-stage handshakes and clapping of hands on shoulders. There's much laughter, suggesting old friends happy at meeting again.

'*Ndimi murikufamba ne GP?*' enquires a wrinkled, twinkly man in a baseball cap. '*Makaenda riini kuSouth?*'

Astonishment turns to us and translates. 'He's saying, "Is that a GP car you're driving?" He's referring to my South African numberplate with GP for Gauteng Province. He wants to know when I went down south.' He addresses his friends again, explaining that he went *kuSouth* last year. Then he draws us in. 'Now, I'm back in my own country and I've brought my friends to show them where I grew up.'

Lynda and I are greeted warmly. 'It's good for Astonishment that he went south to improve his prospects,' confides the man in the cap, switching to English. 'If he'd stayed in Zimbabwe, he wouldn't have had this nice car. Or come back with friends from Britain. But ya, he still looks the same. I don't think crossing the Limpopo has changed him.'

'Sure,' agrees another. 'Sometimes in our culture, if we see someone driving a car, we say, "Ah! This man cannot communicate with us." Even more if they're with white people. But Astonishment, he can talk to anyone. Rich or poor, black or white, it's the same to him. This is a man who has a degree, but at any funeral he'll dig the grave with you, eat from the same plate, sleep on the ground where you sleep. Ya, it's good to see him back.'

We're escorted into the compound. Bridget produces a long, patterned wrap for Lynda to tie around her waist, covering her knee-length skirt. Now she looks acceptably African and Bridget leads her away to fill a couple of buckets from the borehole on the far side of the *kraal*. For me, someone produces a wooden chair, finds a level spot in the shade of one of the huts and urges me to sit. '*Tatenda chaizvo,*' I say in my halting Shona. 'Thank you very much.'

I'm left alone to observe the mourners as they gather, hoping I'm striking a balance between intruding and standing back. Other than the cooking and a group of men digging the grave beyond the *kraal* perimeter, the main action is taking place across the compound where twenty or thirty women, some with babies on their backs, are sitting on the ground alongside the main hut. They're being forcefully addressed by a slender young man in a dazzlingly white shirt. Though I don't know the words, I recognise the gestures and cadences of a sermon. When he stops, someone starts drumming and four or five women in Manyano-style uniforms get to their feet and break into lusty singing. Three small girls in similar dress begin to dance, upper bodies bent forward, elbows thrown back towards the sky and bare feet pounding the sand as if pedalling stationary bicycles. Astonishment tells us later that Uncle Chengeta was not a great churchgoer, but late in his life he started attending Zion Church in a village nearby. As a result, the Zion evangelist and the Zion choir have taken the opportunity to win souls at his funeral.

Elsewhere on the compound, the service is being ignored as others prepare to feed the 3–400 people expected to arrive by tomorrow. There are women in small groups, their hats and headscarfs and bold-print skirts a rampage of clashing colours. One lady's rear declares FREEDOM beneath a picture of a dreadlocked Bob Marley. Looking around I can see ten or twenty bright yellow, identically patterned skirts extolling another Bob. VOTE ZANU-PF, they urge, alongside images of Great Zimbabwe, a cross in a ballot box and Comrade Bob looking slightly surprised to find himself decorating the female bottom in this way. Circling his portrait is ZANU-PF's latest mantra: INDIGENISE, EMPOWER, DEVELOP, EMPLOY. It's a complicated message on a complicated design, but clear enough as a statement of loyalty on the part of the wearer.

When I later ask Astonishment if the skirts and the corresponding T-shirts among the mourners are signs of genuine ZANU-PF support, he doesn't dismiss the possibility. The party has always been strong in country areas like this. But he also points out that these items were handed out by party agents in the recent election. No one's going to turn down free clothing, especially if it offers political protection. Though the 2013 election was largely peaceful, people weren't to know beforehand that it wouldn't be a blood-soaked rerun of 2008. Wearing a Mugabe skirt would have been a small price to pay for staying safe. And even with Mugabe back in power, gatherings like funerals are still carefully watched by agents of the CIO to make sure they don't turn into opposition rallies. The skirt could still be a sensible precaution.

There's a disturbance over by the *sadza* drum. Bridget and Lynda are back from the borehole. Lynda has been drawn into the group of cooks and I see her taking her turn at stirring. The women respond with clapping and ululating laughter. A white woman stirring *sadza* is clearly a cause of wonderment. Then Bridget breaks away and picks up a drum. She offers it to Lynda as if inviting her to play. Lynda laughs and declines. So Bridget finds a seat and starts drumming. As if to make up for not drumming, Lynda starts jiggling to the beat – more disco than tribal, but a good effort. She looks up in surprise to find the women gathered round her in a circle, hooting with merriment. Not for the first time in our marriage, I'm amazed at Lynda's ability to connect with strangers in an instant. Bridget gives her a hug.

'Ya, these ladies were so surprised,' comments Bridget, when we meet up later. 'Here was this white woman coming to a funeral and doing the things that they do. They said to me, "She's a woman in the wrong skin. Underneath, these are black people!"'

The day draws on and people start to eat. Someone fetches a tin plate each for Lynda and me and we settle down to *sadza* with greens and gravy and little lumps of meat. People come and greet us. '*Mhoroi. Makadii?*' they smile. Hello. How are you? To which we reply, as Bridget has briefed us: '*Tiripo. Makadiwo?*' We are well. How are you? Some engage us in English, asking where we're from and what we're doing here. It's all done with extreme Shona politeness and no sense at all that we're busting into someone else's ceremony.

Many want to talk to us about Astonishment. We're approached by Wesley Chimombe, his old teacher from Mutemachani Primary. He recalls a grubby child with one

302

long-sleeved shirt, torn at the elbow, and one pair of oversized shorts down to his knees. 'I remember one day he came to school in a pair of slippers which one of his relatives had given him. Many times he'd had no food, so we gave him some at break time if we could. We could see his abilities and we tried to help him. This hungry, ragged child became our head boy – and look at him now.'

A younger man called Julius settles down with his back against the mud wall and tells how he once had a road accident and ended up lying in pain on the hard floor of his hut after being discharged from hospital. Astonishment found him and went straight home to dig out a foam rubber mattress. 'I was very much touched by this act of compassion, and now feel I must do to others as he has done for me.'

Again, the goodness of the man.

Another, with surprising candour, explains that he always wanted to study espionage and become a state security agent, but he didn't have the right credentials – by which I think he means the right standing in ZANU-PF. So having failed to become a spy, he settled for teaching. Others who shake our hands in the course of the day really are security agents, members of the CIO who want to check us out. At least that's what Astonishment tells us later. Lynda and I have no idea who's an agent and who isn't, but Astonishment knows many of these individuals by sight and can quickly pick out Mugabe's spooks in a crowd.

More people are arriving by foot and in donkey carts and one or two cars, and clouds of dust continue to rise from the grove of gum trees where the gravediggers are battling to gain enough depth in the hard ground to take the coffin. The ceremony is moving on. As the afternoon shadows lengthen, there's a movement of people towards the main hut and a wail of anguish from Chengeta's one surviving wife – Bianca, the original Mrs Mapurisa. She falls writhing to the ground and is tended by keening women. The crowd draws back from the hut as a hearse noses slowly into the compound. It's a white, 4x4 Ford truck, just arrived in Madamombe after collecting the coffin that morning from Driefontein Hospital. The cab bears the undertaker's logo and a faintly unnerving strapline: 'We light your way to final Destiny'. The capital 'D' on 'Destiny' adds its own note of finality.

The hearse stops in front of the hut and the wailing rises to a crescendo. The coffin is removed and carried inside to the sound of weeping and ululation. Here it will remain until the burial the following day, watched over by members of the family. The truck drives slowly away, the drums begin and the church choir strikes up with another exuberant hymn, the singers swaying and clapping and the three little dancers gyrating in the sand. The wailing and the celebration continue simultaneously, charging the scene with extremes of emotion as though the juxtaposition of joy and sorrow might somehow neutralise the grief.

After a time, things quieten down. The crowd is swelling with more arrivals. People are preparing either to bed down on the ground or to stay up all night to drum and dance for Uncle Chengeta. There's more food to be prepared and arrangements still to be made for the burial itself. Astonishment has a long night ahead, but decides at sunset to take us back to the rural home. He'll call and collect us early in the morning.

24

Coming Home

So to Sunday, day two of the funeral. As Astonishment drives us back to Madamombe, he fills us in with developments overnight. Chengeta has remained in the hut in his coffin and been given the all-night vigil required by Shona custom. Meanwhile, word has got back to the local chief that the grave was dug on the day preceding the burial, not on the day itself. This is a break with tradition and a serious matter.

'Why so?' we ask.

'Well, when you dig the grave,' explains Astonishment, 'custom dictates that you must bury the person the same day. This way you avoid any kind of witchcraft infecting the grave overnight. The custom in this case has been flouted and the chief has fined the *kraal* head two goats for allowing it to happen. But those responsible have been claiming mitigating circumstances.'

I ask him what those might be.

'Well, firstly, in view of Zimbabwe's electricity supply, no one knew what condition the body would be in when it arrived from the hospital – whether it had been refrigerated or not. So it might have been necessary to carry out the burial very quickly last night and the grave had to be ready. As it happens, Chengeta's body is still reasonably OK, so the burial can take place today. But there's another problem. Burials are traditionally carried out in the morning when it's cooler and our ancestors are thought to be most present and paying attention. But the ground is so hard the gravediggers could never have finished in time if they'd started today.

'So you see the problem. To be on the safe side, some people remained by the grave all night to ward off any evil influences. But we still wait to hear if the chief will rescind the fine.'

'And how was the night for you?' I ask. 'Did you get any sleep?'

'Hardly any,' smiles Astonishment. 'We're expecting many more people to attend today, so I've had to organise the logistics – like how they'll be fed. A cow was killed and cooked yesterday, but most of it has already been eaten. So we've had to kill a second cow to take us through today. And a cow, as you know, is expensive. Then I had to find utensils and plates for 300 people.'

'So did you have a chance to pay your respects to your uncle?'

'Oh yes. For some of the night, I was keeping watch by the coffin with the other relatives.'

'And what were your thoughts?' I add. 'As you stood there in front of Chengeta's coffin, what was going through your head?'

'That this was a man who'd played a big part in my upbringing. Yes, his life was sometimes a mess and he didn't manage his family very well, and for most of his life until his later years he drank too much. But he also taught me a lot about kindness and taking responsibility. Last night in front of his coffin, I simply said thank you.'

We approach the *kraal*, rattling and bouncing over the bare earth and pulling up at the edge of the huts. As we climb out of the car, I can see immediately that numbers have swollen. The central area is now almost overflowing and we find ourselves peering over people's shoulders at the back of the crowd. Astonishment disappears to talk to the chief who is here to give the main address. Bridget, who has also been up all night, is involved in cooking cow number two. Left alone, we attract a few stares but otherwise seem to be wholly accepted.

It isn't long before the hearse we saw yesterday glides into the compound, ready, finally, to light Chengeta's way to final Destiny. The coffin is carried from the hut, loaded into the back and driven the hundred metres or so to where the grave lies open beneath a temporary awning. Through superhuman efforts, the diggers have managed to get it deep enough. People drift over from the compound and make themselves comfortable on the ground. Lynda and I choose a rock that's not too near and not too far from the action, and wait to see what happens.

Astonishment takes a break from his duties and appears at our side. 'The chief and the security guys have been concerned about your presence,' he murmurs. 'Obviously you're very conspicuous.'

'Really?' says Lynda. 'I can't imagine why.'

'What's been the problem?' I ask.

'They wanted to be satisfied as to why you're here. Remember, we've just had an election in which the rhetoric in these rural areas was very much black against white and all white people being colonial oppressors. And now here you are. Many people are very surprised and don't know how to react. It's the first time in our community that such a thing has happened – a white person joining in the funeral of a black person. The chief and the CIO wanted to know how you and I are connected.'

'And you've told them?'

'Ah, yes. I've told them about your background, Graham, in colonial times. And I've said you're my close friends and good friends of Zimbabwe. So the chief is satisfied and he's endorsed your presence. And because of that, the CIO guys are OK with you being here. The chief appreciates that you've come. He wants you to sit somewhere prominent so he can talk about you in his speech.'

Wondering what's to come, we shift closer in, to another rock. Astonishment slips away and pops up a few minutes later at the front of the crowd. He signals for silence and thanks everyone for coming. Then the chief rises to his feet. He's an imposing man with a boxer's physique, a ready smile and a boldly striped shirt with outsized collars and cuffs. Pinned to his beige corduroy jacket is a brass medallion of office such as I'd last seen hanging round the neck of Chief Siabuwa in 1969. Astonishment has told us he's ZANU-PF – no surprise there – so I wonder if events are about to turn political.

The chief's speech seems to be not much about Chengeta – at least, not to start with. It covers other ground, mostly in Shona but with bursts of English for our benefit. According to Astonishment's summary afterwards, he first addresses the issue of the grave being dug the previous day. Yes, this is a serious breach of custom, but the chief has considered the circumstances and decided to cancel the two-goat fine on the *kraal* head. He then turns his attention to Chengeta's errant son, Muzorodzi. Despite being on the run from the police, Muzorodzi has slipped into the *kraal* and is in the crowd. The chief knows he's here (the CIO have been doing their job) and asks him to stand. We see him only in profile, but his hunched stance suggests a worried man.

'I am aware of the charge of theft against you,' declares the chief. 'I am also aware that some of the stolen money has been recovered. I have spoken to the people you stole from and they have forgiven you. As a result, the police have agreed to pardon you as well. But you must now amend your ways and emulate your cousin, Mr Mapurisa here. Conduct yourself as he conducts himself and all will be well.' There's more to be said to Muzorodzi, but eventually he's given permission to sit down.

The chief then talks about Astonishment, expressing appreciation for all the support he gave to Chengeta in his declining years. 'This man, out of his own pocket, paid for his uncle's medication and treatment. And see how Mr Mapurisa has bettered himself. Here is a man, one of us, who used to be an ordinary young boy, herding cattle and running long distances to school. But this boy was determined to be educated. First, he went from here to Harare. Now he has gone to other countries and is relating to people who are not like us. To people who are white. I wish that more Zimbabweans were like Mr Mapurisa, having international contacts who can come and see what a peaceful country we are. This is what education can do.

'So let me tell you today that not all white people are bad. Take these British friends of Mr Mapurisa's who have come to visit us from afar. I have heard that Mr Jones' father was a pastor here in Zimbabwe – one who supported the liberation struggle and was sent packing by the colonial government because they didn't like what he was doing.' Here he switches to English and turns to face Lynda and me on our rock. We're not hard to spot. 'Mr Jones' father was one of us in our struggle for freedom. And so, I would like to welcome Mr Jones and his wife and ask them to come to the front.'

Surprised to be included so directly, we step forward through the crowd. I take off my crumpled bush hat in respect and we shake his hand. The shaking goes on for some time as the chief continues with his welcome. 'It is an honour for us to have you here and we are grateful that you have come. You must come and set up a business here in Zimbabwe to provide employment for our children. We will give you land and you can easily do business here. We are not political in Zimbabwe. We are a peace-loving country and I want you to take that message home to Europe.'

We sit down, the speech turns to other topics – Chengeta, presumably – and the chief eventually concludes. The coffin is lowered into the hole, the gravediggers shovel furiously at the sandy earth and that appears to be the end of it. As the mourners drift away from the mound that now marks Chengeta's resting place, I'm surprised to see a fine, plump turkey waddling forward as if to take up guard. I hope Chengeta would have been pleased at the send-off he's received.

We decide to find the chief again and thank him for his welcome. We're stopped on the way by several people asking for jobs when we set up our business and try, politely, to dodge the question. The chief is still on the scene, accompanied by his bodyguard. He greets us with more hearty handshakes. Yes, he admits, he did think it was a bad idea when he learned that two white people were coming to the funeral. But having been reassured by Astonishment, he now sees our presence at this African event as symbolic of the unity of black and white. That's why he called us to the front, so that all could see how two *varungu* had entered into local culture, not as colonial leftovers, not as *baas* and madam, but alongside and taking part.

We're flattered. Even moved. Astonishment and Bridget have quietly worked another act of reconciliation. In this faraway patch of Zimbabwe, we feel totally accepted.

So Uncle Chengeta, the nearest Astonishment ever had to a father, has been buried according to the customs of his people. By an accident of timing, Lynda and I have been privileged to play a small part in seeing him off. Back later at the rural home, as the soft African night exerts its magic, the stars blaze and peace descends, we sit with Astonishment and relive the events of the funeral. He might have been cautious initially, but we're grateful to the chief for endorsing our presence. Despite his party's and his President's rhetoric in recent weeks, he has treated us as friends rather than enemies. The description of Dad's contribution to the liberation struggle might have been exaggerated, but we'll let it stand if it helped to break down the racial divide and placate the ZANU-PF spooks.

What we've learned in Zimbabwe is to let the politics go and appreciate the humane, humorous, long-suffering people who deserve far better from their government and who've welcomed us into their lives – chief among them, Astonishment Mapurisa, whose story has so intertwined with mine since little Zondiwe set the process in motion in Victoria Falls.

Settling back in his chair at the rural home, Astonishment speaks of the Madamombe funeral as a point of affirmation for him, personally. Among people who knew him as a barefoot herd boy in tattered shorts, he's now the man of consequence, forging international connections and turning up in a car with friends from Britain. Not that he would put it that way. To him, the contrast between the frightened *murambiwa* and the man we know today is testimony to the power of God to remake lives, however hopeless and insignificant they may appear. And with that transformation has come a God-given mission to heal relationships elsewhere, not least in Madamombe these last two days. Astonishment and Bridget have used our unexpected presence to show their community that people castigated as the enemy can stir the *sadza* and fetch water from the borehole and be part of African life. Not that we did it well or in any way that was at all demanding, but the gesture, so Astonishment tells us, has made its mark on the Madamombe community.

'When we left the funeral,' says Astonishment, 'some people thought I was driving you back to your hotel in Chivhu and dinner at Vic's. They were very surprised to hear you were staying at our rural home. They appreciated that.'

It's a generous sentiment: staying at the rural home is no sacrifice. But if today's events were the culmination of a journey for Astonishment, so they were for me. When I last attended an African funeral, I was sixteen and the burial was that of an unknown child. Unknown to me, anyway, as were the people I stood and observed in Siabuwa village. Then I knew just a narrow segment of the country in which I lived, and I watched the funeral dispassionately as an outsider looking in. Today's funeral has felt like a bookend to the first, a completion. After half a lifetime and all Zimbabwe's intervening turmoil, Chengeta's family and the people of Madamombe have embraced Lynda and me with extraordinary warmth and welcome. Astonishment, in particular, has connected me to my past and opened up the human wealth which to me, then, was alien and out of my experience.

The poles of the magnet have finally, if briefly, touched. I've found the land of my childhood, not in the places I knew but in the people I didn't.

Five years earlier, I'd stepped off the plane at Victoria Falls for the first time in four decades and wondered if I was coming home. Sitting among the mourners at Uncle Chengeta's funeral, a million metaphorical miles from the life I lived as a child, I knew I had.

In Closing

More than five years have passed since we buried Uncle Chengeta. Astonishment, still in Johannesburg, has now set up his own charity (www.youthopportunitiessouthafrica.org) to help disadvantaged youngsters in Soweto to rise above the problems they face and make a positive contribution to their community. It's a mission that in many ways replicates Astonishment's own story, now among a generation of *murambiwas* in urban, twenty-first-century South Africa. Similar work goes on in Zimbabwe where Matthew Rusike Children's Home (www.friendsofmatthewrusike.org) continues to deal with the fallout from so many years of political and economic chaos.

After almost four decades in which Mugabe seemed unshiftable, his fall in November 2017 was more sudden and peaceful than anyone expected. Zimbabweans erupted onto the streets, celebrating noisily and scarcely daring to believe that the tyrant's long reign was over.

Those scenes have given way to a darker mood as the new beginning promised by President Mnangagwa has stalled. After another disputed election in 2018 and the shooting of citizens protesting the result, Zimbabwe's problems continue. The country is short of cash.

Supermarket shelves are empty. Hospitals are without drugs. Roads remain potholed and farms derelict while the ruling party seems as determined as ever to keep its grip on power.

And yet, and yet, Zimbabweans continue to hope.

A decade ago, our guide at Victoria Falls spoke wistfully of God bringing better times after Zimbabwe's season of suffering. He could not have imagined that the season would be so long. For the sake of his afflicted country and all who love it, may his prayer soon be answered.

January 2019

Glossary

Baas	Boss
Baba	Father, older man
Badza	Digging implement, hoe
Bakkie	Pick-up truck
Biltong	Dried meat
Braaivleis (braai)	Barbeque
Bundu	Bush, countryside
Chimbwido	Guerrillas' girl companion
Chongololo	African millipede
Dorp	Small, insignificant town
Fudzamombe	Cattleherd
Gogo	Old woman
Gukurahundi	Early rains; Mugabe's 1980s campaign against the Ndebele
Indaba	Consultation, debate
Iwe	You
Ja	Yes
Jamkoko	Cowherd
Kachasu	Potent African beer
Kaffir	African (offensive)
Kaya	House, servant's quarters
Knobkerrie	Stick, club
Kopje	Hill
Kraal	African village

Laager	Defensive camp
Lekker	Delicious
Lobola	Bride price
Mangwanani	Good morning
Manheru	Good evening
Mubhoyi	Boy (derogatory)
Mudzepete	Hallucinogenic brew
Mufundisi	Pastor, minister
Mujibha	Guerrillas' errand boy
Munt	African (offensive)
*Murambatsvin*a	'Clear out the rubbish'; Mugabe's 2005 campaign against shanty dwellers
Murambiwa	Rejected; rejected person
Murungu	White person
Piccanin	African child (patronising)
Piccanin kaya (PK)	Toilet
Povo	Common people
Pungwe	Guerrillas' re-education session
Sabhuku	Village record keeper
Sadza	Staple African dish made from cornmeal
Sjambok	Heavy leather whip
Stoep	Verandah
Tackies	Canvas shoes
Tickie	Three-pence coin
Varungu	White people

Bibliography

Peter Godwin and Ian Hancock, *Rhodesians Never Die* (London: Macmillan, 2013)

Peter Godwin, *Mukiwa: A White Boy in Africa* (London: Picador, 1997)

Alexandra Fuller, *Don't Let's Go to the Dogs Tonight* (London: Picador Classic, 2015)

T W Baxter and R W S Turner, *Rhodesian Epic* (Cape Town: Howard Timmins, 1966)

Sir Robert Tredgold (ed), *The Matopos* (Lusaka: The Federal Department of Printing and Stationery, 1956)

When Graham Jones returns to Zimbabwe to recapture his idyllic Rhodesian childhood, a chance encounter leads him to meet a one-time child slave called Astonishment. Now dedicated to helping society's most vulnerable, Astonishment grew up on the other side of the racial divide and is set on revisiting his very different past.

As they travel together, this remarkable Zimbabwean shares the incredible story of how he overcame grinding poverty and being sold by relatives as a slave. Both men lay old ghosts to rest as Astonishment forgives and reconciles his divided family and Graham reconnects with the land of his youth – not through the places he knew, but through the people he didn't.

Set against the daily brutalities of racist Rhodesia and Mugabe's bankrupt Zimbabwe, *Astonishment* is a moving account of nostalgia, race and reconciliation that celebrates the transformative power of forgiveness.

'A fascinating portrait of two contrasting societies and what happens when forgiveness and reconciliation replace hatred and division. Intensely moving and evocative.'

HENRY OLONGA, artist, musician and former Zimbabwean international cricketer

Graham Jones grew up in Rhodesia, now Zimbabwe. He studied English at Cambridge before working as a copywriter and speech writer. He's married to Lynda and has three grown-up sons.

CHRISTIAN
BOOK CENTRE PRESTON
£ 8.99

ISBN 9781912726103

9 781912 726103

www.instantapostle.com

Genre: Biography/Memoir

Price: £8.99 / US$16.99